m

Praise for

"At once an intimate, accessible, and deeply analytical examination of gendered experiences of socially structured suffering, care work, and resistance, Buer's ethnography is an important counter-narrative to the increasing stigmatization of pregnant and parenting women who use drugs—and to the overall stigma surrounding Appalachia. In this book Buer skillfully interweaves a critical anthropological unveiling of the policy-driven constraints affecting the women whose lives and families are humanized in the pages, with their own accounts of how it affects them, and what they do about it. Refreshingly un-sensationalized, *Rx Appalachia* comes across as some of the most silenced and marginalized in a region finally telling their own story, with support from a narrator who clearly articulates their context."

—Dr. Bayla Ostrach, author, *Health Policy in a Time of Crisis: Abortion, Austerity, and Access*

"Lesly-Marie Buer's *Rx Appalachia* is a compelling account of substance abuse in Central Appalachia that at last puts race and gender at the forefront of analysis. Buer, a harm reductionist and medical anthropologist, offers a layered portrait of the lives led by women who use drugs and their experiences navigating treatment programs too often shaped by punitive impulses rather than evidence-based research. A rare book that combines a powerful systemic critique within humanely-rendered stories of coping and survival, Rx Appalachia is a clear and accessible primer about the people and places now synonymous with America's new addiction crisis."

—Elizabeth Catte, author of *What You Are Getting Wrong About Appalachia* and *Pure America*

"Lesly-Marie Buer's ethnographic study *Rx Appalachia* examines what happens to women and mothers who use drugs and get caught up in the intertwined therapeutic, rehabilitative, and often punitive practices of public and private addiction recovery programs including drug courts. Buer analyzes the entangled dimensions of care and cruelty, domination and love, family and community, and the discursive and disciplinary techniques that are involved in so-called "rehabilitation" efforts. What good such programs might do is often undercut by inadequate funding and by their tendency to ignore or worsen the stereotypes and the structural and systemic inequalities, constraints, and violence their clients face on a daily basis—often within the programs themselves. The ethnographic site of this brilliant book is Appalachia but it is a must-read for scholars, practitioners, students, concerned citizens, and clients everywhere."

—Dwight B. Billings, emeritus professor, University of Kentucky

"Reproductive justice demands that we provide parents who use drugs with sufficient resources such as housing and access to comprehensive reproductive health care, knowing that parents' well-being is intrinsically linked to that of their children. Dr. Buer makes a strong case for why tax dollars spent on policing and incarceration are harmful and no substitute for adequate social supports and basic human rights. This book makes the case for why we can't simply wait on the state to rectify the many injustices that plague the lives of people and especially women in Appalachia—we must take care of each other now."

—Anna Carella, codirector, Healthy and Free Tennessee

"In this riveting account, Buer defies the media version of the opioid crisis in Appalachia, a story of overnight villains and victims. She listens to the women who for years have navigated punitive and highly gendered and racialized state policies, deeply unequal social structures, and state divestment. She asks women who use drugs—who have been told over and again how to "fix" themselves and to whose standards—what they believe they need for themselves and their care networks of family and friends. Their refreshing narratives intertwine with Buer's careful contextualization to produce a bold vision for harm reduction in Appalachia. A necessary book for those seeking to understand the opioid crisis and the broader political economy of which it is part."

—Jessica Wilkerson, author, *To Live Here, You Have to Fight: How Women Led Appalachian Movements for Social Justice*

"In the midst of the latest drug scare focused on opioids, pregnant women have once again become the objects of state surveillance and control. Lesly-Marie Buer's book arrives just in time to provide information needed to evaluate and challenge government responses that focus on separating families and fixing mothers rather than the economic, social, and public health policies that undermine women's health and lives. With moving accounts by mothers of their desperate efforts to do whatever it takes to get their children back and revelations of sometimes shocking state action—including compelled religious education and prohibitions on needed medical treatment, this beautifully written book is a must-read."

—Lynn Paltrow, executive director, National Advocates for Pregnant Women

"Anyone who does research or practice in rural communities affected by drug use will agree with my feeling that we have long needed this book. This deep ethnographic examination into the lives of women in Appalachia who use drugs serves as a vital antidote to shallow representations of rural drug use in the age of the opioid epidemic. Buer is comprehensive in her approach to understanding not only the histories and inequities that contribute to drug use, but also the ways that the design of public health and social systems to address these health disparities inadvertently can harm those who they are meant to serve. While this book helps us to understand the larger inequities that have led us to here, it also begins to help us understand the path to move forward."

—Claire Snell-Rood, author, *No One Will Let Her Live: Women's Struggle for Well-Being in a Delhi Slum*

"*Rx Appalachia* offers a compelling examination of a region often mischaracterized as a place plagued by inherent violence and dysfuntion. Looking deeply into the lives, care networks, and treatment experiences of women who use drugs, Lesly-Marie Buer reveals the vigilance necessary to overcome the forces of structural violence, as women strive to instate their rights to dignity, healthcare, livelihood, and their childrens' futures."

—Kelly Ray Knight, author of *addicted.pregnant.poor*

mothers rather than the economic, social, and public health policies that undermine women's health and lives. With moving accounts by mothers of their desperate efforts to do whatever it takes to get their children back and revelations of sometimes shocking state action—including compelled religious education and prohibitions on needed medical treatment, this beautifully written book is a must-read."

—Lynn Paltrow, executive director, National Advocates for Pregnant Women

"Anyone who does research or practice in rural communities affected by drug use will agree with my feeling that we have long needed this book. This deep ethnographic examination into the lives of women in Appalachia who use drugs serves as a vital antidote to shallow representations of rural drug use in the age of the opioid epidemic. Buer is comprehensive in her approach to understanding not only the histories and inequities that contribute to drug use, but also the ways that the design of public health and social systems to address these health disparities inadvertently can harm those who they are meant to serve. While this book helps us to understand the larger inequities that have led us to here, it also begins to help us understand the path to move forward."

—Claire Snell-Rood, author, *No One Will Let Her Live: Women's Struggle for Well-Being in a Delhi Slum*

"*Rx Appalachia* offers a compelling examination of a region often mischaracterized as a place plagued by inherent violence and dysfuntion. Looking deeply into the lives, care networks, and treatment experiences of women who use drugs, Lesly-Marie Buer reveals the vigilance necessary to overcome the forces of structural violence, as women strive to instate their rights to dignity, healthcare, livelihood, and their childrens' futures."

—Kelly Ray Knight, author of *addicted.pregnant.poor*

Appalachia

Stories of Treatment
and Survival
in Rural Kentucky

Lesly-Marie Buer

Haymarket Books
Chicago, Illinois

Published in 2020 by
Haymarket Books
P.O. Box 180165
Chicago, IL 60618
773-583-7884
www.haymarketbooks.org
info@haymarketbooks.org

ISBN: 978-1-64259-123-1

Distributed to the trade in the US through Consortium Book Sales
and Distribution (www.cbsd.com) and internationally through In-
gram Publisher Services International (www.ingramcontent.com).

This book was published with the generous support of Lannan Foundation and Wallace Action Fund.

Special discounts are available for bulk purchases by organizations
and institutions. Please email orders@haymarketbooks.org for more
information.

Cover and text design by Eric Kerl.

Printed in Canada by union labor.

Library of Congress Cataloging-in-Publication data is available.

10 9 8 7 6 5 4 3 2 1

For those who led me down this path,
but are gone and sorely missed

I've learned something about times like these.
In times like these you have to grow big enough
inside to hold both the loss and the hope.

—**Ann Pancake**, *Strange as This Weather Has Been*

Contents

Introduction
An Ethnography of Intervention

FEW FAMILIES ARE UNTOUCHED by drug use. My story with use begins before I was alive with an East Tennessee funeral. Two more funerals keep me working on substance use and harm-reduction issues. I often feel pangs from the loss of these three men, two of whom I cared for a decade before they died and one of whom I surely would have loved had he lived to see me born. I am one step removed from these overdose or suicide deaths—it is hard to know the difference at times. I am a few steps removed from many more. I have never lost a parent, sibling, partner, or child to either of these causes, and I hope with all my might I never will. These two feelings, loss and hope, permeate this book.

I learned about substance use before the Drug Abuse Resistance Program (D.A.R.E.) presentation in middle school. I came across an obituary in an old family trunk that elicited a more in-depth explanation of alcohol use than one could ever find in school. I then viewed, and still do at some moments, drug use as a thing that takes people away. Through ordinary experimentation in high school and college, I came to understand use as something that can also bring people together in both conventional and radical ways. I passed this stage of life without incident. Some of those around me were not so privileged. I keep returning to this disparity. Why am I okay? Why are some of my friends trapped in the criminal processing system? Why are others dead? The work that follows is not a testament to personal will but rather an exploration of how people get caught up in systems, especially state programs, and what happens when they do. Getting caught has far more to do with societal understandings of human worth than individual action.

1

The mixture of drug use as cultural spectacle and the very real pain associated with abuse complicates research on the issue. When stereotypes of Appalachia enter the conversation, misinformation balloons. The media coverage of the region where I was raised as well as the epidemiological course of prescription drug use enticed me to return to Appalachia in an effort to better understand the complexities of where my family and I come from. I noticed that most media coverage of Appalachia and drug use focuses on what "experts" have to say. These experts rarely include people actively using drugs. As a person who earned a PhD concentrating on substance use, I benefit from the authority associated with expertise. At the same time, I wanted to center my research on people's experiences with use, ceasing use, and, at times, using again, within state institutions, communities, and cultural ideologies.

During my high school years in southern Appalachia in the late 1990s, the benzodiazepines alprazolam and diazepam, generally known by the brand names Xanax and Valium, were more available than alcohol. Generations older than mine had access to prescription drugs—I often heard stories involving muscle relaxers and sedatives—but the access we had was unprecedented. While we were experimenting with benzodiazepines (benzos), an entirely different medication, OxyContin, dramatically altered regional drug use. In the early 2000s, we began seeing increasing amounts of OxyContin being sold and used. Various forms of oxycodone and hydrocodone, including Percocet and Lortab, were present at every party. Using benzos, pain pills, and Adderall (the attention deficit hyperactivity disorder medication) became as ubiquitous as drinking beer. The statistics show that our use was commonplace. It was not until I started working in Colorado on substance use issues in 2008 that I began hearing about the increases in overdose deaths. The deaths I had already heard about within my circles seemed unsurprising and consistent with my parents' and older sister's remembrance of early deaths among their family and friends. When I returned to

Appalachia in 2011, it felt like a sucker punch of panic and grief as communities were attempting to address an overdose death crisis. Not until I started this research did I fully realize that a whole separate set of interventions, or prescriptions, shaped this region. The antidrug programs I describe continue a line of public and private interventions in Appalachia that reach back to the Frontier Nursing Service (1925), the Tennessee Valley Authority (1933), the United States Forest Service (1905), and the War on Poverty (1964). Both these pharmaceutical and nonpharmaceutical prescriptions represent the idea of pharmakon, those things that have the ability to heal and poison.

Most substance use treatment in the Central Appalachian area where I completed research is regulated and funded by the government. This gives an opportunity to examine how state programs interact with people characterized as both vulnerable and deviant. Those living on the fringe experience increased government surveillance as compared to populations that are economically and racially privileged. Yet state surveillance among and between marginalized populations differs. The women who appear in this ethnography qualify for and at times are coerced to use particular state services because of their gender, race, class, and motherhood status. Through state and quasi-state institutions, the government offers services that are punitive, rehabilitative, and therapeutic. The vast majority of those I spoke with agree that some of these services are needed but that they do not adequately address substance use or the inequalities they face. It is hard to expect a treatment program that is itself economically and politically constrained to overcome a mass of social forces working against its clients.

Three treatment programs are highlighted in this book. All local program, county, and individual names are pseudonyms. These counties have small populations, and I do not want treatment clients, programs, and staff to be negatively affected by claims or descriptions made in this book. Statewide program names and the names of agency directors or politicians making public claims are not pseudonyms. I refer to the first program as "Horizons." Horizons provides intensive outpatient substance use treatment along with case management to approximately 110 women a year. The program is located in a nonprofit, nongovernmental, community mental health center. Horizons was created to address substance use and child maltreatment. The Department for Community Based Services (DCBS) refers the vast majority of clients to Horizons because women who use substances are at risk of permanently losing child custody. The second program, drug court, provides intensive outpatient substance use treatment along with case management to people who have had their criminal cases deferred to drug court. The drug court described here served nine women during my research.

The third type of program offers buprenorphine medication-assisted treatment and is located within private clinics that vary dramatically in the services they offer and the number of clients they serve. All clinics in the area prescribe buprenorphine with naloxone, referred to as bupe. They have drug testing as well as behavioral modification components. State or federal agencies regulate these treatment programs. All are dependent upon government funding streams, whether through direct grants or Medicaid reimbursement. Yet there are fractures among programs, particularly in regard to bupe. Some program staff do not support bupe treatment and consider the drug to be just as harmful as heroin. Other agencies view bupe use as therapeutic, a harm-reduction strategy. Women who use drugs often have to navigate between these conflicting views.

Neither state institutions nor the people who inhabit them work within a vacuum; understanding their political and socioeconomic contexts is critical. Institutions constrict what people do by making some actions politically infeasible or financially impossible. There still remains opportunity for resistance against inequalities within institutions.[1] These crosscutting powers create nuances, where it becomes impossible for the careful observer to glorify or demonize people or places as homogenous, unchanging, or inherently pathological. Individuals differentially encounter oppression and privilege due to their unique social positions, facing divergent opportunities as well as consequences to actions.[2] In this ethnography, the main pathways people use to navigate the unending complexities of drug use, institutions, and marginalization involve forming close alliances with friends, family members, and others in treatment. These alliances often involve intense care work and at times erupt violently. They nonetheless offer an avenue to resistance and change.

Individual and collective action offers a way to cope with and challenge socioeconomic inequalities and government intrusions. Yet people remain limited insofar as their strategies are tied to unequal access to resources.[3] Drug use itself may be a constrained survival strategy. Everyday violence limits the actions of those who use drugs, where people knowingly take risks because there are either no other options or all of the available options pose risks.[4] Direct activism, such as protests and walkouts, is not as often practiced as actions that occur within the "hidden transcript," what James C. Scott conceptualized as actions that take place "off-stage," out of view from those who hold dominant power.[5] Actions within the hidden transcript may include complaints, minor theft, tampering with drug tests, or (in the words of some who are profiled in this book) just "jumping through the hoops" of programs. A focus on survival strategies and constraints reveals the inequalities people navigate, contests depictions of certain people as incapable of action, and provides a platform to make systemic changes in social services and treatment programs.

Activists and political commentators have rightly highlighted the unequal treatment of people who use crack and opioids.[6] The stereotype of the person who uses crack is Black, poor, and urban. The stereotype of the person who uses opioids at this time is white, relatively wealthy, and suburban. I understand the frustration. White, wealthy suburbanites have financial and geographic access to private substance use and mental health facilities that rarely work in cooperation with law enforcement or DCBS. If these folks do come into contact with state agencies, they are often able to pay their way out of negative repercussions through quality legal representation and swift settlement of criminal processing or court fees. When people of color, especially those who are poor, face state agencies, they are more likely to lose custody of their children, to be incarcerated, or to be killed. There is another stereotype looming as well. The person who uses meth is coded as white, poor, and rural. White meth users are labeled "white trash," and are considered polluters of the white race, much like Appalachians in general. White mothers who use meth are particularly criminally prosecuted because they are viewed as physically and socially reproducing cultural rot.[7]

The women I spent time with who are poor, white, and rural were not treated like the children of the elite. Although they primarily use opioids, they are framed similarly to people who use meth. Everything they experienced was heavily tied to the carceral state. Yet, in the words of Grace Howard, this is the "velvet fist" of the state. Many had been to jail, but few had served long-term prison sentences. They feared the police, but generally not death by the police. Instead, they were corralled into treatment programs where they generally lost temporary or permanent child custody. These programs provided few if any social services and frequently could not even provide quality substance use treatment. Most staff taught women that their entire way of being was immoral, from their substance use to their economic strategies and caretaking. Poor, white women see a different side of the state than poor, Black women because they are more often put into programs instead of prison.

Still, the current versions of the programs that poor white women are likely to use do not represent a just alternative to incarceration. A truly just alternative must provide quality health and social services and must address punitive and racist drug policies. An alternative that abides by reproductive justice should ensure that all people who use, irrespective of their gender identity, sexual orientation, or race, have access to these services and that punishment is not particularly levied at women because of their reproductive capacity or caretaking roles.

The complexities and contradictions presented here are meant to push against stereotypes and single narratives that flatten experiences. Programs based on such caricatures inevitably further marginalize people who are poor and use drugs in Appalachia. To acknowledge the importance of ethical research in documenting people's narratives, I explore my positions as well as the positions of those I spoke with. I make notes on the language and sources in the book with the hopes that this work will be used to fight oppression rather than reify stereotypes. My research takes place among people who are on the fringes in an area that is impoverished materially but steeped in rich traditions of storytelling and, at times, unified resistance against the powers that be. Entering a field as contested as this, especially in my home region, presents a series of dilemmas that must be worked through. State intervention in Eastern Kentucky follows popular theoretical models and is often implemented because of the falsely assumed whiteness of Appalachians. But as in other areas of the country, residents living in poverty are viewed as irresponsible and unworthy of social services. State intervention is thus underfunded and often punitive.

Knowledge Sources

A note on sources is in order. Living on the edge and using drugs produce uncertainty. So much of being in a place, ingesting a substance, and caring for others is felt in complex ways that cannot be easily translated through sterile language. Artists often create more fruitful methods of transmitting these moments of being. While I use few sources to lessen the feeling that this is simply a collection of disparate narratives, I draw from one novel more than others. In *Strange as This Weather Has Been*, Ann Pancake pulls together the anxiety and hope I continue to witness in Central Appalachia.[8] While Pancake focuses on mountaintop removal in West Virginia, there are parallels to the counties that I studied. From my previous research in counties where coal mining is a more common occupation, I found there are certainly direct causal pathways between the injuries workers sustain in extractive industries and use of prescription opioids. The connections between mountaintop removal and drug use extend to the strain they put on individuals, families, and communities. Pancake successfully illustrates the dynamics of different types of brutality through accounts of individual experience. Most important, she reveals the messy ways people navigate inequalities in their daily lives that are not as polished or as visible as collective action. I attempt to do similar work here, though without the eloquence of those I quote.

The research for this book took place over four years, from 2013 to 2016. I completed formal interviews and had informal conversations with folks, spent time in Eastern Kentucky communities and agencies, and collected local newspaper articles and program documents. All research activities are centered in the place I refer to as Adams County, Kentucky, but this research took me into organizations and homes across the region. One woman who has grandchildren the same age as my young children helped me gain entry into Adams County. She is the local volunteer director of a nonprofit antidrug coalition and a former grade school teacher. She is raising her grandson because both of his parents use substances and lost custody of him. With one e-mail, she encouraged me to attend community events, found me an apartment to live in through her family, and introduced me to numerous people.

What social scientists call participant observation I would call spending time with people, and my mamaw would call visiting. These descriptions sound less labor-intensive than they actually might be. When I visited my mamaw, there was always lots of gardening, washing dishes, and doing involved, especially for the women. When I set out to learn about Adams County and Eastern Kentucky, I began by volunteering for local organizations that provide services to the people I later interviewed to get a better idea of what resources they have available. I started attending community meetings, holiday celebrations, reunions, and religious events to get a feel for the place. I met people who encouraged me to see other county sites and even guided me through forests as they explained their love for the place and visions for the future. These encounters made it impossible for me to view Adams County or the region as a stagnant snapshot, something a few journalists have been apt to do as photographs of abandoned homes are printed beside headlines proclaiming the area one of the poorest in the United States. Instead, I saw the histories of the region written in the landscape and was drawn into various scenarios of the future that are more hopeful than the headlines would suggest.

Since 2011, I have been going to meetings throughout Appalachia focused on substance use, health, the economy, and community revitalization. In these gatherings, I have observed how those with power discuss national and state policy initiatives, including those focused on substance use. The conversations are fraught with particular understandings of rurality, Appalachia, kinship, and poverty. They provided an important juxtaposition to women's own narratives because it is through relationships with these leaders that women experience private and public interventions.

I spent time with women in their homes, in the community, and in treatment programs. Very often, I simply helped as they completed everyday caretaking and household chores, including running after toddlers on the playground, planning a summer garden, dealing with a litter of puppies, or enjoying nice weather on the porch. These everyday practices revealed how people navigate their health concerns, substance use histories, intimate relationships, and income-generating strategies. I saw how program services and requirements often support women even as they undermine their efforts to maintain a life outside of the drug economy. For instance, women's caretaking responsibilities and time-intensive engagement in treatment often prevented them from obtaining employment, even though the latter is often a requirement for certain phases of treatment.

At other times, we scheduled specific activities, such as attending a parenting class, a children's Christmas celebration, and district court. I spent one day driving Ashley, whose story is highlighted in this book, to food banks where we tried to figure out how she could survive on juice and seafood broth for two weeks. I met with women coming in and out of treatment and occasionally drove them to appointments. My observation in treatment programs was restricted, due to administrators' as well as my concerns over confidentiality. I was able to observe a few drug court group meetings after securing the agreement of drug court participants, the program manager, and the counselor.

I formally interviewed forty people who identify as women and who are over the age of eighteen. All but three identified as non-Latinx white. The remaining three identified as biracial. At the time of my research, neither drug court nor Horizons served any women who identified as an ethnicity other than non-Latinx white or biracial. Of the forty total participants, thirty-three had experiences with Horizons, seventeen with buprenorphine clinics, and fourteen with drug court. All but two had encounters with DCBS. I completed formal second interviews with ten participants, but I informally had multiple conversations with roughly half of the women I interviewed. I interacted with six women repeatedly during my research; we completed several scheduled interviews, visited, chatted briefly, or texted.

I completed thirty-two interviews with people I refer to as gatekeepers because of the power they wield over programs and policies. To be clear, this power varies dramatically among them and changes through time, even during the relatively short period of my fieldwork. Fifteen of these gatekeepers administered programs or provided substance use treatment. I spoke with local and regional DCBS staff, local politicians and judges, health department staff, community activists, law enforcement, and religious leaders. The purpose of these interviews was to understand various viewpoints on the broader socioeconomic and political contexts that situate women's experiences. This information is not meant to override or supersede women's narratives, but it helps explain the multiple contact points women have with the government and the institutional practices and services they are navigating.

Terminology Matters

Words matter. Throughout this book, I made terminology decisions to limit the ways in which this research can be used to advance harmful policies. I take from activists across a variety of platforms a person-first terminology. I find the terms "drug-using women," "addicted," and "women who use drugs" all problematic as descriptors of the people I spent time with. "Drug-using" is the most reductionist in defining women as first and foremost an embodiment of one stigmatized behavior. I do not consistently use the term "addicted" in order to highlight that many who use drugs explicitly do not identify as being addicted, are not labeled as addicted by their service providers, and are caught in state systems because of drastically varying levels of drug use. However, I use the term "addicted" when I discuss other literatures where the authors and their participants use the term or when those I interviewed described themselves in this way. I primarily employ "women who use drugs," while acknowledging that this term may appear as sanitized, as divorced from material and political realities, and as reifying a category based on one individualistic behavior.[9]

I vehemently oppose the use of stigmatizing terms, such as "drug babies," "addicted babies," and "crack babies," to refer to newborns with drug exposure. The last term has roots in racist efforts to criminalize Black bodies and demonize Black communities and families. By its very definition, the term "addiction" should not be applied to infants or young children. I am critical of these terms because they imply lifelong impairments and foster the idea that newborns exposed to substances in utero are genetically inferior. As shown in chapter 2, no evidence supports these claims.

What to call study participants is tricky. The connotation of "informant" as someone who helps law enforcement in prosecuting others makes use of the term inadvisable. The term "clients" is fraught with reductions of individuals to the status of consumers of state services and of individual action to the realm of consumer choice.[10] I nonetheless use this term, especially in discussions of Horizons and buprenorphine clinics, because both those who access program services and providers continuously use it, but most often I use "participants." Yet this term does not indicate the level of coercion most people feel as they process through programs.[11]

Although the vast majority of those with whom I spoke refer to buprenorphine with naloxone as "Suboxone," this is a brand name and not the most accurate term. Thus, I refer to buprenorphine with naloxone when I write "buprenorphine" or "bupe" because most people who speak of buprenorphine are referring to buprenorphine with naloxone. If I am writing about buprenorphine that does not include naloxone, I make this explicit. Subutex is the brand name for bupe without naloxone.

A review of the literature on imprisonment reveals a shift in terminology from "criminal justice" to "criminal processing." Their work and mine shows that the "justice" qualifier is inaccurate.[12] Another terminology issue is related to the state: I intentionally use the term "quasi-state institutions" instead of the more common nongovernmental organizations (NGOs). While some of the programs I examine may consider themselves NGOs, I question the accuracy of the term. All of the treatment programs discussed are privatized to varying degrees, but all are solely or primarily funded by the state. Federal and state policies heavily regulate all these programs.

I use a double understanding of "prescription" to get at two types of prescriptions in Appalachia. The first is of the pharmaceutical kind, including benzos, OxyContin, and bupe. The second is programmatic. Administrators and regulators often see the programs I describe as something more than a place where services are offered— they offer these programs as the only or main answer to issues such as substance use, poverty, and interpersonal violence. These programs are prescribed to fix a problem by people who consider themselves experts and are often located outside of Appalachia.

The love and violence that permeates people's lives and relationships can be hard to grasp. Care networks are complicated spaces where, for those on the fringes especially, everyday forms of brutality become commonplace. In writing of everyday violence, I do not want to make it acceptable, but rather to show how ubiquitous it is. This cruelty is not in any way inherent to individuals living on the margins; it is an embodied and intimate representation of domination. Care networks are the spaces in which people cope with state and police assault. They are also the primary source of interpersonal violence, which itself must be contextualized within deeply ingrained inequalities.

Insider/Outsider Researchers?

All researchers are in particular power positions in relation to the people or things studied. These positions influence how and what data are collected. My location in Adams and surrounding counties and substance use treatment programs blurs the imagined boundaries between "insider" and "outsider." As a white, Appalachian woman in her early to mid-thirties, I share several important characteristics with the treatment participants with whom I spoke. I have personal stories of loss related to overdose death that are not very different from their stories. I share some of the same ambivalences about the region. I could not wait to leave when I turned eighteen and could not wait to return almost as soon as I left. During my fieldwork, I was pregnant, and my growing belly provided an easy conversation starter with people, especially other pregnant women and new parents.

Despite these similarities, the chasm between our experiences due to differences in housing, access to food, transportation, and status with state systems created instances of frustration, embarrassment, fear, and mutual support. The gaps between us differed across participants and through time. I spoke with treatment program participants, political leaders, community activists, and tenured academics. These jumps across social locations required me to move in and out of worlds and integrate multiple perspectives simultaneously, sometimes more successfully than others.[13]

Understandings of being an insider or outsider make researching drug use contentious. Many people have some sort of familiarity with drug use, either personally or through close others. Experience has led some to develop intricate explanations of use that are difficult to articulate, while others become reductive in their logic. This simplification is understandable. These women's stories and the stories of those who provide services demonstrate the messiness and just plain exhaustion of drug use in the fringes. Perhaps being able to reduce is therapeutic in its own right. Though understandable, simplification is not helpful. Agencies, programs, and community members may overlook and thus support the structures that produce the very actions they aim to fight. Who gets to be an expert? The self-identified ex-alcoholic preacher who has been counseling people who use drugs for ten years and maintains that the devil sent buprenorphine? The woman who says she owes her life to bupe? Or the anthropologist who draws on her research and personal feelings of loss? I do not pretend to offer definitive answers to these questions here, but through explanations of my own position and the narratives I heard, I hope to offer contextualized insight.

With program participants, the tensions that arose during our interactions revealed differences in our social positions and my own understanding of what it means to use drugs. I was rarely uncomfortable, but there were moments of fear. The instance that stands out clearest was when I was supposed to meet a participant at the county courthouse for our second interview. She called to say she was running late. She then drove up with an older man and told me to follow her to his house. I obliged the request and became increasingly nervous as we drove further from town, ending up at a remote farm with a few other men in the driveway. I followed her into the living room, the others in the house removed themselves to an out building, and we spoke for a few hours. I became relieved after a few moments. During the interview, this participant relayed her deteriorating relationship with her mother, who worked at the courthouse; she did not want to chance a meeting with her. This was a rational explanation, which was far from the melodramatic crime-drama scenarios running through my mind on the drive.

These tense and sometimes fearful situations never led to harm to me or those I interviewed, to my knowledge. I further realized my privileged position where I used women for their stories. At the same time, I became for a short while incorporated into women's survival strategies. Participants could ask for rides and gain compensation for interviews. Several women asked me to go with them to access resources, from jobs to food bank grocery boxes. In these situations, I provided moral support but also looked like an authority figure to program staff who were gatekeepers to resources. I played a somewhat contradictory role. In some ways I was an arm of these treatment programs, but in others, I was a coconspirator in navigating these programs as well as the injustices that situate women's lives.

In Adams County, I sometimes became an unwitting intermediary between people who used drugs and those who said they wanted to help provide services. Women told me they desperately wanted a local Narcotics Anonymous (NA) style group, and I relayed this information to local church leaders when they asked what they could do to help. This intermediary position was fraught with uncertain fault lines as I attempted to advocate for services women asked for without supporting the negative assumptions local leaders make. In the meeting with church leaders, they dismissed the request for NA and instead said they wanted to have a Bible study for those who use drugs because they believed that drug use is a spiritual and moral problem. When I told several women that the church leaders were going to offer a Bible-based support group rather than NA, they were disappointed and said they would not attend.

Notes on the State and Quasi-state

The state figures prominently in these women's lives. Most use government benefits. All of them experience state intervention through substance use treatment, DCBS, or the criminal processing system. With virtually no services, the county jails are strictly punitive. Conversely, programming within substance use treatment and DCBS is meant to be therapeutic and rehabilitative. Much of the current

political talk and research around substance use encourages a spread
of therapeutic and rehabilitative services to replace incarceration and
additional punitive measures. I found that these "softer" services rely
heavily on coercion and punishment.

Moreover, these services are not just being used to heal but to
transform people in ways unrelated to substance use. Middle- and
upper-class moral understandings of family and work saturate agencies. Programs reify socially constructed gender roles by emphasiz-
ing motherhood and demonizing mothers who use drugs. Like most
US substance use treatment, programs are based on a white, Protestant, capitalist culture that emphasizes self-control, spirituality,
and personal responsibility.[14] Women overwhelmingly want access
to substance use treatment, but most women and a large subset of
staff think programs are underfunded and mismanaged and do not
address people's primary concerns.

Governments are not monoliths with uniform effects; they represent cohesive and conflicting forms that differentially affect segments
of the population. Through various programs, states attempt to manage populations without necessarily addressing people's needs.[15] State
interventions that do not consider larger social patterns exacerbate inequalities by treating certain populations as pathological.[16] Since the
1970s, the US government has used the War on Drugs and stereotypes
of social welfare recipients as "unworthy" of aid because of race and presumed drug use to justify reductions in government welfare spending.
Punitive drug policies are targeted toward people of color and poor people, creating a situation in which the US has the highest incarceration
rate globally.[17] Alternatively, state policies may respond to vulnerability
and fund programs that people advocate for, such as substance use treatment. Such programs have mixed effects on people's lives.[18] Counseling
services, for instance, may only be available during the day, preventing
people from simultaneously attending counseling and holding a day job.

State surveillance is unevenly distributed. Some populations
may be deemed violent and thus the state's suppression is seen as

warranted.[19] At the same time, in the midst of austerity measures, people attempt to use their vulnerabilities to demand rights in the form of state-funded health care and social welfare services.[20] In our society, through reports, movies, and a litany of additional sources, women are dichotomized into "good" and "bad" mothers based on social locations of class, ethnicity, place, education, and religion. Ideal US motherhood is defined by white, middle-class, heterosexual norms of respectability where women are supposed to place fetal and child health above all else.[21] If and how people reproduce is held to be under the purview of the state because women are characterized as being responsible for physically reproducing infants and socializing children.[22]

Because of the perceived unique relationship between women and children, the state makes people who are mothers eligible for particular services while placing all women under suspicion for harming children. Although access to substance use treatment is particularly limited in rural Appalachian Kentucky, state agencies advocate treatment as an alternative to the permanent removal of children from parents who use drugs.[23] Through these efforts to keep mothers and children together, women who have children may be eligible for programs that are unavailable to men or women without young children. Some women want to be involved with treatment and thus view access positively, even if it is state-mandated, as an alternative to incarceration or child removal. Other women experience state-mandated treatment to be equally as coercive and intrusive as incarceration because the government controls their caregiving and survival strategies.

Beyond understandings of motherhood, a second broad theme relating to neoliberalism, individualism, and privatization contextualizes substance use treatment in Appalachian Kentucky. Neoliberalism represents specific systems of domination that have a long trajectory within the history of oppression. I want to avoid alluding to a mythical past where equality prevailed through critiques of the present, because equality has never prevailed for anyone who is not white, male, heteronormative, and wealthy. Neoliberalism frames the

organization of social, political, and economic relations between the
state and its defined citizens; among global corporations, people, and
the environment; and among different sectors of society. Some elite
have pushed neoliberal agendas, so current policies are purposeful
and changeable.

Neoliberalism in part comprises processes that enforce surveillance of the poor and other marginalized populations while
deregulating those in power. Public and private institutions utilize
coercion and auditing of individual behaviors through such entities
as private health insurers, prisons, and social services to support
self-regulation. When operating from a neoliberal stance, these institutions blame negative outcomes on individuals. They downplay
the role of inequalities in creating harm and the role of safety net
services in protecting communities from that harm. The neoliberal
state emphasizes individualized private solutions, such as marriage,
child support, adoption, high-interest loans, and low-wage work, as
the only answer to social problems.[24]

Treatment programs reflect current trends of partially privatizing
social services where governments fund (and in the current study, require) some clients to attend programs that are implemented locally
by quasi-state institutions. This partial privatization does not signal
a retreat of power, but rather a blending of the state with private institutions. The degree of program engagement with the state shifts in
intensity in terms of funding and regulations. Some institutions are
for-profit while others are nonprofit. Programs and their staff are thus
beholden to corporations or board executives as well as the government. These fractured loyalties lead to frustrations among staff who
often feel lost in miscommunications between the multidimensional
bureaucracies. Clients are at times trapped in competing organizational agendas and may be unsure of who is an ally as they attempt to
navigate various agencies. With multiple sources of power influenc-
ing programs, it becomes unclear who is responsible for which decisions. With inconsistent and at times conflicting leadership, staff and

community members are often quick to place the blame of program failures solely on clients.

Treatment programs themselves face heavy surveillance and marginalization. Community members, particularly those who support "tough on crime" efforts, may stigmatize staff for the services they provide.[25] Staff must frame programs in particular ways so they become politically and culturally acceptable enough to maintain funding and legal status.[26] This framing may encourage programs to focus on remaking the individual, which prevents group solidarity, may not address people's most basic concerns, does not change the environment in which people live, and ignores the association of drug use with increasing poverty and homelessness.[27] When clients critique social service programs, their living conditions, or service provider instructions, staff and other clients may dismiss these critiques as being emblematic of an individual's noncompliance with program rules or denial of their addiction.[28] Again, poor health outcomes can be blamed on individual lack of motivation.[29] A focus on individual action ignores the risks that people who use drugs must take to survive, such as desperate income-generating strategies that may increase experiences of sexual and physical assault.[30] Women's gendered economic marginality may instigate involvement with illicit economies and limit the ability to cease deleterious drug use.

While participants' actions through treatment should not be discounted, solely focusing on client compliance serves to "pathologize the behavior of the poor."[31] Structural violence and poverty bleed through quasi-state institutions as workers and clients must contend with these issues within and outside of programs. Structural violence is a system of exploitation where those in power prevent the marginalized from reaching their potential, in some instances causing death, primarily through inequitable resource distribution.[32] Economic, political, religious, cultural, and legal social structures uphold these distribution patterns.[33] Structural violence is partly articulated as an everyday violence that is experienced as shame, stigma, and physical harm or the threat of harm within interpersonal relationships. This everyday violence occurs in interactions with representatives of the state, creating distrust of state institutions among those who are marginalized.[34]

Most overdose deaths may be attributed to structural violence. Many of these deaths could be prevented by an adequate distribution of resources where all individuals have access to employment that pays a living wage and to housing, education, and quality harm-reduction services (e.g., access to the medication naloxone that rapidly reverses overdose). Substance use treatment exists within defunded spaces where staff must operate spartanly to survive, which equates to decreased wages and fewer available services. To curtail negative health outcomes, systems of exploitation must be worked against and the illness itself must be treated simultaneously.[35] In the end, organizations often lack the power to change inequalities and simply help people cope with oppression.[36] Part of structural violence is depriving people of their ability to organize against their own marginalization,[37] yet people develop strategies to make it through. As domination comes into individual lives and families, it is often confronted in these spaces.

I describe throughout how people are caught in frictions within and among state or quasi-state institutions, health-care providers, and those who they care for and who care for them. These spaces provide opportunities for resistance but also for harm. The people who are most successful in taking the least harmful paths through these institutional labyrinths do so by forming or reforming relationships with others who are not using drugs or are using drugs only to a certain degree. Yet these relationships can be difficult to maintain.

Poor, White, and Rural

Like other systems of domination, neoliberalism's ideological success is based on particular characterizations of marginalized populations. The poor have been reductively framed as dependent, immoral, irresponsible, threatening, and thus unworthy of welfare.[38] Supposed cultural differences can become a political tool to retract government-funded health interventions because culture rather than resources becomes the explanation for health inequalities.[39] This focus on culture is predominant in Appalachia, as explored in the next chapter. Welfare reform targets poor mothers and Black mothers whose caretaking responsibilities and marginal status in the workforce are no longer seen as legitimate reasons for their entitlement to state services.[40] The ideals of personal responsibility as well as private solutions to marginality absolve the government and industry from creating viable economic environments. Those in the fringes are expected to survive through their care networks, which include those people who provide material and emotional resources as well as labor to one another, but not necessarily on equitable terms.

Those in privileged social positions accept the existence of everyday violence because they view the marginalized as deserving of suffering. The elite generally do not react against brutality in meaningful ways until it occurs among the privileged,[41] hence the softer rhetoric surrounding prescription opioids, which are characterized as ethnically white and middle-class. Historically, social welfare programs have focused most resources on white working males and their families.[42] Even if policy makers have deemed some populations worthy enough to receive at least minimal social services, the provision of these services subjects people to intense surveillance. This surveillance may include urine- and blood-sample testing, home and work visits, and electronic monitoring. With limited resources, organizations depend on eligibility requirements. These requirements are often based on funding streams, and those who are deemed too needy may be banned. Drug courts often do not work with individuals who lack personal transportation.[43] Along with this transportation requirement, rural Kentucky drug courts generally do not accept individuals with mental health diagnoses or unstable housing. Thus, large segments of the population, arguably the most vulnerable, are ineligible for services precisely because of their vulnerability. People must participate in claims of eligibility where they perform in a series of roles that are at times conflicting. They must be victimized enough to need services, but adequately personally responsible to justify the use of resources. These performances are rooted in understandings of Appalachia that stereotype the region as ethnically white and thus racially privileged, but also as a region that is under suspicion for its poverty.

Determinations of eligibility and worthiness often go beyond one identifier. While most of the people I spoke with are white, programs are available to them not because their lives are portrayed as worthy but because their white children's lives are worthy. The people in these programs are intrusively managed, but, in terms of funding, barely addressed. If people do not have child custody, they might die or just barely survive because their entitlements to resources such as substance use treatment, health care, housing, and food are drastically cut or eliminated. Thus, access to services is tied to whether people are seen as fulfilling their caretaking roles as mothers to white children.

Gendered caretaking roles mesh with neoliberalism's focus on personal responsibility to create a burden of care. Women cycling through treatment as individuals are expected to take care of families, and the primary caretaker in many families is expected to be a woman. To clarify, women's social positions, not some genetic predisposition, situate them in particular care networks.[44] Due to structural violence, care provided by or to women is limited and sporadic. I take an expanded definition of care, an understanding that care is far messier than good intentions or positive outcomes and may be entwined with oppression.[45] Women who use drugs have intensive caretaking responsibilities and are entrenched in cycles of cruelty and care. When they need support, they must place that burden on their family because care through state or quasi-state institutions is not available. Communities may try to support members, but they struggle financially to provide even basic services. Volunteer labor can only do so much. If people do not have a support system, it becomes difficult to navigate state and quasi-state programs.

Receiving and providing care can be joyous, but it is also tedious as well as emotionally and physically draining. Depending on care from those who are obviously strained, whether family or nonfamily, may lessen an individual's feelings of worth and dignity. What feels like cruelty from the inside may look like care from the outside. I find this to be most typical when care takes the form of surveillance of behaviors, whether of drug use or the people with whom one chooses to associate. The same act may feel like state intrusion when performed by a state employee but may feel like care when performed by a beloved family member. A partner's doling out of a daily bupe dose may feel supportive, but driving to a state-sanctioned methadone clinic for a daily dose turns into an insurmountable barrier to treatment. Conversely, what appears to the outsider as assault may be experienced by an individual as a declaration of love or intense care, as when an individual beats an abusive partner. Violence can at times be a demonstration of care and solidarity. At other times, what looks like violence feels like violence, but that violence is as complex as the care with which it intertwines. This is especially true when a parent relies on an abusive partner for material support.

Navigating the Book

In general, people are not randomly caught in state systems. State systems are built to deal with people who have been pushed aside in our neoliberal white capitalist country. Politicians stigmatize the populations that are in state systems to justify underfunding these systems. This turns into an ugly cycle, where marginalized populations are pulled into underfunded systems that inherently further marginalize people.

The relationship between the state and people on the fringes is a global problem, but I am focused on bringing analyses to Appalachia to understand what is happening there and how that applies to other areas nationally and beyond. The narrative that follows is centered on the stories of people who use or used drugs in Central Appalachia, not their family, physicians, or social workers. In no way do I claim to be giving voice to the voiceless—many do well getting their voices heard on their own. What I can offer is a deep analysis of their experiences using broader contexts and theories.

There are many divergences among the people I spoke with, but a few conclusions kept arising. People who look like they can bear children and who use drugs are being particularly punished by their communities and a variety of state agencies. Everyone, irrespective of whether they have children or of their gender identity, should have access to quality health care, food, affordable housing, and other services that make life livable.

I entered this research with a particular set of lenses based on personal experiences and a privileged social position, as well as an understanding that most entities in a life have the ability to inflict pain and provide much-needed support. I outline the setting I entered in chapter 1, because it is also key to understanding the issue. Global trends, national policies, and social ideologies are made meaningful in a particular place. While some view Appalachia as a world apart, the region is entrenched in the same systems that oppress communities across the country. The patterns of domination and resistance in Appalachia are not unique, but they are nonetheless rooted in a specific history of public and private intervention ("prescription").

Talking about substance use began many of my conversations, so it's appropriate to introduce women's narratives in chapter 2 with stories of use. Use never occurs in a vacuum, and how the state responds to substance use among certain people is couched in narratives of those people.

Chapter 3 explores Horizons in terms of what it offers as well as how it is perceived by those processing through, often jumping through the hoops of services designed specifically for mothers who use drugs. Drug court, assessed in chapter 4, takes a different approach; it is rooted in an explicitly punitive model intended to reform individuals into neoliberal Christian citizens. Chapter 5 reveals some of the unexpected results in communities and among people who use drugs that occurred when decisions at the Kentucky state level gave unprecedented access to buprenorphine in Central Appalachia.

These programs are important in people's lives, but what is happening outside of the programs is pertinent and longer lived. In chapter 6, I explore women's care networks in Eastern Kentucky. These networks often put people in a position to be regulated by the state while simultaneously assisting navigations of state institutions. I conclude by melding the information I gleaned from the programs as well as women's lives outside of programs to suggest recommendations for moving forward, especially attempts to provide people services that they ask for.

For those who keep up with issues around Appalachia or drug use, maybe current narratives ring true with your experiences. But maybe they don't. This book in some ways aligns with other work on poverty and the War on Drugs in the United States. In other ways, it represents a counternarrative against depictions of some places and some people as being unable to be productive in any sense of the term. A list of organizations in the appendix shows how Appalachians, people who use drugs, and advocates work for change. For those who may know little about Appalachia or substance use, welcome. These stories from Eastern Kentucky give a more in-depth introduction than those found in any D.A.R.E. or US history courses I had access to in middle and high school. Current narratives on substance use often focus on an individual, family, or community. I use individual stories to implicate the structural forces that are affecting people. This purposively attempts to shift understandings of substance use, and, perhaps more importantly, shift how we, as a society, respond to substance use. Prescriptions at the individual level are not remedying our problems.

Chapter 1
How Did We Get Here?

I OUTLINE THE STEREOTYPES that couch substance use treatment programs, while contesting these stereotypes using research from the region as well as data from Eastern Kentucky. The appearance and increased use of OxyContin reveal the structural, not individual or familial, factors that surround substance use. Yet a focus on the individual defines much of the response to substance use, resulting in the criminalization of individual users rather than the systems that produce use.

Popular descriptions of Appalachia have characterized the place as somehow different from the United States, representing a glorified and, at the same time, degraded culture. From the nineteenth century on, some outside commentators, including Berea College founder William Frost, have revered Appalachia as a bastion of untainted "white" culture. In the most recent iterations largely based on opioid overdoses and the Trump election, the Appalachian myth has been used to highlight the plight of poor whites and to further white nationalist understandings of this country's past, present, and future. The culture of poverty model, which was developed in the 1960s and persists to this day, links poverty not to structural factors but to cultural and familial ones. For those such as J. D. Vance, Appalachia becomes a horror story of a culture that has failed to adapt to modernity and has been overly reliant on government subsidies.[1] Yet the current systems of inequality in the region are no different than those that exist within the rest of the United States. The history and recent socioeconomic indicators from a five-county area in rural Central Appalachia show what extractive industries and public and private disinvestment look like on the ground. One consequence of these forces is a spike in overdose deaths.

While OxyContin takes center stage in people's drug use narratives, benzodiazepines (or benzos) and methamphetamine (or meth) are primary actors as well. Current use is embedded in a decades-long story based on lack of access to quality health care and safe employment, unscrupulous pharmaceutical companies, and gendered inequalities. State and private institutions have respond to off-label pharmaceutical use in a variety of ways, determined by the individual user's class, gender, and race. Pharmaceutical companies found liable in court pay nominal fines in comparison to their profits. People of color as well as men in poverty are incarcerated at unfathomable rates.

The Hate Outside and Within

> Growing up here, you get the message very early on that your place is more backwards than anywhere in America and anybody worth much will get out soon as they can, and that doesn't come only from the outside.
>
> —Ann Pancake, *Strange as This Weather Has Been*

I did not expect to have to address Appalachian stereotypes so bluntly when I began my research. But when speaking to people about it, I became bombarded with questions about incest, poverty, and violence. In the popular imagination, Appalachia is an exceptional space for a variety of purposes, home of exploitive industries, such as timber and coal, and white nationalist identity.[2] Though culture of poverty arguments were first used to attack Black families and communities in the Moynihan Report, ideas from the culture of poverty have plagued Appalachia for decades.[3] Current politicians employ expressions like "generational poverty" and "cycles of poverty" to bolster ideologies that hold that pathological individual, family, and cultural practices cause poverty rather than any local, national, or global political and economic forces. Government subsidies for the poor are thus seen as exacerbating poverty by supporting pathological behaviors. What is too often ignored is that corporate entities, in Appalachia and across the United States, receive more government subsidies than any individual or community in poverty. In that sense, perhaps, subsidies support the pathological behaviors of entities that are considered persons in name only.

The culture of poverty model has too many proponents and applications to be homogenous. People learn the model through various forms that may appear fragmented but come together in different ways to influence understandings of the poor, work, and the family. These ideas are promoted in current scholarly and nonacademic works on the poor and on the Appalachia region by authors who characterize symptoms of poverty as causes of the problem and continue to privilege white elite narratives.[4]

Appalachia is a geography shrouded in blame. Rural Appalachia is blamed for causing poverty, substance use, and assault against women. When suburban areas are considered the norm, rural areas are coded as unregulated and incomprehensible. Health crises are seen as rooted in a combination of geography and culture, rather than financial and political processes. When a culture is characterized as inherent to a place, both the place and those within it are assumed to lack the ability to change.[5] Since OxyContin misuse first became widespread in the region in the late 1990s and early 2000s, parts of the news media as well the medical-scientific community blamed Appalachia for rising rates of prescription drug and opioid use across the United States. Presumed isolation, fear of outsiders, and dependence on government services, especially Medicaid, are taken as the causes of prescription opioid use. These narratives persist despite the investigations of Purdue Pharma's unethical marketing strategies, limited funding for primary health care, little to no mental health and substance use treatment, and industrial exploitation and disinvestment.

Despite economic and ethnic diversity, stereotypes about Appalachians as poor, white, and particularly drug addicted underlie the creation of some substance use treatment programs.[6] Constructions of whiteness confer privilege in the United States, including in Appalachia, but Appalachian whiteness is "marked" as representing inherited cruelty, sexual deviancy, and failed whiteness.[7] The media and government agencies' glorification of Appalachians because of their race and demonization of Appalachians because of their poverty contextualize characterizations of women as victims and perpetuators of a harmful but uniquely traditional culture.[8] Over time, this has lead to health education campaigns that target poor white Appalachian mothers and, more insidiously, promote forced sterilizations of these women.[9] Substance use treatment staff see women's place in rural Central Appalachia as hampering their ability to become good mothers and citizens. Presumptions about women's race because of their location also play into people's pleas for funding substance use treatment. Treatment is represented as saving white children, and incidentally, their parents too.

Appalachians are characterized as fatalistic, doing little to contest their marginalization. This alleged fatalism is a pathway to blame rural cultures or individuals for health problems, instead of examining the larger contexts that produce these conditions.[10] Using the idea of fatalism, state and nonstate actors are able to treat Appalachia as an area in need of intervention, but a type of intervention that can only be created and implemented by those who live outside of the region. Appalachians resist their marginalization, but this may go unseen, either because it occurs within hidden transcripts (the actions that take place off-stage) or is actively erased.[11] There are long traditions of collective activism for such issues as labor rights, land rights, alternatives to extractive industries, and better health and access to health care.[12]

Regional Economy

In an effort to move past assumptions about Appalachia, I briefly describe Central Appalachia's political economy. In contesting these stereotypes, my purpose is not to gloss over the realities, which can be harsh. Appalachia's isolation is overemphasized, at times to make the region appear more exotic or trapped in time.[13]

Yet Central Appalachia, no matter how rural, is intensely connected to the global political economy. How else could the prescription drug OxyContin, marketed by a Connecticut company, and the street drug methamphetamine, manufactured with materials from China, have taken hold of some residents?

The Appalachian Regional Commission (ARC) classifies the vast majority of counties in rural Appalachian Kentucky as economically "distressed." This is the worst category on a five-point scale and is based on unemployment, income, and poverty data.[14] The inclusion of greater numbers of global workers into the workforce has created an industrial shift out of the United States.[15] As in regions globally, neo-liberal forces in Appalachia have encouraged corporate deregulation, nonunionized workforces, decreased wages, and increased pressure on individuals and families, especially women, to take responsibility for safety-net services. Currently, employment in the formal sector that provides a living wage and benefits is limited, especially for women.[16] Factory jobs in Eastern Kentucky rely on just-in-time production and flexible schedules that make it difficult for people to plan for childcare or their household finances.[17]

While some in Appalachia have certainly prospered through time and wealth may have been in some periods more evenly distributed, there have always been racial and class divides, as shown in the Civil War and postwar guerrilla warfare as well as the labor conflicts in the late nineteenth through mid-twentieth centuries.[18] The polarized class economy that persists in rural Central Appalachia is rooted in a political economic context where white male elites, both from within and outside the region, have controlled politics and used local, and at times state and federal, governments to protect their material interests ever since the eighteenth century.[19] Elite land speculation in rural Central Appalachia beginning in the eighteenth century, including corporate absentee ownership, prevents economic diversification, drastically decreases local governments' tax bases, and thus limits the construction and maintenance of infrastructure.[20] The declining ability of subsistence agriculture in the late nineteenth century to support the Appalachian Kentucky population, in large part due to soil depletion and land scarcity, has led to an underemployed labor pool that could be exploited as cheap industrial labor in Appalachia as well as urban centers to which Appalachians migrated. Political corruption continues to create public institutions that cannot effectively address such issues as economic stagnation.[21]

The state has a large but inconsistent presence in Appalachia. At times it has supported industry and elite interests, going so far as to remove indigenous, African American, and poor white populations from lands as well as bombing workers in conflict with coal operators. Public and private institutions have embarked on "civilizing missions" into the mountains as well, which have often been rooted in eugenics, social Darwinism, and culture of poverty models.[22] In Appalachia as elsewhere, Christian missionaries were associated with social uplift and criminal rehabilitation and often predated or accompanied state economic development endeavors.[23]

Appalachia was at the heart of the 1960s War on Poverty, owing in no small part to the region's perceived whiteness. When the mere half-decade government campaign did not eliminate the poverty caused by nearly two centuries of exploitation and destruction, Appalachians became categorized as undeserving of aid because they allegedly wasted tax dollars.[24] Although created after the War on Poverty began, the federal ARC reflects similar concerns over the southern mountains. Since 1965, the ARC has invested billions of dollars in the region. Much of this spending has gone toward infrastructure such as sewer systems and broadband internet. The ARC is a consistent funder of socially progressive programs, including those focused on media arts, drug use prevention and recovery, and community wellness.

With even this brief history, it becomes difficult to attribute current regional failures to stigmatized individuals and families. Centuries of political and economic choices have coalesced to create the environment with which individuals must contend today.

A Local Picture

There is at times a cloud of grief or anxiety in some counties, which certainly presents itself in many of the narratives I explore. In the words of Mrs. Taylor, an older woman in Ann Pancake's novel who experienced the 1972 Buffalo Creek Disaster in Logan County, West Virginia, and lived below a mountain top removal site, "I try to stay off of the nerve medication . . . But this has turned into one nervous place."[25] This ecological catastrophe driven by greed and political ineptitude in many ways mirrors the persistent health catastrophe that is overdose deaths.

This anxiety in some ways presents itself as an intense out-migration, which has been occurring for decades in the counties I have called Adams, Douglas, Eagle, River, and Teller counties (the area of my research). Most people say they leave for higher education or employment; some just want to be in a city. The population density was just thirty-four persons per square mile in 2015, compared to Kentucky's 109 and the US average of ninety-one.[26] There are two small towns and a few more very small towns with one main street about two blocks long. The topography ranges from foothills and river valleys to mountains.

The counties remain primarily non-Latinx white, with 97 percent identifying as such in 2015.[27] Although I witnessed no direct personal conflicts over race or immigration, these issues haunted the area, just as they do the entire United States. The proliferation of Confederate flags in late summer 2015, and in one moment, a Nazi flag, after the white supremacist church shooting in Charleston, South Carolina, and increased visibility of the Black Lives Matter social justice movement is a demonstration of racial tensions in the area. Eastern Kentucky is purposively majority white, with whites having used terrorism to drive Black communities out of the region in the late nineteenth and twentieth centuries. Black populations in Appalachia are more urbanized than whites—hence arguments to concentrate federal or state funding in rural areas in fact privilege whites.[28]

The economic indicators are weak. Unemployment rates run high at around 10 percent.[29] The median household income is about $20,000 less than the Kentucky median and less than half of the US median. The percentage of persons below the poverty line is twice that of the nation. Around 40 percent of people live in poverty in the counties with the worst economic indicators.[30] Coal has been somewhat important in the five counties, but it has never been the primary employer. Currently, the area has five small coal mines. According to locals, extractive industries have been dominant, including timber, oil, salt, and iron. The land speculation and absentee ownership that accompanies these industries is ongoing. The area has an agricultural history based primarily in livestock and tobacco. All of these extractive industries, as well as tobacco farming, have decreased sharply in the last half-century. (One resource that continues to provide, albeit minimally for the families I spoke with, is the forest, where people collect geodes, ginseng, and other roots to sell.) At this time, most employment is in chain stores, local schools, and health care. Retail and fast-food locations offer low-wage employment. Jobs in health care run the gamut from low-wage, physically intense, entry-level positions at nursing homes to high-wage medical providers. Education jobs vary, from bus driver positions to administrators; education is seen as offering the most solidly "middle-class" employment.

The dire employment situation here was highlighted at a local job fair I attended. When I arrived, half of the tables where employers were supposed to be stood empty. A group of young men were trying to find those in charge to ask why employers who advertised did not attend. The vast majority of the staffed tables represented government agencies, telemarketing, or job placement. For the government jobs through DCBS or the Department of Corrections, people who have any criminal or civil records are unqualified. (The rate of incarceration in Kentucky is 869 per 100,000, compared to 698 per 100,000 nationally.[31]) The telemarketing jobs demand flexible hours, pay minimum wage, require certain telephone and internet connections (which may be unavailable in rural areas), and are unstable. The job placement agencies focus on temporary work, and most place people at least two hours away from the counties. I asked all employers if they accept those with past felonies or misdemeanors. Most said they tried to be flexible, but a few said no felonies, a few more said no violent crimes, and some said the person could not have any record at all. Most of the people I interviewed would not have qualified for any of these jobs because of their records, their lack of internet connections, or their inability to leave the counties for months on end because of their family, court, or treatment obligations.

Creating more jobs is the primary directive of all local politicians. Community leaders are working on economic development in the form of tourism and call centers that may perform telemarketing or serve as help desks. Both of these industries offer low-paying, unstable employment. Those who live outside the region often control tourist endeavors and generally employ college-age students who are on summer break from universities that are hours away. Despite the problems with these industries, the efforts of local leadership are important. They have seen what coal, prisons, and factories can do to a county. These industries may bring in employment for a little while, but the jobs are not great and are controlled by those who have no interest in the community. When they leave, the county is devastated. A natural gas fracking company was attempting to enter Adams County during my research; most community members were against the company. They did not cite environmental concerns, but concerns that the jobs being advertised are temporary and low-wage. Leaders desperately want locally owned small businesses that take the community into consideration, because if they fail, only a few jobs are lost. This has led to wide support of an entrepreneurship business model.

Other factors tied to income, such as food and housing, are primary stressors for families. The expense of rental housing is equivalent to more urban areas in central and northern Kentucky because of low availability. Housing affordability is exacerbated by the low median income. Most agencies consider housing unaffordable if households must spend more than 30 percent of their gross income on rent or a mortgage. Between 2011 and 2015, as much as 57 percent of renting households faced unaffordable housing in the five counties as compared to 52 percent of US households and 47 percent of Kentucky households.[32] During the same time period, a greater percentage of residents in the five counties lived in households where the mortgage was unaffordable (37 percent) as compared to Kentucky (26 percent) and the United States (33 percent). Rental housing is expensive and hard to find without personal connections. People who lack these connections are homeless or live in dilapidated conditions. Several I spoke with paid at least $200 a month for a trailer with no electricity or running water and large holes in the flooring, ceiling, and walls.

For the five counties, 37 percent of households utilize the Supplemental Nutrition Assistance Program (SNAP), as compared to 17 percent of Kentucky and 13 percent of US households.[33] Eligibility for SNAP in Kentucky is based on citizenship, work, wealth, and income requirements that shift according to household size. Despite SNAP qualification, 20 percent of residents lack adequate access to food.[34] Food remains difficult to get due to lack of local availability, and SNAP often does not cover everyone in the household who needs food assistance.

That many residents, whether living in poverty or not, rely on government monies through salaries or benefits creates complex relationships between people and government. At the local level, those working within state programs may follow state guidelines or deviate from those rules in ways that help or harm clients. Local communities often fight or support the state in unexpected and seemingly conflicting ways that may have more to do with the local face of an elected official or program than with state policies. Those in this five-county area expressed hostile feelings toward the government because they do not think the state is doing enough to curb substance use.

Local, quality health care remains a problem, but there has been a historical shift in services in the last five years. The US Health Resources and Services Administration designates the area as medically underserved and as health-professional-shortage areas for primary, mental health, and dental care. Depending on county of residence, the life expectancy in this area is six to nine years less than the national average.[35] Health-care reform is at the center of current debates in the United States regarding the role and effect of programs such as Medicaid: are they part of the state's responsibility for its citizens or do they create a corrosive dependence upon government. The 2010 Patient Protection and Affordable Care Act (ACA) expands health coverage to US citizens who previously did not have private health insurance, did not qualify for public health coverage under Medicaid, or were underinsured. The 2008 Mental Health Parity and Addiction Equity Act prevents health insurers from imposing stricter benefit limitations on mental health care and addiction services as compared to medical and surgical services.[36] This act along with the ACA provides access to forms of health care that were often not covered by previous private or public plans. Substance use and mental health treatment are now deemed "essential" and must be included in insurance offered through ACA marketplaces and Medicaid.

Kentucky decided to implement Medicaid expansion as part of the ACA, which went into effect on January 1, 2014. Prior to 2014, Kentucky Medicaid only covered substance use treatment for pregnant women and youth below the age of eighteen. With the expanded coverage, substance use treatment is covered for all Kentucky Medicaid members and those in ACA insurance exchanges. This coverage has greatly helped people who use drugs and those seeking treatment. The uninsured rate for opioid-related hospitalizations in Kentucky dropped 90 percent from 2013, the year before Medicaid expansion, to 2015, the year after implementation. During this same time period in Kentucky, there was a 700 percent increase in Medicaid beneficiaries being treated for substance use.[37]

The Kentucky governor at the time, Matt Bevin, successfully requested to modify expansion in order to institute sliding-scale monthly premiums, work requirements for adult Medicaid recipients, and up to six-month coverage lock-out periods if an adult fails to renew enrollment or to pay the premiums. Bevin also implemented removal of eligibility for nonemergency medical transportation to adults, which limits people's transportation access to mental health care and substance use treatment. Out of 462,000 Kentucky Medicaid enrollees, 95,000 are estimated to have been dropped because of failure to pay or not meeting employment requirements.[38] Of forty female participants in the current research, thirty-four had either Medicaid or private insurance through the ACA exchange. Only three had private insurance through their partner's or parents' insurance and one had Medicare. Only two were uninsured. Horizons staff informed me that, had my fieldwork been completed before implementation of Medicaid expansion and ACA, at least half would have been uninsured. This high uninsurance rate may return due to Governor Bevin's rolling back expansion in Kentucky.

Even for the insured, health-care access remains a constant problem. This lack of access is due in part to scarcity of providers and overburdened systems in rural areas, especially mental health systems. There are often extra administrative duties and more restricted formularies associated with Medicaid as opposed to strictly private insurance plans, which may result in fewer providers who accept Medicaid.[39] A majority of those I interviewed cannot afford the co-payments for health care or prescription medication. Others do not have transportation; some risk losing their jobs if they take time off work. Some avoid seeking care because of their negative experiences with providers.

People in this research have major health concerns, especially depression and anxiety, which they associated with poverty, intense care work (both paid and unpaid), domestic violence, and grief from the death of loved ones. Six had attempted suicide, four within the year previous to our interview. About a quarter experienced chronic pain from occupational injuries, car accidents, or injuries from domestic violence. Several were prescribed pain medications, and a few talked about selling some of their medications to survive financially. There is little access to nonopioid pain management in the area, such as physical therapy.

Almost a quarter said they test positive for acute hepatitis C. This is unsurprising given that Kentucky regularly has the highest rate in the nation. All said they contracted the virus through injection drug use. While all were concerned about having the virus, most attempted to ignore their status because there was no locally available treatment and they could not afford the treatment available an hour away. At the time of research, new hepatitis C treatments, including Harvoni and Zepatier, were in the news because of their costs (up to $94,500 for a treatment course).[40] Insurance providers were arguing that they should not have to pay for such a drug, especially for people who inject drugs and who may become reinfected with hepatitis C. People make do with no treatment, attempt to use new needles when they inject, and use bleach to clean their house to keep those they live with from contracting the virus. These strategies may be changing, as new syringe services programs opened through the health departments in four of the five counties in 2017.

The Persistent Overdose Catastrophe

I start this analysis of Purdue Pharma and OxyContin, a high-powered opioid prescription pain reliever, with a quote from a substance use treatment provider in Central Appalachia who was at the forefront of legal actions against Purdue by a coalition of treatment providers, physicians, people in recovery, and families of people who died of drug overdoses:

> Already Purdue Pharma was targeting communities where they could market OxyContin. And of course if you look at the way they were going to market it, they were going to market it right to communities like ours with a high Medicaid rate, a lot of legitimate pain because we have logging and the coal mine. Well they were

making hand over fist with money. They wanted to profit, profit, profit. So they were so upset about us that they flew in there, the director of Purdue, the medical director, the attorney, everybody on their staff came and asked if they could meet with a few of us here. So we did meet with them and of course their whole purpose was to sell their drug; like how important this was and so forth. They thought they would manipulate us and they were going to offer money to the community. Oh, it was just crazy; it's just like everybody else does for us. And anyway we met with them just to listen and of course they realized when they were with us, they were against a brick wall with us. Because they weren't moving us at all. We just kept challenging them because we were so angry.

Beginning in the 1980s, patients, clinicians, and researchers began to address issues of undertreated pain in the United States, especially non-malignant chronic pain. Through the 1980s and 1990s, a series of letters to the editor and opinion articles as well as recommendations from the American Pain Society shifted the medical culture in the country to view prescription opioids as beneficial to all pain patients, regardless of pain intensity, and unlikely to be abused. With this endorsement of prescription opioids, health insurance companies stopped funding more holistic pain treatments, such as occupational and psychological therapy, and increasingly covered opioids as opposed to nonopioid pharmaceuticals.[41] The milligrams of opioids prescribed in the United States increased dramatically due to more people being prescribed for longer periods of time and with higher doses.[42]

    With hindsight, but even with a lay understanding of addiction, this process of pain pharmaceuticalization seems unbelievable. The World Health Organization had been warning about the addictive capacity of oxycodone since 1957.[43] Why were clinicians eager to increase opioid prescriptions when evidence of addiction far outweighed the few opinion pieces and letters to the editor that stated otherwise? Part of this has to do with chronic pain being a complicated complaint that may require multiple forms of intervention, which is frustrating to patients as well as clinicians who are increasingly being given less time to work with patients by administrators and health insurance companies. There are few other options for chronic pain treatment in resource-poor areas, including Central Appalachia.

Enter the pharmaceutical companies. Companies may have close relationships with clinicians where they bestow economic rewards, produce clinical research knowledge, and provide access to this knowledge.[44] Rural providers in particular, located in small practices at a distance from research universities, may not have another avenue to access this expertise. Companies are more inclined to create new and expensive products focused on such issues as chronic pain because these patients have a chronic condition and many of them are insured.[45]

Marketing soon follows. Modern pharmaceutical advertising began in the 1950s with Arthur Sackler, whose family later bought Purdue Pharma. With Sackler's marketing of the first billion-dollar drug, Valium, drug companies heightened their investment in medications that address diseases with generalized symptoms, like anxiety, depression, and chronic pain. Through marketing, pharmaceutical companies and sales representatives often downplay the possible side effects and risks of prescription drugs to clinicians and patients in order to increase sales.[46] Exacerbating this phenomenon is that companies generally recommend the highest tolerable dose as the best standard of care.[47] Beyond clinicians, direct-to-consumer advertising has created an environment in which taking pharmaceuticals becomes a matter of personal choice where individuals demand and expect prescriptions when they visit their provider. Direct-to-consumer advertising, unique to the United States and New Zealand, dramatically increases drug consumption as compared to those countries that do not have the practice.[48] In terms of prescription opioids, lack of regulation for pharmaceutical development and marketing both served as an impetus to exploding opioid use as well as to exacerbate use once it began.[49] The trajectories of Purdue Pharma and, later, buprenorphine make this clear.

Purdue Pharma surpassed all marketing norms with OxyContin. At times, drug companies exploit human bodies for profit, as exemplified by Purdue Pharma's actions. Purdue aggressively marketed Oxy-Contin to clinicians in the United States by covering the expenses for more than five thousand physicians, nurses, and pharmacists to attend all-expenses-paid trips to resorts to learn about OxyContin. The company set up another twenty thousand free educational programs for physicians between 1996 and 2002, where Purdue continuously dismissed the addiction risk of OxyContin. Purdue provided physicians with over thirty-four thousand starter vouchers and coupons for OxyContin to give to patients.[50]

According to their own research with OxyContin, Purdue knew the addiction risk to be higher than it alluded to in its marketing.[51] The company could be confident from a history of weakly enforced regulations that its illegal marketing would be met with fines that could be considered part of its operating expenses in relation to the size of its profits. Purdue knowingly spread the false claim that the effect of OxyContin lasts twelve hours, which gave the drug a competitive edge over nonextended-release options. It reality, it generally relieves pain from four to eight hours; instant-release oxycodone is known to relieve pain from four to six hours. As part of this myth, Purdue encouraged prescribers to not decrease the time interval between pills but to increase the dosage of pills.[52]

OxyContin hit Appalachia hard in the early 2000s. Purdue Pharma's intensive and illegal marketing in the region led to higher rates of prescriptions for and increased use of OxyContin.[53] Currently, Kentucky's estimates of illicit drug use, nonmedical use of prescription pain relievers, and illicit drug dependence reflect national trends.[54] Yet the five-county area has elevated numbers relating to prescription opioid use and some of its consequences. The counties have some of the highest rates of opioid prescriptions per capita in the United States.[55] From 2006 to 2015, deaths due to drug overdose stood at 42 per 100,000, more than triple the national rate of 13 per 100,000.[56]

As noted by advocates for harm reduction and for the rights of people who use drugs, the problem here is not necessarily use but rather overdose deaths. With these increased deaths in the area over the past two decades, it's not really an epidemic or a crisis—it's an ongoing catastrophe. This catastrophe reveals failures on several fronts and will not be undone until particular actions are taken.

Prescription drugs, primarily prescription opioids and benzos, have been the main drug used in the area for at least fifteen years. While these drugs are created licitly, they travel through underground networks as illicit drugs. Treatment program clients argued that as the number of increasingly expensive prescription drugs dwindles due to tighter regulations, people begin using other drugs—primarily meth or bupe—they can obtain through illegal and legal networks.

I asked women which drugs they used most often. Of the forty I interviewed, twenty-eight named prescription opioids. Around five each said meth, cannabis, benzos, and alcohol. A few more named cocaine, heroin, and crack. About half had injected drugs. Five did not name a substance because they said they were never addicted to anything, but only used cannabis or prescription opioids occasionally. Several continued to use cannabis, primarily because it helped with their anxiety and they regarded it as a drug that should be legal in Kentucky, as it is in other states. None of the women I talked to said they were currently taking illicit prescription opioids. Three were taking meth and two were injecting illicit bupe at the time of our interview.

Pharmaceuticals in the form of prescription opioids and benzos remain a primary component of drug use in the area, but in some ways the past use is as important as the current market. Even those who primarily prefer meth, cannabis, or other drugs still use pharmaceuticals from time to time. Most of those who identify as users of meth, cocaine, and heroin ingested pharmaceuticals long before they moved to these drugs. One woman exemplifies how OxyContin changed people's drug use:

What really got me, when I was taking just the Percocet [acet-
aminophen/oxycodone], I took them as prescribed for three years
straight. If I missed one, I wouldn't even realize I missed it. One
day I was out of Percocet and me and this person went and got an
OxyContin. We snorted it and ever since, I was pain free for three
days, my body was numb, I had energy, I couldn't sleep. I was like a
wired animal. When I crashed, I crashed. That pill made me feel so
good. I was like, I need that today. When I look back, if I had never
done that, I might not have gotten on those pills.

Without minimizing the effects of OxyContin marketing, other
factors contextualize use in Central Appalachia. According to a few
treatment providers, prescription pain relievers have been widely
used for decades in the region due to the activities of another unscrupulous industry. Coal company doctors would prescribe pain
relievers to miners to keep them working instead of addressing underlying health concerns, which may have required more expensive
and extensive treatment. This indicates that overuse of prescription
pain relievers may simultaneously be tied to lack of access to certain
types of medical care.

This pharmaceuticalization of health, where health is equated
with access to prescription medications, is a global phenomenon
pushed by transnational corporations.[57] A focus on prescribing and
consuming pharmaceuticals downplays the ways in which housing,
food insecurity, and economic inequalities alter health.[58] Pharmaceuticals make money for a corporation; these other issues are not
(or not as) profitable. Yet pharmaceuticalization is not evenly distributed. There are more prescription opioids among whites because they
are more likely to have the health insurance to attain prescriptions.[59]
Those with health insurance may have abundant access to pharmaceuticals that are part of insurance drug formularies, while uninsured
or underinsured people may not be able to afford medications they
are prescribed. Pain also goes undertreated among people of color,
so this group is less likely to have prescriptions for opioids, even for
legitimate concerns.[60]

The people I spoke with who had mental health concerns were especially frustrated. For conditions such as depression or bipolar disorder, lengthy experimentation may be required to find the drugs that work best for the individual. If the most appropriate medication is not on their insurance drug formulary, they may be left with a drug that has unbearable side effects, including addiction. Several women were prescribed benzos for a host of mental health issues because their insurance did not cover other options for their diagnosis. One woman was prescribed a selective serotonin reuptake inhibitor that was not covered by her insurance, so she did not take the $600-a-month medication. Another was prescribed the antidepressant bupropion, but did not have transportation to renew her prescription with a clinician or to a pharmacy. Instead, she took her neighbor's bupropion, which he did not use. (After telling me this, she laughingly said, "Sharing is caring.")

Sometimes people feign pain to acquire pills. People who use drugs have told me stories of paying prescribers large sums of cash to obtain pharmaceuticals. They offer tales of lengthy road trips driving around the Southeast and Midwest to find profuse prescribers and loosely regulated pharmacies. I have heard one narrative repeatedly, of people driving to a Deep South state to get a prescription and then up to a northern midwestern state to have it filled. More often than adventure stories, though, are those of car accidents, surgeries, occupational accidents, and untreated or mistreated mental health issues, which lead to people's use.

Researchers, clinicians, law enforcement, and prosecutors agree that the entrance of OxyContin onto the market intensified drug use in Appalachia.[61] Not only did Purdue Pharma make profits from OxyContin, but companies, including Purdue, make money from the pharmaceuticals used to treat substance use and one of the primary comorbidities to it, hepatitis C. This persistent catastrophe is a neoliberal story, where corporations are underregulated, the poor are overregulated, financial gains are privatized, and financial and human losses are socialized. I may contest the idea of cycles of poverty in Appalachia, but there are certainly running patterns in the region. The cycles here are more akin to corporate misdeeds, low-quality services, private and public disinvestment, and (ultimately) bad outcomes.

Federal and Local Responses

Courts have ordered pharmaceutical companies to pay stiff fines for their roles in creating the crisis, but even steep fines pale in comparison to the profits they reap. As of 2017, Purdue and its top three executives had paid $654.5 million in fines for downplaying OxyContin's risk for diversion and abuse; their OxyContin revenues had totalled around $31 billion.[62] Kentucky, along with other Appalachian states, sued Purdue. The Sackler family, which owns Purdue, is in negotiations with local and state governments to settle over two thousand additional lawsuits against the company, yet the results are unclear as of mid-2019.[63] In 2017, two large drug distributors, Cardinal Health and McKesson Corporation, and several small distributors agreed to pay hundreds of millions of dollars in fines to the federal government and Central Appalachian states for failing to report suspicious pain medication orders to the Drug Enforcement Agency (DEA).[64] An Oklahoma judge ordered Johnson & Johnson in 2019 to pay $572 million for its role in opioid use.[65] Law enforcement has closed pharmacies and jailed doctors for overprescribing or misprescribing pain relievers. These actions are not unique to Appalachia; evidence indicates similar pharmaceutical company and drug distributor misconduct in Maine and on Cherokee Nation lands in Oklahoma.[66] Individuals outside of the pharmaceutical industry are those who are truly criminalized. People who use drugs are seen as the problem, whereas pharmaceutical companies are seen as having a problem drug.[67]

The War on Drugs is linked to moral arguments that individualize drug use, criminalize people of color and the poor, and support diminishing social services. Increased US incarceration rates are not a response to more crime (which actually decreased), but rather to the marginalization of populations through the withdrawal of welfare

services and the restructuring of work.[68] The disappearance of many
social services does not signal the withdrawal of the state. Instead, the
government spends public dollars on penal institutions and welfare
entitlements for the rich rather than services for the poor.[69] Government services that are available have become more punitive. Intense
surveillance, interrogation, and sanctions have spread to welfare offices and beyond.[70]

Individualized understandings of drug use are consequential
throughout the United States. Over fifty years ago, Howard Becker
argued that deviance is not about individual behavior, but about how
those in power publicly label other's behaviors as wrong and act upon
those labels.[71] This othering process is an assault. Policies based on
stereotypes of people who use drugs that do not acknowledge the
context in which they use drugs isolate people through application of
stigma.[72] Stigma threatens people's abilities to engage in activities that
make them feel like moral persons, such as caretaking, employment,
and spirituality. Stigma thus threatens an individual's personhood. At
the same time, rebuttals to stigma often include people attempting to
remain engaged in those activities.[73] People may not seek treatment
services in order to avoid stigma.[74] With such pronounced societal
stigma, substance use treatment is underfunded and often overlooks
inequalities clients face, such as unemployment and homelessness.[75]

The government deals with people who use drugs differently
based on race, class, gender, and place. Substances that have been
associated with people of color are harshly regulated. Even though
the word lacks specificity, I use the term "cannabis" in this book because prohibitionists created the term "marijuana" to link the drug
with people from Mexico. Prohibitionists correctly assumed this la-
beling would lead to cannabis illegalization. For years, I have heard
federal, state, and local law enforcement refer to drugs used in Appalachia as "Mexican" meth or "Mexican" heroin, without explanation
of distribution networks or end users. It is not a coincidence that a
few weeks before the Immigration and Customs Enforcement raids

in Morristown, Tennessee, on April 5, 2018, I heard a local substance use treatment provider rail against "Mexican" meth and immigrants.

Crack has become notoriously racialized. While cocaine and crack have similar effects on the body, crack use and distribution are more heavily punished because crack is identified with poor African Americans and cocaine with rich whites. Prior to the 2010 Fair Sentencing Act, there was a 100:1 ratio disparity in prosecuting crack versus powder cocaine federal infractions; now it is 18:1. As opioids have reached increasing numbers of white people, treatment has come to be seen as the answer to drug use rather than incarceration.[76]

Economic class and division of labor affect how drug use is understood. Working-class drug use is blamed on individual moral failure, and upper-middle-class drug use is blamed on a broken system that requires owners and high-wage employees to overextend themselves.[77] Yet the poor and minorities face the brunt of punishment for their supposed individual failures, while no one is significantly punished for creating and perpetuating a broken system.

Gender intersects with class-based inequalities to affect women's experiences of substance use. Women more often face sexual and domestic assault, become involved in drug economies because of their lower wages in the formal sector, and face more sharply critical public opinion and interventions assigned to those who are responsible for childbearing.[78] Women in several states have been prosecuted and imprisoned for using drugs while pregnant.[79] Before the law sunset, prosecutors and law enforcement systematically jailed Tennessee women who were pregnant and tested positive for drugs, explicitly punishing those who have the ability to become pregnant more than those who do not. Women differentially experience gendered oppression based on their class, ethnicity, and role in the drug economy.[80] Women of color are more likely to be arrested, charged with drug-related crimes, and serve more time as compared to white women.[81]

Incarceration is often catastrophic for individuals, families, and communities. Incarceration creates debt, as inmates accrue court fees and child support arrears. Inmates cannot have meaningful employment while incarcerated and are often prevented from ever attaining a job that pays a living wage due to felony records. Mass incarceration strains the care networks of vulnerable communities, limiting navigations of economic and social injustices.[82] Prisons and jails produce bad community outcomes in the places they are located through numerous pathways, from providing low-wage and dangerous employment to burdening local infrastructure.[83] These facilities are located in low-income urban and rural areas. Other forms of state intrusion may also be damaging. All of the forms of state intervention I describe are targeted at people who are already on the fringes. These interventions more often than not exacerbate their low social positions and limited material resources.

Although federal guidelines and national rhetoric shape responses to drug use, state governments and local actions matter. Kentucky policy makers responded to OxyContin misuse with a number of initiatives, including the introduction of Kentucky All Schedule Prescription Electronic Reporting (KASPER). The KASPER prescription monitoring program was established to collect data on the dispensing of scheduled prescription drugs through pharmacies and other providers in order to expose overprescribers and so-called "doctor shoppers," people who elicited prescriptions from multiple clinicians. Additional initiatives and programs abide by Kentucky's law enforcement, treatment, and prevention/education three-pronged approach. All of these responses are focused on the individual, whether through incarceration or educating grade school students. For the counties, most government and private actions are defined by a lack of resources. Service providers and some clients say the intensive outpatient model available through Horizons, drug court, and bupe programs does not address the needs of many who are just ceasing drug use. This model is really better as a maintenance model after people have sought detoxification services and inpatient treatment. Detoxification programs are located two to three hours away from the five counties. According to Horizons staff and those who have tried to access such services, waiting lists vary from a few days to a few months, and people are often denied service after they have already traveled hours to the program.

For people who use drugs in Adams County, the closest inpatient treatment is located two hours away. Kentucky facilities generally have multimonth waiting lists, and many programs do not accept Medicaid because of low reimbursement rates or delayed reimbursement for services. There are only two treatment programs in the state where women can bring their children. Several providers said that people were not willing to leave their county to seek inpatient treatment. Several women said they would leave if they could get into a treatment program that accepted their insurance and allowed them to bring their children. Others chose to access services outside of their home community so neighbors and family did not see them going into particular buildings.

Neighborhood location and race are the primary determinants of state surveillance in urban areas. In rural Central Appalachia, stigma that is attached to individuals based on their reputations, which often begin construction in elementary or middle school, and their family's reputation, which may go back generations, defines interactions with local government officials. People who use drugs argue and service providers concede that DCBS, law enforcement, and judges repeatedly target certain individuals because of their family's "bad name" or because of their past. Community employers refuse to hire people based on their (or their family's) reputation, even if they do not have a criminal record and have not used drugs for years. One woman told me that after an arrest, one is more likely to be arrested again and that harassment is ongoing: "There for a long time, after I straightened up, I kept getting pulled over every time I came to town because I have a bad name. And it was constant. The police down there have certain people they just hate."

All of those I spoke with are stigmatized because they have used drugs *and* are going through a program for it. This indicates to the community that they must have been using enough to get into trouble. Some said they were using a lot and consider themselves addicted. By all accounts, others just got caught in hard situations and happened to test positive for something once. Women embody the stigma associated with female drug use and are further stigmatized because of the marks inscribed on their bodies. Some of these marks are directly tied to substance use, like track marks on the arm from injection drug use. Other marks are identified with drugs but often have more to do with other issues. Sissy, whose stories appear repeatedly in the following chapters, is missing most of her teeth. Community members automatically assume that she is on meth and are not shy to tell her this. She defines herself as being addicted to opioids but insists that she has never touched meth. She said her teeth rotted because she never had fluoridated water or access to dental care.

In the sociopolitical context of people's lives, their families, communities, and the state scrutinize their bodies. People who use drugs but do not inject continually degrade people who inject for wearing long-sleeves in the summer to cover track marks. Since the local jail uniforms are short-sleeved, one woman described the "walk of shame going to court with track marks" when inmates are walked from the jail transfer vans into the courthouse. Once you take that walk, the entire community knows you inject. Ashley feels that she is treated differently by health care providers, particularly when her arm is used as a teaching tool:

> I'm thankful I ain't got track marks, but I tell you what, I went to the hospital right after I stopped using and I had track marks. There was a nurse who asked if she could bring a training nurse in so she could look at my track marks and see what they looked like. And one of them was actually just a sore where I had scratched you know, I told you I get nervous and scratch, and she had thought it was a track mark. I just let her do her thing because she was trying to teach and I'm totally for teaching, but yeah, I think people treat me different.

Most detrimentally, law enforcement and DCBS regard track marks as proof of drug use. Several people are pulled over frequently, just so the police can examine their arms. DCBS threatens people with child removal if they notice track marks on mothers or pregnant people, even if the marks have scarred. Ashley told me about a time when she was examined by her DCBS caseworker at Horizons: "[The caseworker] showed up today and I had to show her my arms, like, 'Look, there ain't no marks, I promise you, I'm not doing it.' But I had to take my socks off and show her my feet and everything. You talk about embarrassing."

Overall, local officials and state agency workers blamed opioid use on individual behaviors and Appalachian cultural values they see as destructive. The local DCBS administrator connected drug use with laziness and reliance on disability as well as a loss of the cultural values of hard work and noble suffering. This creates a situation in which she ignores the harm that emanates from cuts to government services. I asked her about diminishing government welfare programs: "Yeah, you know what? People know how to survive, with limited income that they have. They just know how to survive. They'll come out on top."

Others link drug use to lack of education and an Appalachian culture that does not value it. When I asked a Horizons clinician if education level is an issue, she said that lack of education causes poverty and drug use. She went on to blame individuals, families, and "Appalachian" cultural values for this deficiency:

> They don't have a GED [General Equivalency Diploma]. Some of them don't even have the intellect to pass a GED so you have got people dropping out of school early because of the poverty; because of their families probably not encouraging them to go. They don't have any kind of degrees or education and they'll tell them, I've heard it more than once, several, a whole lot of times; you know, "Go out and get your own check now. You're 19, 18, you need to get your own check now." And so it's a generational thing of staying on disability or Social Security.

Several DCBS administrators and Horizons clinicians blamed women's marginalization on their lack of intellect, which for them is rooted in harmful Appalachian cultural practices and genetics.

This idea that education in itself will save Appalachia is not new.[84] Some strands of public health have a history of focusing on education rather than social or environmental factors, including in Appalachia.[85] Every single woman I spoke with except one wanted an education and all hoped their children would make it to college. The single exception does not have (or want) her GED, she has severe dyslexia, and she is one of the few women I interviewed who consistently has full-time employment with benefits. She does not see benefit in a GED for herself. But hers was a lone opinion: overall, the women and their families valued education.

Gatekeepers characterized drug use in other individualized ways, at times playing into Appalachian stereotypes. Service providers and most clients agree that lack of available jobs that pay a living wage is a large motivator for entering the illicit drug economy. Inversely, local Adams County politicians blame drug users for industries not relocating to the area. They said the employers do not think they can find enough local workers to pass drug tests. Blaming certain sectors of the community for lack of private investment is certainly not unique to Appalachia, and people who use drugs often become the national scapegoats. One employer in a non-Appalachian urban area said she no longer hired anyone from Eastern Kentucky because she assumed they used drugs. Others connect drug use to the stereotyped inherent lawlessness of Appalachians. Horizons staff members showed clients the film *The Wild and Wonderful Whites of West Virginia*, which outlines members of a family who are all involved in illegal behaviors, in an attempt to explain drug use in the area.

In this place, people are incarcerated based on their drug use as well as their class and reputation. Yet their gender and ethnicity often turn encounters with the state from incarceration into encounters with DCBS and substance use treatment. Their positions as mothers to white children qualifies them for this shift. One of the state's most damaging responses to substance use is the criminalization of people who use drugs. Though my research and interview questions were centered on substance use treatment, women at times recentered the conversations on law enforcement, incarceration, and DCBS.

Encounters with law enforcement and DCBS generally precede treatment. These state responses have several characteristics in common. The criminal processing system, DCBS, and substance use treatment in this area rely on punitive measures. They are all intrusive, focused on personal responsibility, and profoundly underfunded and understaffed. The rhetoric of personal responsibility and noncompliance forecloses the possibility of people explicitly and openly critiquing agencies, yet these agencies create underground and often unorganized networks of resistance. These programs blur lines between sanction and access to desirable and useful services, from material resources to counseling.

In the end, people who are mired in inequalities are swept into institutions that are marginalized and marginalizing. Even when people accept the discourse of personal responsibility, they nonetheless feel stuck in these systems, as expressed by one woman when I asked her about experiences with government agencies:

> Well, I done everything to get myself in the messes I've been in. You know it's nobody's fault than my own. But my God, it seems like once you've been through this, where do you go for help? Like right now, I'm clean, my husband, he could pass a drug test, but how do I go about getting my kids back? [crying] I mean I just don't know where to pick up and go.

Despite the often times softer rhetoric applied to whites who use drugs, those in the five counties may have more frequent contact with the criminal processing system as compared to other Kentuckians. In examining jail incarceration rates in 2015, the rate in the counties was 865 per 100,000, compared to 665 in Kentucky and 326 in the United States.[86] Of the forty, fourteen women with whom I spoke had served time at the Adams regional jail and eight were incarcerated at another county or regional jail. The regional jail is located in Adams County and imprisons women in all the counties except one. The regional jail, according to women who have been incarcerated at various facilities, is comparable to other county jails. Women are sent to the regional jail during pretrial and presentencing periods if they have not posted bail. Generally, if they are sentenced to less than one year of incarceration, no matter the charge, they are kept at the regional jail. For sentences longer than one year, they may be sent to state or federal facilities, depending on the charge.

The gatekeepers to the jail are local police. Like other programs in the area, police departments are underfunded and continuously have positions cut or remain unfilled after a retirement. Reflecting trends across the country, these departments are controversial. One police department paid hundreds of thousands of dollars for a settlement in a brutality case the year before my research. During my research, a fiscal court judge had an editorial published in the county newspaper critiquing the police department for using excessive force on inmates when the police were bringing them into court.

Only two clients I spoke with and one Horizons peer support had been to prison. All three had also been to county or regional jails. They agreed that prison has better conditions than regional or county jails because you receive more medical and substance use treatment services and are allowed to be outside. At the regional jail, incarcerated women are locked down in their cells almost twenty-four hours a day. Inmates have no outside time and are only allowed out of their cells for brief visitations. Male inmates are allowed outside for work release. Service providers, especially those in drug court, talk about incarceration as a moment that can be a "rock bottom" for people that forces them to change. Only three women talked about incarceration in this way.

For most, the regional jail exacerbates their marginalized positions in numerous ways. People lose housing and income streams while incarcerated, must pay booking and drug screening fees, and live in crowded and unhealthy conditions. One woman I met who eventually entered drug court lost a factory job that paid a living wage and her house went into foreclosure when she was incarcerated for a nonviolent drug offense. Like others who had been incarcerated, she was disenrolled from SNAP when she was imprisoned and had difficulty reenrolling. She described the regional jail as "nasty" and has insisted on being regularly tested for HIV and hepatitis C since she was released. Several women living in her pod disclosed their hepatitis C status to the other inmates with which they shared close quarters in an effort to prevent transmission. She practiced tattooing within the jail as an economic survival strategy. She used the money to pay for her court fees and toiletries and food items in the jail commissary.

"The jail has killed us." That was the response of the Adams County fiscal court judge when I asked him about county services. The jail uses most of the local budget. Adams County government has had to reduce budgets for every program funded through the county to pay for inmates, including the budgets for county roads, parks, and schools. The judge said he would like the county government to do more in terms of substance use treatment and housing, but their funding is going to the jail.

According to drug court staff, clients, and the local newspapers, the regional jail generally has a quarter to a third more inmates than it is built to house. None of those who were incarcerated received any substance use treatment, psychiatric services, or job training or placement while in Adams County jail. The most extensive health care that is regularly applied is people being given the medication they are already prescribed prior to incarceration. Some people, if they know the guards, may receive acetaminophen, clonidine, and the antihistamine diphenhydramine to help with withdrawal symptoms. Yet people are often prevented from taking their prescriptions, like medication for hypertension. During my research, the local newspaper reported that a man died at the jail because he did not receive timely medical care for a ruptured spleen. Most people are scared to go to the regional jail because they fear they will die or at least get sick there.

One woman who had a court date approaching with almost certain jail time following was visibly shaking when she told me about going back to the jail. She listed a number of deaths there, including two women who died of overdoses. Her father died at the jail in the early 1990s. He was in his early thirties, and jail officials told her family that he died of a sudden heart attack. She was later told by several people, including a former corrections officer, that her father was injected with something and then died. She remained convinced that a jail staff member murdered her father. A research assistant who works with many individuals incarcerated in county and regional jails throughout Eastern Kentucky told me that people simply do not get health care at jails until they are dying. She attributed this lack of care to inadequate funding as well as general disregard for inmate well-being. She knew several women who had hysterectomies because they had infections that went untreated for years while incarcerated, despite their complaints of pelvic pain. She worked with another woman who had complained about being sick for well over a year before she received health care. The woman was diagnosed with stage IV cancer and died within two weeks of diagnosis.

People develop strategies that involve using their kin for making it through the criminal processing system. Most have family members transfer money into the commissary while they are jailed, so they have access to better foods and toiletries. If people know they will not be allowed to take their prescribed medication, especially bupe, they or their family will smuggle the medication in. Within some kin networks, if one person is arrested, then someone who has an outstanding warrant will turn themselves in so they can serve their time together.

Once released, people must find housing and employment, often through their family. Joining statewide social justice organizations is also a strategy after release. Frustration can motivate larger scale social action beyond individual navigation. When I asked Alisha about convicted felons not having the right to vote in Kentucky unless they petition the governor for the restoration of that right on a case-by-case basis, she said:

> I disagree one hundred percent. So what I feel doesn't matter? I have never missed a vote until I became a felon. It really bothers me. Now you can apply for your voting rights back. I will go to the steps of Frankfort and picket for my rights to vote. When I called Frankfort, the lady told me it was a procedure like having a child, but none of the good things. She said, "It's all of the bad things."

When I spoke with her a few months later, Alisha had joined a statewide social justice organization to campaign for felon voting rights. In 2017, this organization successfully convinced groups of legislators in the Kentucky House of Representatives and Senate to draft bills to restore felon voting rights more easily. While these bills have been successful in the House, they continue to fail in the Senate.[87]

Incarceration is not the beginning of anyone's story, and it is rarely the end. People come from and go back into communities and care networks. Six women's stories with drug use reveal where it began with them, and I tended to catch them in the midst of their dealings with a related state agency that is no less steeped in prejudiced understandings of Appalachia, poverty, and motherhood than the criminal processing system.

Chapter 2
Facing the State

S tereotypes as well as attempts to use incarceration and pharmaceuticals to treat a spectrum of social ills rely on flattening human experience. I offer a few in-depth stories as a political gesture meant to complicate individual lives and the institutions where they take place. "Institutions" refers to state or quasi-state agencies within which women are located, primarily substance use treatment and DCBS, as well as familial institutions. By examining family, I don't want to reify the positions women at times hold in the family, but instead question these positions and what they come to mean for people.

Women who use drugs and Appalachian women are often presented as unable to produce anything meaningful, such as ideas for policies and programs. These stories thus serve a second purpose. They highlight the value of women's experiences, beliefs, and theorizing. The people whose narratives follow provided me space to work through ideas and ask questions in ways that would be impossible in others spaces. I ran theories past three of the women who are introduced in this chapter (Sissy, Alisha, and Katie). They provided constructive criticism that challenged me to rethink assumptions. While these narratives display common themes heard throughout my research, they are not definitive examples of what it means to be a woman who uses drugs in rural Appalachia. No one is, which is why policies determined to generalize based on stigmatized identities are ineffective. Some people are more articulate than others, and those I outline below more often have this gift. I also tended to spend more time with these six people, which means I had heartier stories.

Their introductions here begin in the same way our interviews began, with stories of their drug use. In this setting, people have limited access to formal employment. The available positions are often physically and psychologically straining, whether they are being hired as caregivers in nursing homes or as correctional officers. Work in the home, often caring for children, elderly family members, and partners, is no less intense. People do not have adequate access to medical care for common health concerns or occupational injuries. When they are able to seek health care, they are generally prescribed pharmaceuticals and offered no other health or social services.

OxyContin and buprenorphine are the drugs people talk about in this area, whether it is community members, clinicians, or people who use drugs. Some "street" drugs have been available in rural Eastern Kentucky for decades, especially cannabis and meth. Despite increasing meth use, OxyContin remains at center discursively. During this research, most people had not used OxyContin for nearly five years. The pill was reformulated in 2010 to make it harder to break down for inhalation and injection. People who used prescription opioids illicitly quickly replaced the controlled-release OxyContin with instant-release oxycodone pills, which continue to be one of the main drugs on the street. Drug use originates in bodies and relationships. The consequences of drug use are found within these sites as well.

Women's encounters with the state are often experienced through a motherhood identity. The people in this study have access to programs specifically designed for mothers with substance use problems. These programs are rooted in a history of state interventions in the lives of Appalachian women, who are presumed to be white and poor. The primary purpose of these interventions has been to save white children, not necessarily to relieve the suffering of adults living in poverty. While women who have children may be uniquely eligible for some programs, state-sponsored sanction through DCBS is particularly leveled at mothers.

I witnessed negative characterizations of women who use drugs among community members and service providers. These characterizations were often articulated through discussions of neonatal abstinence syndrome. Ideas surrounding women who use drugs, Appalachian women, the culture of poverty, addiction as a moral failure, and addiction as a brain disease culminated to produce characterizations of Appalachian mothers who use drugs as genetically and morally flawed beings who are chronic victims of trauma and perpetuators of addiction and poverty. While I do not deny women's experiences of trauma, simply treating women who use drugs as victims or as "bad" mothers is reductionist and unhelpful. In these ways, being a mother can carry risks of state intrusion, but women have also used this identity as a source of power to challenge marginalization. The care that flows through relationships, between parents and children but also between people and all those for whom they care, is strength.

Stories of Substance Use

Writing about drug use is a tricky thing, especially in Appalachia. Some tend to be fascinated with the things they find damaging or even disgusting. There is a long history of photographers in, and sometimes of, the mountains taking staged pictures to emphasize the supposed degraded peculiarity of Appalachians. These types of images, along with depictions of decrepit homes and cars, continue to populate articles and blog posts about the five counties. These images are certainly not unique to the region. Certain organizations thrive off "poverty porn," showing emaciated children of color in an undisclosed place that is understood to be far from the United States, both geographically and politically. Similar pictures and descriptions litter blogs and articles on drug use as well—images of adults overdosing in a West Virginia car, while a child screams in the backseat, brightly lit snapshots of a newborn who has been exposed to alcohol.

These images dehumanize, victimize, and sanitize. Descriptions that focus entirely on drug use risk doing the same thing. One of the ideas in the Federal Bureau of Investigation and DEA documentary *Chasing the Dragon: The Life of an Opiate Addict* is that people who use drugs are inhuman.[1] They may have been human before they began use and while in long-term recovery, but when using, they are anything but. People in these images, whether identified as Appalachian or as people who use drugs, are characterized as victims, doing little to change anything. They are in need of outside intervention by an organization that changes individual selves, that "uplifts." They are not, however, victims of anything or anyone but themselves or their families. The context of their lives is sanitized, scrubbed clean of any structural violence.

When first entering the realm of drug use, the use itself seems like an exotic ritual, hence all the snapshots of arms with needles hanging out of them. This ritual is worth understanding because it leads to important methods of harm reduction. Yet the ritual becomes quickly mundane, and everything that is happening around it become the pieces that matter. Drug use may only be a small part of the story, and I present it as exactly that here. People are using in the context of ongoing family dynamics, policy changes, and economic shifts. There are interventions targeted at people who use drugs in an effort to alter use. Law enforcement and DCBS are usually the first agencies people come in contact with. By going beyond use and documenting how people interact with the agencies that are trying to change them, I take a step back from these still images to see the staging. There are systems of violence that stifle programs and everyone in them, removing any predisposition to view these stories as sanitized. Clients, and arguably many staff, are trying their best to do what they can, making emotional and rational decisions that are in every way human.

Sissy: Strength in Relationships

The person I refer to as Sissy exemplifies the name. Sissy is a mostly southern colloquialism for sister. While Sissy may be used in many families, especially when children are young, I have found that the name generally survives to adulthood for those who show a cheerful warmth to folks beyond their household. The name for me connotes affection that is easily won, but not without wisdom of who will reciprocate. Unfortunately the name turns derogative when applied to men. Female strength becomes male weakness where care and care work is undervalued.

A Horizons case manager gave Sissy my number, and she reached out within a few days. Sissy and her family live in a singlewide trailer. A winter storm made it seem like night the first day I arrived at her house. As I scrambled inside the trailer with a puppy at my heels through pouring rain, I was thankful for the comfort I found inside. Once I visited with Sissy through the seasons, I realized her home was an enormous resource for her family, including nearly one hundred acres of inherited land with a large garden, a few barns, waterfalls, and walking trails. I do not include these details to glorify some bucolic other, but to emphasize Sissy's land resources.

We were always accompanied by her infant and then toddler daughter, a puppy turned dog, and a few cats. While these could be seen as distractions, they proved quite the opposite. If not for her daughter, we would not have spent as much time discussing caretaking strategies and providing for children on one low-income job. If not for the dog, I would have missed the conversation on how Sissy's neighborhood relationships and gardening techniques are centered around dogs more than anything else. Sissy did not shy away from detailing her self-defined problems, but she also highlighted the happy coincidences she saw in her life. Her youngest daughter and puppy, for example, were born on the same day.

Sissy's drug use was rooted in a relationship. She started using with a previous husband who she met and lived with in central Kentucky.

> But he was the one, he would be doing whatever and say, "Hey do some of this, it will make you feel better" when I was having a draggy day. He did whatever he could get his hands on, whether

it was an OxyContin, speed, cocaine, crank [meth]. Three or four years we were together, because there's a lot of ups and downs when you're doing that kind of stuff, we would split up and get back together. I won't say that he didn't love me, and I loved him, but nobody's going to survive doing that kind of stuff, but that is what got me, and I'm not blaming it on him, I take full responsibility for it, but that is what lead me into being an everyday user.

She ended that relationship and found support and stability with her natal family, her new husband, and their infant daughter.

Ashley: Complexity of Concerns without Support

Ashley's narrative reveals the complexities people must face when attempting to navigate a multitude of issues, including addiction, mental health concerns, domestic violence, and social isolation. I met Ashley at Horizons and went to her house a few days later for our first interview. Dogs dominated the first moments of our interaction, as I had to first avoid running over a pack and then had to sprint from them to make it into her house without being bitten. Ashley barely leaves her house anymore for fear of the neighbor's half-dozen dogs. She used to walk to neighbors' houses and to church, until she was bitten twice. She blames the dogs for her loss of connection to the neighborhood because she no longer feels safe walking to visit other people or attend events.

I had a hard time keeping up with Ashley, both physically and mentally. In the half-dozen times I was at her house, she ran from room to room and subject to subject. She was sometimes trying to give me objects, like books or clothes. She was sometimes showing me that she had enough resources for her children. At other times she was revealing bare cabinets to convince me that we needed to go to the food banks, and quickly. When I first met her, our relationship became a bit exhausting, with late night phone calls and last minute requests. Then she started a new romantic relationship, and I did not hear from her very often.

Ashley grew up in a single-parent home with a mother who was diagnosed with bipolar disorder. Ashley, her sister, and her mother remained locked in their house for days. Ashley's mother was unable to get out of bed and unwilling to let her daughters out of the house without her oversight. Ashley has similar struggles with mental health issues. She said she has posttraumatic stress disorder (PTSD), bipolar disorder, attention deficit hyperactivity disorder (ADHD), and physical pain.

Ashley spent considerable time documenting much of what she told me, displaying notebooks of materials from Horizons, the court system, and medical providers. She was the first (but not the only) person I spoke with who detailed every prescription bottle and box in her medicine cabinet, including buprenorphine, the selective serotonin reuptake inhibitor Lexapro, Abilify for her bipolar disorder, the antidepressant Remeron, and Neurontin, which she uses to treat pain. I think this documentation was in part to convince me and others of her story, but it was also to help her. Ashley keeps videos and pictures saved on her phone with time stamps to help her organize her past. She remembers events well, but has difficulty thinking about them on a timeline. I could not follow some of her stories because it was not clear what happened when or after what, just that these things happened. Ashley has had dozens of different jobs primarily in restaurants and retail, but her mental health often led her to either being fired or quitting. During the year or so in which I saw her somewhat regularly, Ashley never had an income.

She directly connected some of her mental health concerns, particularly PTSD, with previous relationships with men. Her father was an abusive alcoholic when she was a child. Her first husband was verbally abusive. Ashley spent six years with her children's abusive father. After a particularly violent episode where he punched her in the head repeatedly, Ashley's friend called the police and he was incarcerated for six months. After that incarceration, he ceased the physical abuse. Since he has custody of their children and gives some money to Ashley, he is still able to exert influence over her life, even though he is engaged to someone else and lives hours away.

Ashley lived most of her life outside of the five-county area, where she used heroin and to a lesser degree crack. She began using powder cocaine with her first mother-in-law on a military base in North Carolina. They grew bored during the day, would snort cocaine, and then would clean the house for hours. Ashley divorced due to her husband's infidelity and began dating her children's dad in Ohio. With this change in relationships and geography came a shift in drug use, from cocaine to crack and heroin. Ashley attempted to cease use for years. She moved to Adams County to get away from heroin and be closer to her dad's family. Ashley found a new appreciation for meth when she came to the county. In our first interview, she spent time describing meth as the worst drug someone could take. When I talked to her for the last time, she was using meth weekly. Unlike Sissy, who often treated giving up drugs like just another thing she made it through, consequential but not defining, Ashley considers herself addicted. Either addiction or attempts at stopping use dominate her life, along with a general lack of resources.

Katie: Battling Loves

I met Katie through a local nonprofit where her mother volunteers. Katie looks like the epitome of white, middle-class "normal" with the air of someone who knows everything about a place. She lives close to the county seat in Adams, and I saw her the most of anyone I interviewed. She would catch me up on local news and then introduce me to anyone she knew, which was generally everyone in sight. Katie says she loves heroin ("Pills never took me to the places that heroin did"). Katie also loves her daughter intensely. These loves come in conflict. My interactions with Katie are important because she most frankly discussed treatment and returns to drug use. We completed an interview a week before she began using pharmaceuticals illicitly. I unknowingly attended a Christmas children's toy giveaway with her while she was using. I then spoke with her several times after she had ceased use, once at a court hearing for a driving under the influence (DUI) charge she received.

Katie's father used alcohol and was abusive during her early childhood, creating instability in the household. Her drug use began with a prescription to alprazolam when she was fifteen after a sexual assault, and she continued on to OxyContin, instant-release oxycodone, and then heroin when she moved out of the area. The rising price of instant-release oxycodone and widespread availability of heroin made the switch logical. She was also with a boyfriend who favored the drug. Katie used heroin in central Kentucky for five years and Houston, Texas, for four more.

Maggie: Gendered Violence

Maggie contacted me through Katie. Yet another interview started with dogs, this time with me talking to Maggie in her yard as we prevented the dogs from going after the mail truck. Although I never met him, the sounds of her teenage son playing video games provided the backdrop to the only interview I completed at Maggie's house. Maggie was excited about participant observation. I did not have to explain to her what it was; she had been assigned to sit at Walmart for a few hours for her introduction to anthropology course in college.

Maggie has roots in a family that is well resourced in Adams County. Since her entire drug using tenure had been spent in the county, she had insightful knowledge of the drug scene. Maggie informed me that I lived across the street from a set of apartments where you could buy most drugs that were available in the area. I never saw anything, until my last interview, which took me inside those apartments. She had survived single incidents of assault as well as long-term gendered violence. Although these experiences are not unique for the women I spoke with, Maggie explored this issue in more depth than anyone else.

I had talked to Maggie for about thirty minutes before I asked her about drug use. When I began the question, she paused and then asked if she could smoke. She shakily chain-smoked for the rest of our interview. For her, the story of her drug use cannot be untangled from gendered violence. Maggie got pregnant when she was sixteen and married the father of her oldest son. They were happy for a few years, during which time she completed three years of college. Her father-in-law then became terminally ill. Her husband began drinking and misusing his father's pain medication. When Maggie's father-in-law died, the inheritance to his son was multiple bottles of OxyContin eighty-milligram tablets. As her husband's grief and addiction worsened, he started beating her. The most abusive night she remembers involved her sitting restrained with her then young son screaming and her husband pointing an assault rifle at her head for hours until he was drunk enough to pass out. She endured brutality for years after this incident. She later caught her then-twenty-five-year-old husband having sex with a fourteen-year-old, and she divorced him. The violence against herself she could take, but not the violence against other women.

Once she was divorced, her cousin set her up on a blind date, who met her at a bar with his friends. Her memories only come in snapshots after that, after she was drugged, of her being carried to a car, of a house with guns and knives, of being raped. She woke the next morning before the men did, and Maggie thinks that saved her life. She ran down a gravel road, seemingly forever, until she found an exit, from that situation at least.

> I finally got to the road and this little old man picked me up and took me to my car and after that, I just didn't care. I figured if I went to the hospital, they would want to know who it was and why I didn't know who it was and what do you tell somebody? I should have known who it was, but, well you don't expect people to be that bad. But I just came back home and I just went all to pieces and I didn't even think about that for a long time. I just did any drug I came across and I was like that for years.

We talked about the relationship between violence against women and drug use among women. Maggie said she would not have started using if not for this kidnapping and gang rape, but she went further. She did not think her husband would have become violent if not for his alcohol and drug use.

About ten years into using pharmaceuticals regularly, Maggie was looking for methadone one night, which by then was the main drug she used. She could find neither methadone nor any prescription opioids that evening. She started withdrawing from pharmaceuticals, smoked some meth with a group of folks, and proceeded to go home and clean her house all night. She woke up the next morning and realized how cheap meth was. Five dollars' worth kept her going for a week at the beginning. She stopped sleeping and eating and began distributing meth to four or five sellers. Maggie sent her sons to live with her parents. The only reason she was able to keep her house was because her parents paid her utility bills and fed the dogs. Even though she was distributing meth, not selling (a distinction Maggie made clear) she was running out of money. She sold everything in her house. This was enough to cause her parents to step in and take drastic action.

Alisha: Family History of Illicit Drug Use

The local drug court administrator gave Alisha my information. She was excited to meet and talk about her opinions of drug court and drug policies. I would not want to be on an opposing side of a debate with her. Alisha is concise and successfully melds data and personal narratives to make her point. She volunteered as a peer mentor with a local nonprofit that contracted with the criminal processing system to provide outpatient substance use treatment services. After watching her in this role, Alisha seemed to have the perfect balance of empathy and willingness to engage people in hard reflections of themselves.

Alisha is one of the few I spoke with who has a family history intimately tied to illicit drugs. This history altered both her entrance into use and made her strategies in dealing with state interventions more embedded in family connections than some other people's. Alisha has been in or had family involved with a state system for her entire life, whether DCBS, jail, or prison. She is thus one of the most adept at navigating these mazes as well as illicit economies. This is not to say that others do not experience interventions through or with family; the centering of Alisha's use within her family is just the most intense.

Familial and intimate relationships supported Alisha's continued use and cessation of use. Her parents divorced when she was a teenager. Her father fought for and won custody, but he was not prepared to care for the children. She took on the burden of care work for her younger siblings. When Alisha was sixteen, one of her father's friends began giving her cocaine, which helped her make it through long days of school and care work. He later raped Alisha. In that same year, her father was incarcerated for two months, and she remained in charge of her younger siblings, while also working to pay their bills.

After the rape, Alisha visited a psychiatrist and was prescribed alprazolam. She took this medication for years. At eighteen, Alisha became pregnant with her daughter while living with her dad and stepmother. Her father began drinking and turned mean. He forced her out of the house, making her unhoused for the first half of her pregnancy. Her stepmother eventually negotiated to have Alisha move back into their home. Alisha has an abusive ex-husband, who continues to terrorize her, at some points pulling her hair and pushing her when he sees her in public. When she divorced, she began using oxycodone. As she became immersed in oxycodone, her father, who no longer drank, began taking care of her children. The police eventually arrested her for drug trafficking, which landed her in drug court.

Star: Family as Source of Support and Crises

I met Star in Teller County when I was visiting Alisha. Unfortunately, she was having extraordinarily bad days both times I met her. During our first encounter, she was coming to see Alisha, the peer mentor, to try to figure out a way to lessen the consequences of a DUI charge she recently received for physician-prescribed benzos. The second time, as I was driving to see her, she texted me to meet her at the local health clinic. When I arrived, she jumped in my car and began telling me of her sister's sexual assault the night before. Her sister did not have a history of drug use, but came into the house late after a date, unable to function and then began convulsing. Neither Star nor her sister wanted to go the local hospital because they feared the staff would call in law enforcement to arrest her sister for being intoxicated. They instead went to a local clinic where Star had a close relationship with the providers. Star was with her sister at the clinic helping her get a physical exam. I sat with Star for a little while, and she insisted she still wanted to do an interview. We later went to her house, and I talked to Star, her son, and her husband for a few hours.

Star has a large family support system, not unlike Sissy, but Star tends to be the center of giving support, whereas Sissy had more shoulders to lean on. Star's husband was also a drug court graduate, and she takes care of her three children, sister, and mother. This entangled care network offers support, but at times propels Star into crisis. Her story is another example of how people develop survival strategies according to their geographic location, ability to rely on state services, and care networks.

Star said her entry into drug use was unremarkable, beginning in high school with experimentation and slowly progressing from there. She extensively described her recent use of benzos, when she received the DUI. She situated this "lapse" in the context of her father's death:

> I've relapsed once in the five years. My dad died of a drug overdose. I was angry. I literally went out, got nerve medication [benzodiazepines], not what I normally use, but a nerve medicine just to kind of like calm me down. I didn't have a relapse. Me and my counselor came to it, I had a lapse, because I didn't like go back and destroy my life up. I went back to the doctor, willingly went to the doctor and got nerve medication knowing it was going to make me feel different. I wanted that. I was never hooked on that before. And I done it three days and went to jail for six days [for the DUI], come home, and I've not done it since.

In terms of drug use history, there are common threads in the forty women's narratives demonstrating how use intersects with the body as well as relationships with others. The stories most rooted in the body belong to seven women who did not begin using until their late twenties or early thirties. They were prescribed opioids as pain medication following surgeries, car accidents, or occupational injuries. One woman, for instance, was a paramedic who broke dozens of bones when she was crushed by an ambulance. She took opioids as prescribed for over a year. When her physician told her she could never return to being a paramedic due to her injuries, she began using more opioids than she was prescribed.

Relationships with family or friends led others into use in their preteens. The fact that this was the beginning story for only three women goes against the narrative favored by a few gatekeepers—namely, that all drug use results from a dysfunctional family with parents who have mental health issues and give their children drugs at a very young age. Almost a quarter of interviewees began using in their early twenties, and they usually started taking prescription drugs with an intimate partner who was also using. Over a third of participants started experimenting with cannabis, alcohol, or benzodiazepines with friends in their mid- to late teens. Their use did not progress past experimentation on weekends until they were in their mid-twenties. Women attributed this progression to being in physical or emotional pain, experiences with intense domestic or sexual assault, and being around others who were using more, especially intimate partners. Emotional pain was most often associated with children being removed, loved ones dying, or partners leaving.

No women in this study had adequate access to mental health care even though most discussed having depression or anxiety, which they attributed to their social conditions and experiences with interpersonal violence. Nearly a quarter of those I interviewed had chronic pain due to physical injuries, primarily from occupational accidents and domestic violence. Structural violence is articulated in these women's lives as anxiety, depression, and physical pain, often caused by gendered inequalities and hazardous working conditions. Self-care through drug use was their primary strategy in dealing with these effects.

Effects of Drug Use on Fetuses and Children

I focus on motherhood because agencies and those within their confines did, whether treatment clients, community members, or gatekeepers. I am not concerned here with understandings of kinship or care that focus solely on biology, as these have been soundly critiqued.[2] Both social and biological connections create feelings of kinship. Pregnancy as well as cultural understandings of the biological body infiltrate women's lives. Having or appearing to have a uterus opens women to a host of state and societal surveillance that is concerned with fetal health. Women who use drugs face more complicated stigma than men who use drugs, as well as a subjective reality that induces anxiety when they find they are pregnant. Yet even physical processes that appear purely biological include social understandings. Pregnant people are connected to fetuses via umbilical cords, but how the public and those in power perceive this connection has as much to do with policies toward pregnant women as the biology of the umbilical cord itself.

Despite calls by medical providers and public health workers to end alarmist reports and policies regarding prenatal drug exposure, women's reproductive rights have been suspended because all women, whether pregnant or not, are seen as possible vectors for the spread of neonatal abstinence syndrome or fetal alcohol syndrome disorder. These conditions are often exaggerated and assumed to produce costly, disabled children who are burdens to families and society.[3] In a community meeting that is geared toward a variety of health issues, I heard a litany of stereotypes against children allegedly born with neonatal abstinence syndrome—that they are uniformly impulsive and irrational and will corrupt the children around them.

The exact effects of maternal substance use, particularly opioid and methamphetamine use, on long-term child health outcomes remains an open question. To date, few longitudinal studies have been conducted to address this question, and it is difficult to parse the effects of prenatal drug exposure from other factors that affect neonatal, child, and maternal health, such as poverty, homelessness, state violence, and interpersonal violence.[4] Prenatal opioid exposure can lead to neonatal abstinence syndrome and prematurity in neonates and *may* negatively affect some child health outcomes.[5] In their review of available studies, Behnke and Smith show that prenatal opioid exposure is associated with minor long-term effects on behavior, but there have been no documented long-term effects on physical growth.[6] The most recent research on the effects of opioid exposure on neonates through age three shows no adverse effects of opioid exposure at age three.[7]

Some studies have found that cocaine and methamphetamine exposure have subtle negative effects on neonatal health by increasing rates of prematurity and low birth weight, but it is unclear if these negative effects extend beyond the neonatal stage.[8] In one data set that has been analyzed by various groups of researchers, prenatal methamphetamine exposure was associated with anxiety, depression, and ADHD problems in children aged three to five.[9] Reporting on this same data set, Smith et al. note that methamphetamine exposure was associated with poorer fine motor skill performance among one-year-olds, but all effects had disappeared by age three.[10] Yet these studies do not control for some confounding factors that could be important, such as housing status, food security, and parental incarceration. Another analysis of these data suggests that serious negative neonatal health effects are not due to meth exposure, but to these other factors, as well as lack of prenatal care and poverty.[11]

Much remains unknown about the effects of maternal drug use on long-term child outcomes and how these effects interact with experiences of structural and interpersonal violence. A mythology that stereotypes pregnant women who use drugs, especially poor women and women of color, and blames them for harming children and society has nonetheless emerged. Focusing on women's bodies as a toxic space while ignoring the toxicity of an environment mired in inequalities and cruelty irrationally blames individuals for factors outside their control and leads to interventions that marginalize them.

Interventions in White Motherhood

Cultural understandings of motherhood and additional gendered responsibilities, rather than evidence-based research on the effects of substance use, shape women's experiences with interventionist agencies in Appalachia. These entanglements are nothing new; there is a history of child removal and forced sterilizations in Appalachia, acts that have been based on ethnicity, class, and marriage status.[12] In terms of public health, Mary Breckinridge founded the Frontier Nursing Service in the 1920s to provide maternal and child health care. While Appalachian women were seeking access to such resources, Breckinridge blurred lines between provision of medical care and moral crusading. She defined only some women as "worthy" recipients of aid and this worthiness was often based on their rural whiteness.[13] Similar positions pervade current strategies in the region.

A concentration on the harms of drug use on children led to frustrations in my research; it seemed as though every time I spoke with community members, they would ignore what I said and immediately begin talking about the children as "innocent victims." I observe characterizations of women who use drugs as "bad" mothers continuously, whether it is in the local or national news, at community or state policy meetings, or in health care settings. My premature daughter was placed in a neonatal intensive care unit that is within the service area of the five counties. I talked to the nurses about drug use and neonatal abstinence syndrome. They sighed and rolled their eyes, and one nurse told me that she was tired of seeing babies prenatally exposed to drugs because of "a series of personal and generational decisions." Women said they felt the juxtaposition of "good" versus "bad" mothers from family members and the community long before they entered treatment. Alisha compared how women are treated in the community versus men: "I think they put that label like she doesn't care about her kids. Dads get off easy. So I always feel like the mom's judged more than the dad is. I think they put it on us like we can't make a mistake. Dad can make up for that lost time."

Community programs may incentivize attendance by giving women a few material resources, such as diapers and children's toys. More important to the organizations according to providers, services are meant to educate new mothers on how to avoid risky behaviors that may harm fetuses and newborns. A primary example of this is community baby showers. Pregnant women or new moms are invited to attend through newspaper advertisements to acquire diapers, a diaper bag, and several door prizes. Participants are given lunch and asked to sit through a slide presentation. The vast majority of the presentation I witnessed used scare tactics, such as alarming pictures of infants with fetal alcohol syndrome disorder, to demonstrate how a mother's behaviors can hurt their fetus, especially smoking, alcohol use, and drug use. The presenter defined pregnant women's bodies as sites of fetal risk and possible toxicity, a word she used repeatedly. Even when discussing postpartum depression and domestic violence, the information was couched in terms of what behaviors may hurt a fetus or newborn, not how women may be harmed. Though the presentation was developed by an organization that exclusively serves rural Appalachia and primarily targets women in poverty, all presentation images represented affluent women in pastel sweater sets with pearls. Most suggestions were urban-based. Women were encouraged to find "mommy and me" groups, which are even difficult to find in the metropolitan areas closest to the five-county region. At the end of the presentation, women were given a "Making Healthy Choices" packet, which focuses almost exclusively on healthy choices for the fetus or newborn. For example, when describing depression and postpartum depression, the list of possible negative outcomes does not mention women at all:

> Ongoing feelings of depression can put your baby at risk of being born too early or too small. If you are having these feelings, it is important to talk to your doctor!
>
> Postpartum depression may get in the way of you being able to care for and feel close to your baby!

The packet explains that children should be women's motivation to change risky behaviors. There are several pictures of babies with the caption: "Remember WHO you are making the change for!" Fixed within this information is the belief that if women continue drug use, then they cannot care about children.

Kentucky researchers and service providers repeatedly argue, despite the absence of data, that Appalachian children have disabilities because of maternal drug use. A presentation by two clinicians based at a Kentucky university blamed Appalachian women's drug use and promiscuity for creating hoards of children who are over-prescribed ADHD medications. Mothers supposedly sedate their children with these medications, because moms just want to get high and hang out with their "boyfriend or boyfriends," insinuating hypersexuality conduct as well. (Anyone who has ever used these drugs without having ADHD knows that the last thing they do is sedate.) The clinicians went on to describe their program. They take children to a summer camp where they are baptized and put in contact with "positive" male role models, generally law enforcement. These presenters made clear that their assumptions did not come from actual research, but from what they imagined children's home life to be.

With discussions of Appalachia come assumptions about race. An allusion to Appalachians' whiteness frequently appeared at regional or statewide meetings, where speeches about Appalachia as uniquely "Scots-Irish" spread a common racial myth. A local treatment program administrator contended that we must increase funding for treatment and naloxone because now opioid use affects everyone, including rural young people. Though he did not mention race, every picture he showed was of young white people. A nurse in the five-county area blamed the spread of drug use on urban areas:

> In the past, you thought you didn't get exposed. If you raised your
> children here, you didn't get the exposure to bigger city problems.
> That's not the case anymore. You thought if you were in a small

town, that you didn't have the problems that the bigger cities have, but it's in the small towns now.

In combination with her discussions of crack, I understood "bigger city problems" to be located in urban communities of color. Characterizations of women who use drugs and Appalachian women have a genetic component. Women who use drugs are seen as having a brain disease rooted in genetics and as possibly harming the genetics of their offspring. Appalachian women are seen as genetically unique because of their allegedly shared ethnicity. Current understandings of genetics and especially epigenomics come in here. Epigenomics is the study of epigenetic modifications, or alterations due to mechanisms other than changes in DNA sequence, on cellular genetic material. Epigenomics is often concerned with epigene–environment interactions. Epigenetic research can be used to combat some people's obsession with DNA where they believe everything is based on genetics by underscoring the effects of the environment on genetics. At the same time, epigenomics may be used to further disentangle bodies from social and political contexts in order to blame undesired behaviors on faulty biology. Much epigenetic research focuses exclusively on the intrauterine and young childhood environments, placing the burden of change on pregnant women and new mothers to implement healthy behaviors. This focus may promote state programs that target pregnant women for behavior changes that are unattainable in their social environments, invariably producing maternal frustration and reiterating belief systems that blame poor mothers and families for poverty. Epigenetic research risks individualizing inequalities as simply a product of problematic familial and personal behaviors that can be changed with education and market-based approaches instead of the state encouraging populationwide programs, such as reduced incarceration and more investment in equitable economic development and infrastructure.[14]

In her discussion of the possible effects of ongoing epigenetic research, Maurizio Meloni notes that, "*Bad habits can become bad biology,* and the indelible scars of past environmental exposures can give rise to ideas of specific groups being 'too damaged' (because of persisting bad social experiences) to be rescued."[15] Moral fervor when merged with shallow understandings of epigenetics creates a social environment in which addiction can be viewed as an unending moral failure that women can supposedly pass down to their children through a risky fetal environment and heredity. This view supports scenarios of coerced sterilization, performed through such organizations as Project Prevention in North Carolina, and imprisonment of pregnant women who use drugs.

Drug use in Appalachia has been described as a "genetic scourge" because it is assumed that use is passed through generations, emanating from and in turn causing poor genetics. Drug use and assumed prenatal drug exposure become framed as a culture of addiction that supposedly creates a genetic underclass of children. Like the culture of poverty model, values, reproduction, and genetics are used to explain poverty or drug use instead of structural forces. In the rhetoric I have witnessed in communities, some community leaders and policy makers continue to view addiction as a moral failure despite the vast social science and biomedicine literature to the contrary. What is most concerning is that people are taking small pieces of biomedical research on epigenetics and addiction as a brain disease, combining biomedical with moral failure understandings of addictions, and using this combination to frame addiction as a moral failure that has a basis in prenatal drug exposure, neurochemistry, and genetics. Moreover, as they deny the influences of structures of power, they use the chronicity implied by epigenetic, genetic, and neurochemical models to remove the possibility of people who use drugs or their "damaged" children being able to change. Women who use drugs and the children they have while using become "lost generations."

In this understanding of addiction, the only way to change drug use and its consequences in Appalachia is to focus services on preventing prenatal drug exposure and drug use among children.

Most community substance use programs in this five-county area, whether run by local groups, county churches, or regional organizations, only have programming for preventing substance use among children. When children are removed from a home, state resources such as SNAP end, turning the lens away from adult suffering. Even though the vast majority of community organizations focus on children, community leaders I spoke with generally said that they needed more substance use prevention programs for children. While this is important, I argue that it should not be the only focus.

These understandings of drug use and motherhood promote individualized interventions that ignore the effects of structural inequalities, such as housing instability and poor nutrition, on the health of women, infants, and children. Policies that separate fetal from maternal health treat women as risks to the fetus, dismiss the complexities of women's experiences, and ignore the efforts that women have made throughout time to take care of their own health as well as the health of fetuses and children.[16] Further, efforts to constrain reproductive rights are rarely applied evenly across a population, with poor women and women of color facing the harshest infringements.[17]

Custody

Limited funding, conservative policies, and societal stigma of client populations bind what agencies and staff can do. Many employees did their best to make services helpful. Some enacted policies they disagreed with because they saw no other option. A few exacerbated the harm their agencies inflicted by violating regulations. It is unfair and unproductive to view all DCBS caseworkers as "baby snatchers," a term I heard more often from DCBS staff than community members. Yet DCBS, like the criminal processing system, needs to be heavily scrutinized. Imprisoning people and removing their children are enormous exercises of state power in which bias occurs. Caseworkers may be more likely to see patterns of neglect among marginalized parents; others may view these same patterns as ordinary and unremarkable or not consider them patterns at all, just normal life.[18]

Mass child removal has similar effects on communities as mass incarceration, hampering meaningful family connections and collective social action.[19] Child removal often results in a loss of personal and political identity. Women lose their relationship with the removed children and their political identity as mothers who have the right to protect their children. Other research shows that removal can stifle women's efforts to lessen or stop drug use.[20]

Unlike their male relatives and friends who were more likely to have come in frequent contact with the criminal processing system, these women had DCBS in their lives. Only two I spoke with lacked experience with DCBS because their drug use did not coincide with having children in their home. No one disputed that DCBS is a necessary service for protecting children from harm. Yet agreement over the institution, including how policies were implemented locally, ended there.

As might be expected, those who have had their children removed rarely have positive things to say about DCBS. Katie, one of the few exceptions, said she had a good experience because her caseworker was new and not "wore out with the system." The caseworker listened and regularly checked in via text message in a way that felt nonintrusive and caring. Katie doubted that other caseworkers who had been at the agency longer would do this, since they were overburdened with work. Although Star had problems with DCBS, one caseworker in Teller County was exceptional: "We have one good worker, but she actually quit because of that. Because she felt that they was picking on drug addicts, instead of help them save their lives and their children, they wanted to come and take them. She wasn't for that."

Family, drug use, and class are intertwined in dealings with DCBS in this rural setting. If women can find local family members who are willing to take their children, for instance, they are more likely to be able to spend time with their children freely, instead of only during official DCBS visiting times. If, however, there are no local family members available, children are often sent hours away.

I saw Ashley between several of her family court dates. She raised two children who are now preschool-aged as a single mother for most of their lives because their father was incarcerated. Her children and their father initially moved to Adams County with Ashley, but then he moved to another state because he could not find employment. Adams County DCBS removed Ashley's children from her home because of an anonymous caller who said they heard "slapping sounds" in the house. (Ashley says the children's occupational therapist told her to clap her hands to get her children's attention, and that was where the sounds were coming from.) Her children were sent to live with their father in another state.

Ashley's relationship with DCBS was defined by stress and drug use. She blamed her sporadic uses on the continued loss of her children. "Just all the pressure. The pressure of not knowing. Everybody else is in control whether I get my kids back or not, so it makes it kind of hard." Not being around her kids is devastating. She has reminders of them everywhere, including two fully set up bedrooms and a play area. Ashley was trying to use the court system to regain full custody. She showed me her children's father's criminal record as well as a newspaper article about his thefts of large quantities of metals from factories. These materials were part of a folder Ashley (who could not afford a lawyer) was building to argue against his having full custody. When I last spoke with her, he technically had joint custody, but effectively full custody because he would not drive the children to Kentucky to see Ashley, and she had no means of transportation to visit her children.

Ashley's case for regaining full custody was ultimately halted because of two positive drug tests, one for cannabis and one for meth. She started using right before her court date.

Ashley: It's like just what my social worker said, "You self-sabotage. You do great up until it's time for court." Then as soon as it hits court, I backslide. Every single time. And I think it's just the stress of it all. Of knowing that I'm going to go to court and then they can say, "Yes, you're getting your babies back or no, you're not."

Lesly-Marie: So wasn't your last court date in October?

Ashley: It was this month on the 19th and I missed it. I completely forgot about it. Who does that? But I feel myself starting to fall until I get this deep depression and I don't know what's causing it. I went four days without taking a bath the other day. I just sat on the couch and all I do is sleep. So I feel it coming on and I'm just trying to prepare myself to be forceful to myself about taking a bath, getting up, and doing stuff because if I don't, I lay on this couch and I won't ever get up.

Ashley was prescribed a selective serotonin reuptake inhibitor and an antidepressant. She questioned the effectiveness of these drugs and lamented her limited access to nonpharmaceutical services, such as counseling, to treat her depression and anxiety. Using cannabis and meth became the most available and effective way to cope with her mental health and child loss.

One way to avoid DCBS is not having children for them to take. While Ashley is fighting to regain custody of her two oldest, she permanently placed her youngest son with a friend.

I have a third child and I was taking Subutex when he was born. I ended up giving him to my friend when he was born because my mom passed away two months before he was born and I knew I couldn't handle the attention. I loved that baby so much that I knew I couldn't give him what he needed and my best friend could. I see him every week and we decided that we were going to tell him that he is so fortunate because some people don't have a mom at all and he has two moms that love him.

Before Maggie sold her belongings to pay for meth, she expressed interest in buprenorphine treatment to her parents. The day her father walked into her bare house was the same day he marched into a local bupe clinic and demanded that Maggie be seen immediately. A few weeks after she entered the bupe program, DCBS searched her home, placed her sons with her parents who live a quarter mile down the road, and mandated her to attend Horizons. Not unlike most, Maggie felt DCBS used deception in removing her children, but the closeness of her family and the ability to pay for a lawyer made the struggle through the DCBS case tolerable. As soon as DCBS removed her children and placed them with her parents, she spent every day with her kids, going against DCBS orders. This physical and emotional closeness prevented her from being cut off, an advantage Ashley didn't have.

Maggie argued that DCBS actions are hard to navigate because caseworkers are untruthful.

> **Maggie:** [The caseworker] did see like week-old track marks on my arms. I said, "I haven't used in a week," and when I said that, that sealed my fate. Thankfully my mom was here and thankfully she was able to sign and take my sons, but, gosh, I couldn't imagine if I didn't have mom there to took them. It's really bad how they do people. I know they're here to help, but the initial them being here and telling you it's all going to be okay, we won't do this unless we have to, then you sign these papers. The minute you sign they say, "Get the kid." That's terrible. And I'm sure all the other girls you've talked to could tell you the same thing.
>
> **Lesly-Marie:** Yeah, so you felt like it wasn't explained to you?
>
> **Maggie:** Oh no, it's not explained, and you're so tore up, you can't read ten pages of writing. And I tried to read over it and I'm pretty educated, and I couldn't understand it. And I know some people couldn't understand it, so no, it's not explained. And it's explained in a deceitful way if anything.

Family help with custody can go even farther, but not without complexities. Alisha has connections to county judges and the DCBS office through her parents. She unofficially worked with DCBS, without record of her involvement and without losing child custody. Alisha's mother went so far as to quit her job as a social worker so there would be no conflicts with Alisha's case. Her mother's help brought its own coercion. She was able to stay out of DCBS, but her mother asked her to sign a notarized contract stating that she could only have custody of her son if she completed drug court. Alisha's daughter, who is two years older than her son, would only live with

Alisha if she chose to. At the time of my research, Alisha's son lived with her, but her daughter did not.

What Does it Mean for Women to be "Good" Mothers?

Women almost always agree that they cannot provide what they consider "quality" childcare when using moderately or heavily. Yet they navigate this dichotomy of "good" versus "bad" mothers by finding ways to preserve their feeling of being a "good" mother while continuing drug use. This involves not using in front of their children and providing for their children's needs as well as wants. Star demonstrated this, as well as her anger that DCBS charged her with neglect and dependency.

> I just told the judge straight out, neglect to me sounds like someone who beats their kids, don't feed their children, leaves them unattended. I neglected myself, not my children. I mean my mind wasn't there, but I never harmed my kids. My kids were always still fed. They had a roof over their head. All that and I tried to hide my use from them too.

Star still had conflicting feelings. She was frustrated with DCBS and did not think she deserved to be sanctioned through a court system. She also spoke of guilt. For her, graduation from drug court, continued work on not using, and devotion to her family and to God were atonement for her drug use.

Once they had ceased use, the women I spoke with began building cases that they are "good" mothers. Although these cases are certainly used with DCBS, they are also displayed to treatment providers and others who enter their lives, including anthropologists. When I was in women's homes, it was not uncommon for them to immediately start showing me pictures of their children, their kids' rooms, and boxes of toys and children's clothes. They explained that I could see as well as anyone that they provide for their children and that the kids were not deprived of things.

When I entered Ashley's house for our first interview, she took me to her daughter's and then son's rooms to show me that they not only had enough toys, clothes, and nice beds, but were "spoiled." In the kitchen, she showed me that although she did not have enough food for herself, she always tried to have food that the kids would eat, like toaster pastries, in case they came for a visit. Ashley spent substantial time reviewing the folder she planned to take to her next court date for child custody. She had pages with the number of drug tests she had passed through treatment and dozens of documents from community members stating that she is a "good" mom. She told me how her children's occupational therapist testified on her behalf during a previous court date. Ashley kept explaining that she volunteers in the community and at the local school, demonstrating that she is not only a "good" mother, but a citizen who contributes to the community.

Women became frustrated with DCBS because they were under increased surveillance as compared to their male partners or husbands. One quote exemplified this frustration:

> So how's it fair that I have to go take a drug test and have to be supervised to be around [my son], but his daddy doesn't have to take no drug test. Shouldn't he have to be drug tested? It ain't fair, it's not right. I mean I've raised that baby since he was a newborn. His daddy has not done nothing.

Several women said their abusive ex-husbands threatened to use DCBS against them. If they threatened to report domestic violence to the police, their ex-husbands counter-threatened to falsely tell DCBS that the women were abusing the children.

Class intersects with gender to determine who DCBS questions as being a "good" mother. Alisha said that socioeconomic status more than drug use determined whom DCBS referred to treatment. She works closely with DCBS caseworkers as part of her volunteering, and she maintained that most of the people she councils do not have drug problems, but live in "run-down" housing. She argued this is not their fault because they live where they can afford and the landlords do not maintain properties. It is nonetheless part of their DCBS case plan to attend outpatient substance use treatment programs because

DCBS in that county assumes that all parents who they come in contact with are drug addicts, regardless of the reality.

The vast majority of women I spoke with view DCBS as another system that makes them feel intruded upon without helping them in any way. Although her children were back in the home after being removed, what made Star truly angry was that DCBS made determinations about her children's welfare based on a once-monthly fifteen-minute home visit. She said this demonstrates her caseworker's lack of care of her family's well-being. Star cares, but her caseworker does not, so why does the person who does not offer care have such power?

The focus of DCBS on women's behaviors results in them being disciplined if they contact DCBS when they are trying to perform as "good" mothers who protect their children. One woman called the agency because her children's father and uncle, who did not live in the home, molested her children. DCBS gave her a drug test and removed the children from her home. What concerns women the most is when they feel their kids are placed in harmful environments when they are removed. Some women trust their parents to be quality caregivers; others do not. These kin are called upon to take custody and prevent foster care, but women do not trust these people who may have problematic or even violent histories. One woman's children were placed with their father's family, who let them see their physically and sexually abusive father.

Some service providers avow that removing children from the home is beneficial to women because it forces them to a "rock bottom"; most women do not agree. While they may enter treatment because of removal, they find the removal process to harm their progression more than it helps. Child loss is devastating and it limits the emotional support women receive from children. They talk about "losing their mind" and feeling the loss as a death. Women outlined effects on their health, especially depression symptoms and anxiety. Several attempted suicide soon after removal. They more often than not increased drug use as their main available form of self-care. Without their children, they saw no reason to cease use.

Women feel shame that their children may blame themselves for removal, that the burden of childcare is placed on their family, and that they miss their children's developmental stages or have to view these stages "from behind the glass" at jail visitations. When children are removed, participants miss connections they have with other humans; as one woman stated, "Before I was a drug addict I was a mother. I'm not happy being a drug addict at all. There's no happiness to it. I've learned that through experience. If this is my life, this isn't my life. There's got to be so much more to it." Mothers wanted to return to a life where they had consistent relationships with their kids, but they often could not imagine how to make that happen.

This leads to one of the major hurdles in treatment: treatment not only removes drugs from a life, but generally removes a person from those in their care network. Only three women said that loss of child custody was good motivation for them to actually do well in treatment. When these three did not have child custody, however, all had their children placed with their parents and could see their kids whenever they wanted, alleviating much of the pain of separation.

DCBS administrators and caseworkers were fully aware that their presence in homes is usually unwanted and sometimes unwarranted. Administrators said they are making efforts to improve DCBS's standing in communities, yet the agency is stifled politically and economically. The federal Adoption and Safe Families Act of 1997 (ASFA) decreases chances of family reunification by encouraging swift adoption. Legal reunification timelines are relatively short in terms of how long it may take a parent to decrease or stop drug use. Parental rights are terminated if children have lived in foster care for fifteen of the last twenty-two months. The combination of the ASFA with the passage of welfare reform in 1996 created a turning point from DCBS focusing on child poverty and social inequalities to potential abuse and neglect.[21] DCBS policies that are solely based on protecting children from parental harm reflect the bind in which caseworkers find themselves as they are expected to protect children and preserve families, which may be conflicting missions, all within a resource-depleted and politically overdetermined environment.[22]

A state administrator who coordinates services with DCBS argued in our interview that DCBS's funding structure has traditionally favored child removal. She is working on family-first initiatives with Kentucky and the federal government. These policies are aimed at increasing the flexibility of funds reserved for foster care. With the current system, children must be placed in foster care before they receive certain services. Those within Kentucky DCBS administration want to alter these restrictions so they may use funds to garner services for children while they are still in the home, thus decreasing removal rates. They supported the Family First Prevention Services Act, which failed at the federal level in 2016. The administrator I spoke with blamed this failure on lobbyists from group homes that house foster children. As this administrator contests the swift adoptions supported by the ASFA, Governor Bevin prioritized the further shortening of adoption times.[23]

DCBS county offices are materially deprived. When I asked a local DCBS administrator what was preventing her office from carrying out their mission, she said:

> There's always room for improvement. I mean we're short-staffed. I have three workers for this entire county. There are six people for two counties. We are overworked, exhausted, and it doesn't take long for workers to get burned out. We just want to make sure we don't make critical mistakes.

While I was at a regional DCBS meeting, county representatives reported that several offices in Eastern Kentucky did not have Internet and three to four caseworkers had to share cell phones. During the relatively brief duration of my research, two county offices were relocated because the walls of their buildings began to fall apart. In the context of limited funding, program staff feel they must take actions to save money and cannot offer wraparound services that they think families need. Governor Bevin acknowledged the high caseload and low pay of DCBS workers and promised a 10 to 20 percent pay increase for workers beginning July 1, 2018.[24] Yet in the same budget, he eliminated seventy state programs, some of which provide the educational and in-home early childhood programs that caseworkers want to offer families.

In order to truly improve maternal and child health, efforts should be made to improve the conditions in which people on the fringes live instead of focusing on the singular behavior of drug use (or of any singular behavior for that matter). I am wary of recommendations to assign more responsibilities to DCBS and law enforcement, because neither institution has demonstrated the ability to handle the complexities of substance use or poverty. In my experiences working with people who use drugs in three states, these institutions more often exacerbate biases and poor material realities than alleviate them. I hope that with strong leadership and policy shifts, these trends can change, but no one can be expected to trust institutions that have a chronic history of problematic behavior.

Chapter 3
The Therapeutic State

THREE SUBSTANCE USE treatment options—therapeutic, rehabilitative, and punitive—reveal various facets of state intervention. All are government funded and regulated. Because of the perceived unique relationship between women and children, women who use drugs have increased access to substance use treatment in this place. Women who are pregnant or are mothers of young children qualify for services. Horizons primarily serves women who have DCBS cases and programming is focused on parenting. "Number of drug-free babies" is an outcome measure of Kentucky drug courts and reflects the prioritization of admitting pregnant women into the program. When women are no longer pregnant, services disappear. Ashley lost access to methadone: "It was right after my daughter was born, and I couldn't pay for the methadone. Legally, they can't take you off of it when you're pregnant because it can kill your kid, but as soon as I had my baby, they tapered me down five milligrams a day. I got sick as a dog." Some of these programs make clear that the primary client being served is the fetus or newborn, not the adult.

Family court usually mandates Horizons. Women are unlikely to retain or receive child custody if they withdraw from the program. The criminal processing system orders drug court and those who fail are incarcerated. There are areas of discordance and confluence between programs, communities, and clients. These gaps provide opportunities and obstacles, as women in treatment are required to navigate multiple mazes that have contradictory overlays. Most important, the state is not monolithic, and neither are people's encounters with it.

I interviewed women who find aspects of treatment programs to be emotionally and at times materially supportive and parts of the program pointless and marginalizing. Most clients agree that these treatment programs are needed, but do not adequately address substance use or inequalities. These services in some ways meet needs, and in others provide more "hoops to jump through," in the words of several clients.

Horizons (often called the "parenting class" by locals) aims to reform mothers to more closely align with middle- and upper class ideals of motherhood. When the program goes "too far" in advocating for women or promoting harm-reduction strategies, it finds itself in conflict with DCBS and drug court, agencies that are punitive and view their clients as women who harm children. Employees at times felt censured by administrators when they complained about limited funding and the institution's inaction in fighting discrimination against people who use drugs. Making it through treatment becomes a matter of getting the resources one can through a chaotic agency and a broken system.

Reforming Mothers

While drug court is directly funded by the state, the bulk of funding for Horizons and bupe clinics is from Medicaid. Prior to the passage of the Affordable Care Act and Medicaid expansion, two Kentucky state departments distributed Temporary Assistance for Needy Families (TANF) and Children's Bureau block grant monies to Horizons. As Medicaid expansion increasingly reimbursed for services, these block grants dwindled. Medicaid expansion did not increase funding into Horizons, it just shifted funding from one source to another. The program was underfunded before expansion, and it has remained underfunded since. Horizons is no longer beholden to TANF program guidelines; it offers services that Medicaid reimburses.

The shift in accountability from TANF to Medicaid is worth noting. TANF was created as part of the 1996 Personal Responsibility and Work Opportunity Reconciliation Act, commonly called "welfare reform," to replace Aid to Families with Dependent Children, Job Opportunities and Basic Skills Training, and Emergency Assistance. TANF eliminated open-ended federal entitlement programs for poor families and replaced these programs with block grants for states to provide time-limited assistance to poor families who had to meet work requirements. States are allowed to use TANF dollars for the following purposes:

- to provide assistance to poor families so children may remain in the home; to reduce dependency on government entitlement programs by promoting "job preparation, work, and marriage";
- to prevent out-of-wedlock pregnancies; and
- to encourage two-parent families.[1]

Judgment of families in poverty, single-parent families, and families of color seep through these goals and through programs aligned with TANF. Several upper-level administrators expressed relief in getting out from under these guidelines. Yet relying on Medicaid created chaos for the administration and staff, because they have to consistently shift what they are able to offer according to decisions made at the federal or state levels.

Treatment at Horizons consistently involves group therapy and random drug testing. Women have access to individual therapy a few times a month and Narcotics Anonymous twelve-step style support groups irregularly. The most often repeated goals in program documents are to place children back in the home and to "reduce dependence on public assistance by addressing barriers to self-sufficiency." Staff explained that they do not want clients to rely on the community mental health center or social services, such as SNAP and Kentucky Transitional Assistance Program (K-TAP). These goals obviously go far beyond substance use in an effort to produce a particular type of middle-class mother who is not burdened by socioeconomic inequalities. Staff use parenting books as a primary source of program materials. The group counseling room is set up with a large table and a side area with children's toys, cribs, and bouncers. These items are used to help women practice parenting techniques and they may bring young children to Horizons while completing certain program requirements, such as drug testing.

Group sessions include a range of activities, from learning about parenting, coping skills, addiction, nutrition, relationships, and job readiness. Individual therapy deals with substance use, mental health issues, domestic violence, and parenting. Case management services that focus on poverty and domestic violence aim to assist women in accessing transportation, education, employment training, legal services, and medical care. Clients must participate in groups and case management throughout the program. Although not described by staff, clients talked about watching movies, coloring, and doing errands with case managers during group session times. I observed numerous smoke breaks and informal moments to talk.

Clients are expected to attend three to six hours a day from one to five days a week depending on the program phase. Horizons is divided into three phases and women have access to aftercare once they graduate from phase three. Each phase lasts approximately two to three months. Some clients may take substantially longer due to individual circumstances. Phase one is the most intensive where participants must attend three group-counseling sessions per week. In phase two, clients taper to two. Participants only have to attend one group per week in phase three. In all phases, they attend two hours of individual counseling sessions per month. Almost everyone involved agreed that these two hours are inadequate to deal with any serious concerns.

Phase "graduation" is based on attendance records, drug screenings, and staff ratings of clients. Women must attend at least 90 percent of group and individual sessions and have negative drug screens for thirty days. Staff ratings are subjectively based on women's attitudes in treatment, including whether they speak in counseling sessions, have a pleasant demeanor, and attempt to reach goals outlined in individualized plans. Three-quarters of clients who graduate all three phases remain in the program for at least one year. Graduating may positively affect their DCBS case; for those who do not have custody, graduating might lead to increased child visitations. Alternatively, if they do not graduate a phase or are even demoted, they may lose visitation rights or permanent custody. If participants complete Horizons, they are told they will regain child custody if it has been lost, but this doesn't always happen. Completion of Horizons is usually part of women's DCBS case plan. A caseworker develops the plan as a series of steps parents must take to demonstrate progress. Horizons staff estimate that DCBS refers 90 percent of the clients to the treatment program; the remaining 10 percent may not have been directly referred by DCBS but usually have an open or closed case with child removal. Horizons staff think that these 10 percent enroll in treatment because they hope DCBS will view Horizons graduation positively.

Fathers usually do not have to attend treatment at all as part of their DCBS case plans. When they do attend, the program is housed within the same community mental health center as Horizons. The fathers' program is for one hour a week for eight weeks with no drug tests. Although DCBS can request drug tests, it is not a regular part of men's treatment through the mental health center. Staff brush off this discrepancy between women's and men's treatment by explaining that they had to fight for the men's program to exist at all. Before the Affordable Care Act and Medicaid expansion, the Horizons TANF grant did not provide funding for men's treatment. Although the mental health center is now largely funded through Medicaid reimbursement, administrators are unsure of the stability of expansion due to Governor Bevin's actions against it. They are reluctant to begin a men's program when they do not know whether the women's program will survive expansion dismantlement. Two staff justified the discrepancy by arguing that mothers are more important than fathers in terms of caregiving. Fathers need to spend their time working, not in treatment: "If the men are working, we don't want to have them here three days a week; they need to be working and doing what they can." This assumes financial support from fathers and highly gendered caretaking roles.

Horizons and DCBS are in communication daily. A Horizons administrator talked about the importance of collaboration between substance use treatment and DCBS because these two systems are "old advisories, in some ways." There is intense emotion tied to DCBS because many caseworkers enter the profession to make sure "babies are safe." Caseworkers can thus come from the perspective that parents are simply the people who hurt children.

There can be some judgment that [people who use drugs] don't even deserve to be a parent or if they really loved their children, they would put those drugs down. So we work hard to build an awareness on the substance abuse treatment side that child safety is incredibly important. And then we also work hard on the child welfare side to, first of all, give [DCBS] hope, to show [DCBS] people in recovery so that they can see that people in addiction really can get better. That can help break down a lot of the stigma and discrimination that can come out of some of those beliefs that the parent has a moral failing.

Despite her efforts, I witnessed adversarial moments in an interagency meeting, with all Horizons staff seated against one wall, all DCBS staff seated on the opposite wall, and administrators complaining about poor communication. Staff from each agency claimed that they knew women and families better than the other agency, and hence their agency should be the ones to allocate joint funding.

Nevertheless, deep connections between DCBS and two of the three substance use treatment options in the area, Horizons and drug court, mean that child custody in addition to incarceration represent the main consequences for not progressing through treatment. This accentuated women's frustrations with treatment. At the same time, the vast majority of treatment clients cited regaining custody after removal as a primary motivator for entering Horizons and drug court. They see progressing through the programs as "working for your kid." But women face a double stigma when they receive drug tests that suggest they used or do not show up for treatment. They are seen as not only failing sobriety, but failing their children. This stigma comes from other women in treatment, just as much as from the community and treatment staff, as shown in Katie's conflict with another Horizons client:

> You know one day she was sitting there and she said, "Well this is just a complete waste of my time to be sitting here." And I looked at her and I said, "Really? Well where else would you be?" She said, "Well I don't know, at home." And I said, "What have you got going on at home? You've got three children and you don't have custody of none of them. So being here is a waste of time, so therefore you're saying being here fighting for them is a waste of time so they're a waste of time." I can't help it; stuff like that just burns me up. So she said, "Well no." And I said, "Well then being here shouldn't be a waste of your time."

Some staff shared these sentiments as well; they viewed child separation as not about removing children from danger, but about punishing parents for their drug use. In these ways, DCBS and substance use treatment do not represent a softening of drug policies, but an extension of carceral reactions to drug use where parents who use drugs especially are demonized as societal and familial failures.

Constrained Programming

The state and federal governments continually reduced Horizons funding when the program relied on block grants. Currently, if Horizons cannot bill Medicaid for a service, they have difficulty offering that service. Case management has suffered the most with shifts in funding. Horizons as well as additional regional safety-net programs are unable to meet people's needs in terms of housing, health care, transportation, and food. One case manager, whose position focused on client needs, claimed to have no budget, which made it impossible for her to perform her job. Her job then was limited to encouraging personal responsibility among clients.

> Technically a case manager is there to help a client find resources to cover their needs, but when you don't have any funds, there's

not a whole lot you can do to help them other than fill out applications and take them to the store. We do transportation some. We try to help them to be responsible. When they first get in here, [we] try to encourage them to keep their doctors' appointments.

In 2014, she received $2,000 to provide services. That amount dropped to $100 in 2015 to help twenty clients. Sissy commended this case manager for being handy with duct tape and super glue, fixing air conditioners and car engines. But of course, duct tape and super glue do little to keep an unrenovated 1960s trailer inhabitable.

In response to changing Medicaid reimbursement structures, Horizons has shifted from offering more individual counseling services through a licensed clinician who is better paid to offering more group counseling through low-wage peer support staff who are less trained. In Horizons, peer support is offered by former clients who have at least their GED and six months of on-the-job training. Their position includes leading some group sessions, regularly checking in with clients, and trying to provide some case management services, such as clothing and food boxes. Administrators are excited by the prospects of peer support staff as role models, serving as liaisons between clients and clinicians, and offering former clients a method of employment. For several administrators, the position also offers a new avenue of surveillance. They hope that peer support staff, with their experience with drug use, DCBS, and Horizons as clients, will be able to "call out" women for behavior that might not be noticeable to clinicians.

The role of peer support and other lay providers has been widely debated. Peer support staff are experts and may legitimize the knowledge of those who lack professional degrees. The peer support system may be a pathway for career development and allow those most affected by programs to have a stake in those programs. Peer support may offer a bridge between the community and clinical settings that are coercive and intimidating.[2] Yet service providers argue that having professional resources, such as credentials, assist them in maximizing the acquirement of resources for their program and their clients.[3] Relying on peer support rather than licensed practitioners can be a way to reduce costs, but this may sacrifice the quality of treatment and the quality of employment treatment programs are able to offer local residents since peer support staff are paid so little.

Almost a third of clients whom I interviewed agree that peer support staff are helpful because they share similar backgrounds. Several said they only stayed at Horizons because peer support staff members care about clients. Yet Katie and Maggie complained that peer support staff are too untrained to be helpful. Katie faulted peer support for not providing enough structure, as when she described the group sessions they moderated: "It's coloring. You know we're all mostly twenty-five and older. There is no structure to coloring and that all falls back on the staff in my eyes. Being lazy. This is therapy. It's not kindergarten." Some of these staff do not know how to connect women to resources or how to effectively lead group counseling sessions. Other women had previously used drugs with peer support staff, and a few even said that particular peer support staff members were the ones who introduced them to illicit drugs. This made working with peer support tense.

During my research, there was a peer support scandal. Two staff were being coercive in ways that clients found uncomfortable and inappropriate. They were primarily using threats and trading favors to obtain women's prescribed pharmaceuticals. A staff member gave Maggie an ultimatum: to either share her bupe or be given a positive drug screen. Maggie went directly to the peer support's supervisor. The supervisor investigated these claims, found evidence to support the story, and relocated the staff member to another program unrelated to substance use. The supervisor found evidence of a second peer support's misconduct. The second staff member resigned. Maggie and another woman dropped out of the program following the scandal because they felt they could no longer trust Horizons. In many ways, this is another instance of structural violence bleeding into women's lives through underfunded health care. Peer support are not paid a living wage and are in emotionally stressful jobs. They face similar barriers to accessing adequate substance use and mental health services as clients. Outside of Horizons, many are in the same position as clients in regards to housing, criminal records, and family responsibilities. The pressures they face come to bear on their clients.

Overall, staffing is an issue. In one year (2015 to 2016), the Adams County Horizons had five different clinicians. The clinician not only runs individual counseling sessions, but directs programming by creating rules and deciding on how group and individual counseling sessions are implemented. When I spoke to them, these clinicians cited a number of reasons for quitting: retirement, terminal illness, low wages, and rural location.

Former staff maintained that the chaos I witnessed was longstanding. Communication between administration and staff is poor. Poor wages lead to constant turnover. Many health care providers are unwilling to relocate to a rural area, where they think their partners may be unable to find employment and where they at times unfairly assume schools are low achieving. Administrators claimed Horizons loses clients when they do not have stable and quality personnel. If there is staff turnover, women will just leave because they are tired of retelling their story.

Clients are well aware of Horizons's economic marginalization and inability to offer needed services. Some women are in a constant state of panic because they do not have housing or food. Although women are targeted for state intervention and have access to resources because they are socially designated as caregivers, treatment programs nonetheless fail to provide the resources they need. Women often miss treatment because they do not have childcare. Horizons staff are frustrated by the absurdity of asking mothers to choose between treatment and working to earn money to house and feed their families. Yet programs do this as they make demands for therapy and drug testing that do not accommodate job schedules.

When they complained about lack of services, clients were rarely complaining about the staff per se. Clients were quick to justify clinician departures from Horizons, stating that clinicians were not paid enough through the program. Still, a large minority of those I spoke with who had experiences with Horizons said staff turnover negatively affected their progress through treatment. Every time they had a new clinician, they had to build rapport with another person and learn a new set of program rules.

Horizons staff find themselves constricted mediators between communities, various state agencies, and clients. The relationship between Horizons and communities is tense; every person I spoke with, whether pastor, local government, or teacher, had an opinion about the program. While those who had personal experience with Horizons had generally favorable views, other community members see it as too lenient because they think people who use drugs need to be harshly punished. This in part leads to the community stigma of Horizons. According to a case manager, the negative characterization keeps mothers from attending: "Now it's so stereotyped that if you're in this program you're a 'loser mother' and you're in trouble with the social worker. To the point that for some people, even if they wanted help, they wouldn't come into the program."

Horizons administrators ensure they work within state guidelines and structure the program to survive in a changing financial landscape, but they push these guidelines to serve people in ways they see as progressive. When distributing gas cards for transportation, they did not examine how clients used these cards because they assumed that people know how to use their resources. Most staff have nuanced understandings of sobriety and the usefulness of treatment. They supported people entering bupe and methadone clinics. One case manager defined success as a substantial decrease in use, even if clients continued to use cannabis to sleep. Yet staff had to report to DCBS and at times drug court, which created tensions both between the programs and between Horizons and their clients.

Gatekeepers cited stigma as a major barrier to accessing treatment. Hints of this appeared in women's narratives. Yet most of the women I spoke with identified lack of material resources and poor quality of care to be major shortcomings of the program. I am not arguing that stigma is not a felt problem, but it often presents as small cuts; lack of resources has the ability to eviscerate more quickly and wholly. Stigma undoubtedly has a hand in decreasing available resources at federal, state, and local levels. People who use drugs often do not talk about this societal-level stigma, however. They talk about the economic marginalization they feel while in these treatment programs.

Every person I spoke to with substance use concerns agreed that treatment should be more widely available. People make do with these programs, but they do not necessarily think that currently available services are helpful or adequate. A Horizons and buprenorphine client's statement probably reflect most clients' sentiments: "They should have done more." Sometimes they find enough mutual support with peers to attempt to create their own program.

Staff also make do. I think Horizons administrators and staff were the most understanding of people's marginalized positions and made the most effort to address people's concerns. Yet Horizons has little political support and meager funding to tackle such issues as unemployment and housing. From what I saw, I am convinced that staff do as much as they can. In these constrained positions, it is hardly fair to expect staff to be able to fully resist the systems that marginalize their programs, their clients, and themselves.

Meeting Needs and Jumping through Hoops

All the women I spoke with who had lost child custody wanted to regain that right through Horizons. About a third talked about ceasing drug use. A few more wanted to go back to school and to attain quality, affordable housing. Issues of child custody dominated our interactions. It is unsurprising, then, that the vast majority of clients identified assistance in regaining custody as one of the most beneficial services provided by Horizons. If women make it through Horizons, they are more likely to be reunited with their children. According to program documents, about half of all the women who enter Horizons regain custody when they graduate, while just over a third regain custody if they do not enter the program.

Every client I interviewed valued case management services but commented about its inadequate funding. The vast majority also found individual and group counseling sessions helpful overall. Due to drug use, caretaking responsibilities, and concerns over basic resources, people may not have had the time or energy to work through traumas. Many felt like this was the first instance in a long time where they were able to focus on caring for themselves. For Ashley, Horizons provided a safe space to talk through the emotional and physical pain resulting from prolonged domestic violence. Individual counseling was helpful. "Because of my mental health and because the abuse I went through with my baby's father where he hit on me. I wanted to tell somebody. I know what it feels like to want to say something and not be able to say it because you know you're going to get beat down."

Another client framed counseling as providing time to deal with the guilt that often comes with being a parent who uses drugs. Horizons can become a place of forgiveness. "It hurts me so bad because I carry that guilt and shame. I've done so much wrong to my kids and it hurts me so bad. Your kids are just like a ball, the counselor tells us, they jump up and go on. So why should we keep punishing ourselves?" The women I spoke with repeatedly lingered over this shame and guilt. After spending time with them over the course of their treatment, I can only see harm resulting from programs that further push this shame.

People are limited in their self-care strategies, and one way to deal with the guilt they feel may be substance use. Women said learning coping strategies was the most beneficial aspect of counseling. These strategies ranged from learning about self-esteem to practicing breathing techniques to reduce anxiety. They equated these strategies with reducing substance use as well as learning how to be "normal," a state of being they associated with abstinence from drugs, hard work, and a taming of emotional responses to challenging circumstances. While several Horizons staff defined substance use as a disordered form of coping that then resulted in harm, I see causation differently here. I do not think inadequate coping mechanisms, nor women's supposedly heightened emotions, are the cause of marginalization. Importantly, even coping mechanisms that the dominant culture considers "healthy," such as time intensive work in the formal sector and in fulfilling caretaking responsibilities, may exacerbate women's stress and poor health.[4] Horizons counseling sessions often helped women learn ways to cope with marginalization that are not as destructive as intense substance use. In my view, however, this is necessary but not sufficient because it does not address what causes marginalization in the first place.

Parents wanted help to get their children back in their home and valued time spent working through trauma, but their feelings about some aspects of the program were more nuanced. The idea of being normal resurfaced again and again. In treatment programming, whether described in documents or pictured in presentations, this normal is dressed in khakis, holding a smiling white toddler, and cooking a nutritious meal. Normal is working a well-paid full-time position while the kids are in school or at the grandparents'. Normal is being involved in the church and the school, but that is where social action ends. Normal does not have tattoos, bruises, or track marks. Normal has no personal, familial, or communal baggage. Most of these women said they want to become normal, but they contested these strict white middle-class notions of normal. The women (and some of the staff) I spoke with developed their own understandings of success, which put them at odds with treatment programs and other state agencies. Their normal was more radical in terms of its valuation of what they saw as working-class culture, which is a mix of benevolence, self-sufficiency, and deep commitments of care between people in the community.

Women took issue with how "normal" care was defined in Horizons. While some found the parenting modules helpful in giving them ideas, like making child bath time enjoyable, the majority said the parenting materials were useless because parenting was not their problem. The legal consequences of substance use were their main concern. They wanted to focus on their own lives, their grief, and their healing before they once again shouldered caretaking responsibilities. Some made fun of the parenting modules, calling them a "waste of time." Others were offended, saying that program materials were so basic that staff must think they were "stupid"; others did not agree with how the materials define a "good" parent. One woman was annoyed with the material because she thought it promoted consumerism and middle-class norms that she could not and did not want to meet:

> The textbook was like, if your kid is good you can take him out to McDonald's and buy him that. I'm sitting here looking at them saying, "I don't do that." And they say, "You have to reward your child for being good." You can look at them and say, "Good job." To me, it made me feel as if they were telling me to go out and buy, buy, buy. You can't do that for a child and that was one of my problems. I can't buy my thirteen-year-old video games after he mows the grass. Daddy has a good job but he still doesn't have it that way. You don't do things like that.

Most women said that while Horizons focused on their parenting, it did very little to support that role beyond education. Those who could not see their children or, conversely, those who had child custody but did not have reliable childcare, had the hardest time making it through. Katie labeled herself "blessed" and "privileged" because of her parents' provision of childcare. She attributed her initial success in Horizons to this support as well as her ability to see her daughter every day, even when she did not have custody.

The connection between Horizons and DCBS complicates women's navigations of therapy. Staff and clients are not sure what kind of information Horizons staff report to DCBS. According to duty-to-report laws, staff are supposed to notify DCBS of anything that could immediately harm children, but this leaves room for personal judgment. In our first interview, Ashley said that you have to be "smart" about what you say in treatment, but you still want to be "open and honest":

> You don't want to say something and have them get wind of it and them see it the wrong way. And then you don't get your kids back. These people have control over whether you have your kids or not. So you just gotta be smart about stuff.... I'm still open. I've always been an open and honest person. Secrets don't make friends and you know secrets end up eating at you. And I don't want to live that kind of life, I did that when I was using.

Although she described Horizons positively in our first interview, by the time we got to our second interview four months later, Ashley was frustrated. She felt disconnected from the staff because she thought they had told DCBS about issues that arose in individual counseling sessions that they should not have. She knew Horizons had to report her reactive drug screens to DCBS, but she did not know Horizons staff would report that Ashley was injecting her physician-prescribed bupe. Since Ashley's children were not in her custody and lived hours away, her injection of bupe could hardly pose harm to her children. With this report, she became reticent in class, speaking only when necessary. When I asked her a second time to identify the most helpful thing about Horizons, she said the free lunch every day. Maggie valued individual counseling. While Ashley only had access to individual counseling through Horizons, Maggie also received individual counseling through a bupe program where she felt more comfortable opening up. She did not think what she said would be repeated to DCBS because unlike the Horizons counselors, the bupe counselors do not have regular meetings with DCBS staff.

Horizons was at times less effective because programming did not make space for or materially support everyday caretaking, even though it focused on parenting. Some staff also seemed oblivious to the deep connection between Horizons and DCBS. Katie claimed that the Horizons program in a county next to Adams did not adequately address the intrusion of DCBS into its clients' lives.

> In [that] county, the clinician and the peer support specialist; nei-
> ther one of them have children. That bothers me. The clinician over
> there, if she hears from an outsider that you've been around some-
> body that she's heard you talk about in group, like an ex-boyfriend,
> she will not phase you into phase two; she will hold you in phase
> one. She says that she feels like that you need more time, but they
> also don't understand how crucial it is for these children to be with
> their parents either. I mean if they're passing their drug screens and
> they're coming to group, you know maybe it's not affecting them if
> they're talking to somebody from their past or whatever.

While this presents a problematic explanation of who can and cannot have empathy for others or understand care networks, it nonetheless shows that women are often critical of programs if they do not think program staff are taking into consideration women's care for their children.

Half of the clients I spoke to appreciated Horizons's flexibility in addressing people as individuals with specific needs requiring various responses. The other half equated this flexibility and individualization with a program that was biased and too lenient for some. Many found the program confusing, because they heard different rules and policies according to which client or staff member they were speaking to. With the focus on the individual, someone who was not progressing through treatment was blamed for not working program steps. This individualization may leave one of the greatest resources in treatment untapped, which is the collective strategizing and empathy built within group. While most thought they were supposed to be focusing on themselves throughout treatment, women also feared that the amount of time they spent in the program would negatively affect familial relationships.

Further ambiguities around the effectiveness of treatment were tied to relationships. A constant tension in all the programs was whether being around other people who use(d) drugs is beneficial or toxic. Fellow participants can be supportive, but people are being asked to expend more of themselves to care for each other. Seeing

participants ahead of them in the process can serve as a source of inspiration, and seeing other participants who are still heavily using can
show what they do not want to do again. Most important, people see
people going through similar struggles and they are provided a space
to talk about problems. These conversations help build human connection and allow people to collectively create strategies for navigating the mazes of addiction, relationships, trauma, and treatment. Yet
when others come to the program while using, this can be a trigger
that makes people want to use. As they share hopes and wins, they
also share frustrations, which can exacerbate everyone's stress. Group
can also be a place to find people to use with.

When I asked Sissy about the best parts of Horizons, relationships took center stage:

> Definitely, the girls. They helped. At the same time, it was like go-
> ing through a land mine field. You never knew when one of them
> would freak out on you because they had had a bad day in court.
> They were a blessing and a curse at the same time, like most things.
> Get a bunch of girls together and emotion is going to come out
> eventually, I mean that's the way it is. Especially when we were
> going through the things we were going through. Me too, there's
> days I went in there crying, too, not just them.

While she valued her friendships through Horizons, Ashley cited
other participants as being the biggest hurdle to ceasing use.

> It makes it hard. Like there was a girl, we were in the middle of
> class and we look over, and she's passed out. She came to class high
> as hell. So seeing that stuff sucks. I can't get high, so why the hell
> can you? [laughs] And some of those girls I really care about, and
> I'm seeing them hurt themselves and living that life and it sucks.

It is not only seeing others use that is difficult, but Horizons asked
Ashley to continue to care for those who may overdose, die, and
abandon her. After her children and their father moved out of the
area and with few established relationships nearby, Ashley had a limited network of supportive people. Ashley had one close friend, but

she died of an overdose. Ashley's mom had died a few years earlier and another close friend she lived with died of an overdose as well. "I think that's another reason I don't really hang out with anybody is because everyone I've ever loved usually overdoses, you know what I mean? Or they're still using and I can't be around them."

The care work that is built into the program feels good and supportive; at the same time, it is draining, explosive, and even dangerous, as when someone breaks confidentiality. For several people, relationships outside of treatment were torn apart when a staff member or client repeated something that was said in counseling sessions. While the work performed is remunerated in some ways, primarily relying on women's voluntary care work continues gendered exploitation. At best, the (mostly female) staff receives low wages.

For some, the treatment staff offer the best support because they are stable. For others, the treatment staff are somewhat irrelevant; others in the program are important. Katie, Maggie, and another client grew close as they processed through Horizons. They decided to start their own twelve-step support group with regular meetings, a Facebook page, picnics for those in recovery, and regular lantern releases at a local park to remember those who died from overdoses in the community. They wanted to start a twelve-step group because the closest regular meeting is roughly an hour and a half away. When I left the field, there was momentum and it seemed as though they were reaching people in the community who wanted to stop or decrease their drug use but did not have access to or want to go to other types of treatment. They were searching for funding to create more intense outpatient and even inpatient programs, but the granting process is so complicated that they did not know where to begin. While much of treatment in the United States is based on grassroots models that were developed more than a half-century ago, these models are difficult to follow in resource-poor areas and with complicated granting and insurance procedures. Appalachians facing substance use issues are striving for collective change, but their efforts are materially and bureaucratically bound.

For some, Horizons just felt like another unorganized maze they had to wander through because they happened to get caught using and were not wealthy enough to afford a lawyer who could get them out of the program. Sissy told me, "I just jumped through the hoops you know, played their game so to speak, I mean it's really not that hard to do what they ask and get your child back and still be an addict." Several called Horizons a "joke" after they were asked to color and watch fictional movies during group sessions. Others asked me during interviews about the purpose of Horizons, even after they had graduated or been in the program for months. Some thought they knew why the program existed: to dredge up the past and create another source of shame. They thus repudiated Horizons for forcing them to continually look back, instead of forward; as one client put it, "I didn't feel like talking. I wanted to talk about things that would help. The past is the past, it can't change. I want to talk about the future."

Horizons was created to reform mothers who use drugs and are at risk of losing child custody. Like many programs before it that focused on altering Appalachian mothers through education, there is much talk of parenting without much support of caretaking. Staff often do what they can, but their actions are stifled by funding streams, program policies, and societal acceptance of particular social service and public health programs. At times, staff themselves stigmatize mothers who use drugs. Sometimes staff make mistakes. Peer support and case managers in particular face similar issues with drug use, economic marginalization, and intense caretaking as clients. From what I saw, most Horizons administrators and staff members try to be empathetic and to offer an alternative to drug treatment outside of criminalization. Drug court, on the other hand, is born out of mass incarceration and a massive effort to criminalize substances and those who use them under the guise of the War on Drugs.

Chapter 4
Punitive Rehabilitation

D RUG COURT IS CLEARLY TIED to coercive governmental power. The state of Kentucky administers and (under) funds the program. Limits on funding and treatment capacity have led to a program that minimizes complications by admitting people who are most likely to graduate from the program. Those with mental health concerns or lack of resources in the form of housing and transportation, especially in rural areas, remain incarcerated. Drug court is not about decriminalization. Politicians, administrators, and staff view drug court as a practical program to get people out of expensive and overcrowded jails. The threat of incarceration hangs over participants' heads constantly. These folks are not in a jail or prison, but they are nevertheless criminalized.

The aim of drug court is to rehabilitate people who are labeled as deviant and is thus tied to particular understandings of citizenship where people's lives are centered on licit, paid work and personal responsibility. It is heavily influenced by some Christian models of recovery that equate government laws and hard work (even exploitive work) with God's will. In these ways, the multicounty program I describe in this chapter furthers a missionary history of reforming Appalachians, generally without challenging structural violence.

The Drug Court Model
Drug courts have primarily evolved in the United States because state and local governments are concerned with rising prison costs. Some policy makers have also begun to understand addiction as a medical disease that requires therapeutic services, not prison time. Kentucky

politicians from the federal level, including Senator Rand Paul, to the
county level promote alternatives to incarceration, like drug court. At
a state meeting I attended the secretary of the Justice and Public Safety
Cabinet described overpopulated prison and jail populations as a "public health disaster." He argued that incarceration is not working in Kentucky and that the state must treat addiction as a disease.

The spread of the drug court model has occurred simultaneously with a growing interest in restorative justice, which focuses
on assuming personal responsibility for negative deeds, expressing
remorse, and taking action to mitigate the effect of former behavior
on others.[1] Drug court does incorporate rehabilitative and therapeutic components, but it nonetheless continues a focus on punitive
measures through threats of incarceration and child removal if the
offender does not comply with the program. Efforts to funnel those
who use drugs into coercive treatment rather than jails represent an
individualized response to drug use that does not address the social
conditions in which use occurs.[2]

Drug court is the strictest of the programs, but people who had
graduated cited the structure as helpful in making it through the first
several months of treatment. Star talked extensively about the ups
and downs of drug court, buprenorphine, and drug use, but she never
failed to praise the highly structured nature of drug court. Star is not
new to recovery. She graduated from drug court more than five years
ago and is now on bupe. She valued most aspects of drug court, especially the drug court judge:

> He's awesome. I hated him at the beginning. I felt like he took my
> life away, but actually, it was me that done that, and I was grateful
> for him. He realized my husband and I had a problem. When I was
> in drug court, I was like in heaven. Now, I would love to be back
> in drug court, even if I had to sacrifice the rules. I didn't never get
> one sanction. I was determined to get my kids back. Also having
> the people around you, your friends. Cause once you get into drug
> court, become good friends, you're like a family. You don't want to
> let the other person down, so that was another reason that kept me

clean. I wanted to show all the rest of them that I was in it to win it and I wanted to get them to do the same.

Star thrived in drug court in large part because of the connections she made with staff and other participants. These connections helped her learn how to be a social person without drug use, and particularly how to fulfil the roles—as a "mother, wife, friend"—that she identified as important. Her close relationship with other participants allowed them to collectively call for drug tests in their home county so that they did not have to take a two-hour round-trip drive to test every morning. In addition to the collective action, Star attributed her success to her care for her children; she is convinced that she was never sanctioned because she took good care of her children. If Star thrived because she cared, what does this imply about those who do not succeed?

While Star framed her children as motivation to graduate from drug court, both Star and Alisha cited childcare as a hurdle to treatment completion. When Alisha was drug tested at six in the morning, she had to wake up her toddler son and drag him to the screening. Due to the strain she had already placed on her family, Alisha found very little support for drug court within her care network. The county attorney offered her drug court after a trafficking arrest. Alisha's mother was against the program because she didn't want to provide childcare to her grandchildren while Alisha attended the program. Alisha's grandmother told her that it was easier to care for an inmate, who at least stays in one place and is housed and fed, than it is to care for a drug court participant. Her grandmother had already spent much of her retirement savings on sending Alisha to treatment centers throughout Kentucky and Tennessee.

Alisha was successful in drug court. She partially attributed this success to the program and community mental health center staff. For her, the material support rather than counseling was vital. She was a client in the community mental health center program she currently volunteers for. The program in her home county is unique in that it

offers housing and paid internal jobs. For the duration of her participation in the drug court program and after her graduation, she and
her son lived in a program apartment, which gave them stable housing
as well as another source of support. Mothers are able to live in the
apartments by themselves, with their children, or with their children
and partner. Group sessions are held daily on the premises, creating a
sense of community among apartment residents and with others who
attend groups. She worked in a garden where clients are paid eight
dollars an hour, which gave her enough income to settle her court fees.

Approximately seven hundred women a year enter Kentucky
drug courts. Program sizes vary dramatically across the state due to
population size and the drug court administrative team. The drug
court I focused on is located in Adams County and serves two additional counties. The drug court team helps the judge decide which
cases should be admitted to and terminated from the program. The
team generally includes the prosecutor and defense attorney, as well
as representatives from DCBS, the community mental health center,
and law enforcement. Eligibility for drug court is based on medical,
criminal, and drug use histories. All participants must be nonviolent,
non-sex offenders who have committed drug or drug-related crimes
and admit drug abuse.

Participants cannot have chronic conditions that require medication that interferes with drug screenings. According to state-level administrators, drug court does not admit people who have co-occurring
substance use and mental health concerns that require medication because of interference of pharmaceuticals with drug screenings as well
as drug court's inability to provide participants with appropriate care.
Administrators insist that they do not want to "set people up to fail,"
especially in rural areas where mental health care is lacking. This policy
leaves those who are arguably the most vulnerable to languish in local
jails, where they receive no services.

Kentucky budgets enough to cover the basic drug court program,
but specific courts can apply for federal grants to offer expanded

services. Adams County did not have such a grant at the time of my research. I did speak to a judge who oversaw a drug court with a federal grant to offer case management for housing and transportation. In his view, substance use resulted from unemployment and a general lack of resources, which is why he applied for such a grant. According to his program's basic outcome data, the case management services dramatically increased the program's effectiveness. He said that people could more easily cease use when they had transportation and were not as concerned with homelessness.

Similarly to Horizons, drug court treatment consists of group therapy, individual therapy, and case management. Drug court and community mental health center staff led mandatory twelve-step group therapy sessions for participants. The twelve-step model considers alcohol or drug addiction a chronic illness. According to the model, sobriety occurs when individuals become more honest and display this honesty in public narratives of their addiction.[3] Despite the reliance on community mental health center staff to offer twelve-step sessions to clients, the local program administrator referred few women to the center's Horizons program. She did not agree with Horizons's tolerance of buprenorphine therapy for its clients. The therapeutic use of bupe created factions among those in the counties. The rift between Horizons and drug court is just an example of this larger debate.

In addition to group therapy at the community mental health center, participants are required to attend a self-help group session outside of drug court and the community mental health center. Since there are no local options for self-help groups, drug court contracts with a local pastor to provide twelve-step Bible-based group therapy sessions once a week. While belief in a higher power is part of traditional twelve-step programs, the Bible-based program focuses on this point and defines the higher power as a Christian God. Drug court contracts with the community mental health center to provide individual counseling as well. Case management is focused on helping participants meet program requirements. Like most treatment programs, drug court has random drug testing and attendance policies. Unlike Horizons and bupe programs, drug court requires clients to have housing, transportation, and either employment or volunteer work. Another unique aspect to the program requirements is that participants pay restitution and court fees.

Like the Horizons program, drug court is broken into three phases—the "stabilization phase," the "education phase," and the "self-motivation phase"—and programming is based on creating an individualized program plan. Making it through drug court graduation is more onerous than Horizons, with added employment requirements and more time-intensive treatment involvement. Participants must call drug court at six every morning to find out whether they will be randomly tested for drugs that day, and they have daily curfews requiring a call-in to drug court staff. For those living in Douglas County, participants must drive to Adams County to have a drug test. When participants are late for a screen, cannot produce enough urine, or drink too much water and have diluted urine, the test is counted as an automatic reactive drug screen, and they are sanctioned, which generally means jail time. Drug court is designed to last eighteen months for felonies and fifteen months for misdemeanors.

While client progression through Horizons affects DCBS cases, progression through drug court determines both DCBS cases and incarceration. If women have an open DCBS case, moving into higher or lower drug court phases affects visitation and custody. If participants fail certain drug court requirements, they can be sanctioned with jail time or terminated from the program. If terminated, participants are imprisoned for the entire time that was deferred from their criminal cases when they entered drug court. Drug court may allow someone to forego incarceration if they graduate, but they may still be charged with a felony that remains on their record and can limit housing and employment options.

Drug court's connection to DCBS and incarceration complicates what women feel they are allowed to say in counseling sessions. Several of those I spoke with argued that censoring one's words in counseling makes healing from trauma more difficult. Alisha felt betrayed when the counselor broke confidentiality to inform on her to the drug court administrator and judge:

> **Alisha:** I felt uncomfortable sometimes when the counselor shared things I had shared in confidentiality. I had signed a waiver that he could share, but it made me uncomfortable, so I stopped my individual counseling at that point. I removed myself from drug court. I didn't attend as many [Narcotics Anonymous] and [Alcoholics Anonymous] as I had been attending. I just did the bare minimum to get me by.
>
> **Lesly-Marie:** Did you not understand that he could share that?
>
> **Alisha:** No. He said that unless it would harm myself or another person, it would not be shared with drug court.

Several drug court staff agreed that fear of incarceration is the incentive for clients to enter and graduate from the program, and they believed that drug penalties have to remain stiff to act as a deterrent. Staff lamented the Kentucky legislature's passing House Bill 463 in 2011 to curb the number of inmates coming into prison and jails. This effort included reducing sentences for minor drug crimes unrelated to trafficking. Staff said the bill made penalties too easy on people who use drugs, revealing their reliance on criminalization policies. Those with a criminal conviction could spend less time incarcerated than it would take them to process through drug court. Those eligible for drug court decided to serve their jail time rather than enter drug court.

A former drug court judge disagreed with this analysis, saying he had seen more people in drug court with the passage of House Bill 463. The Adams County administrator complained that she had not had a new person enter drug court for over eighteen months. Although she blamed House Bill 463 at local meetings, she later told me that the relatively new Adams County drug court judge was not allowing enough people to enter drug court. Apparently, he deemed people ineligible for drug court if they had a past or current theft or burglary charge. When a new judge enters drug court the program can drastically change. (This is also the case when a new clinician joins Horizons.) The administrator admitted that publicly chiding a local judge was dangerous for her own employment as well as for the drug court program; he could shut it down at any moment.

Finding fault with House Bill 463 is problematic because Kentucky continues to have one of the highest incarceration rates in the country. Other bills have expanded the criminalization of substance use. In 2015, Kentucky passed Senate Bill 192, nicknamed the "Heroin Bill," in an effort to curb increases in opioid use and overdoses. The bill included some progressive legislation that supports harm-reduction services. Harm-reduction programs are meant to decrease the dangers associated with substance use by providing such services as syringe access programs, naloxone distribution, basic health services, and, in other countries, safer drug consumption facilities. Kentucky has arguably had the most successful and rapid implementation of syringe access programs in the United States.

On the other hand, Senate Bill 192 provides for stiffer criminal penalties for trafficking and drug paraphernalia (e.g., syringes, cookers). Those facing trafficking charges can be charged with homicide if drugs they sold aided in the overdose death of a person. Although prosecutions have been unsuccessful, women who miscarry and test positive for drugs are particularly targeted in this legislation. A woman's parental rights can be terminated if she tests positive for drugs during pregnancy, does not access prenatal care, and does not enroll in and remain compliant with a substance use treatment program.

Much like Horizons staff, drug court staff are mediators between the state government, local governments, communities, and clients. In Adams County, both funding issues and the judge threaten the program's viability. Prior to the beginning of fiscal year 2016, the local administrator, as well as other community members, were panicked that drug court would be defunded due to low participant numbers.

At the last moment, state officials notified Adams County officials that drug court would be funded for at least two more years.

Rural administrators have to implement urbancentric state guidelines. The requirement that all participants have their own transportation is made more difficult in vast areas of Kentucky where there is no public transportation and where services are geographically dispersed. The transportation requirement was one of Alisha's largest hurdles; she noted, "I almost slipped back to bad behaviors to manipulate someone to give me a ride to drug court."

Another drug court graduate was never sanctioned for having a reactive drug screen, but she was set back in the program and incarcerated for being repeatedly late to screens. The drug court administrator required her to work the second shift in a factory so she could make it to the morning screens. On the days she worked, she drove eighty miles to work, worked for at least twelve hours, drove back home, rested for an hour and a half, and finally drove thirty miles to her drug test. When we completed our interview, she had been awake for several days as a result of her job and drug court obligations.

Community buy-in of drug court wanes. Although some participants permanently cease drug use, others do not. No law enforcement personnel were involved in Adams County drug court, which is an anomaly for Kentucky. The local administrator said they "have lost interest." A former judge attributes this loss of buy-in to a misunderstanding of drug use in the community and among certain service providers.

> Drug court has successes, drug court has failures. I learned a long time ago, success isn't always a black or white situation. When I first started this, I thought I could if not save the world, at least save the county. And now I don't know if I can save one individual because you have so many setbacks. Sometimes if you just keep them alive, you've made a win. And you've got to accept the cliché, relapse is a part of recovery. So I try not to get too high on a success or too down on a failure, I just try to live with it. And we've had a number of drug-free babies. And my job is to yell and scream and hold people accountable. Most people come into drug court, if not virtually

all of them, come in to get out of jail. That is reality. We are not going to turn their lives around. Only they can turn their lives around.

The judge did seem overly concerned with people's reproduction and has a Bobby Knight-type reputation, but he delicately talked about the context of drug use as well as the limits of individual accountability. He said he was not wed to the drug court model and would do whatever he could to help his community. He expressed the sentiment common among drug court staff: drug court is an imperfect system but that it nonetheless offers the best option the county government had to address substance use.

> I've seen results of some studies that show drug court has higher degrees of success than other things. I think of all the things I've seen, drug court is the best thing going, with all its imperfections. If anybody wants to complain and wants to come talk to me with a better idea, I'll listen, and I'll try it if it's within my capabilities. And I'm not sure what's best; this appears to be. I can tell you one damn thing though, it ain't best just to do nothing and just ignore the problem and push it under the table.

He highlighted one primary imperfection he saw in drug court: lack of funding at the state and federal levels. He was the judge who claimed his drug court was more successful than others when he applied for and received a Substance Abuse and Mental Health Services Administration (SAMHSA) grant to provide case management services. He repeatedly said that drug use is a symptom of poverty and marginalization, not the cause. He recognized that drug court participants should be assisted in attaining resources if they are expected to succeed. Yet his drug court lost the grant, and he was no longer able to provide those services. He saw this as a great hindrance. Like other programs, drug court faces a similar cultural and economic marginalization as its clients.

Some service providers outside of drug court view the program as harsh and stopped supporting the program. A local housing authority director indicated:

I just really get so frustrated that it's easier for these individuals to get their drugs than it is to get help. Programs make it so difficult to get their help. They're like, "Well if they get out here and work for a pill, they can work for their sobriety." But I think it should be a little easier than getting a pill.

A few Horizons and DCBS staff agreed with this assessment. A former prosecutor said that the drug court requirement that participants have their own transportation and pay court fees is an obstacle to participation. The highly involved nature of drug court may create situations in which it becomes more costly in terms of time and finances than incarceration or continued drug use.

Promoting a Protestant Work Ethic

Drug court administrators want participants to stop using drugs, but they have other goals as well. Primarily, they want participants to maintain employment. Through employment, administrators expect people to reduce criminal activity, to pay restitution and child support, to learn personal responsibility, and to become self-motivated "productive citizens," which involves community activity. For the Adams County drug court, community activity was centered around church and Bible study. A final expectation of women is that they have "drug-free" babies.

Max Weber famously articulated the links between Protestant Christianity and the spread of capitalism.[4] In order for people to work harder for no increased benefits, at least to themselves, they must buy into their work. Protestants have done this through the idea of a "calling" to a profession. Working hard and even thriving within a capitalist system becomes an ethical mandate handed down by God. Although many people no longer believe in a Christian God, this mandate is handed down by our culture. The failure of some is explained by painting the poor and other marginalized populations as moral derelicts. In this scheme, the only way for someone who lives on the edge to become materially or morally rich is to work in the capitalist economy nonstop and without complaint. "God helps those who help themselves. . . . Thus the sanctification of life could almost assume the character of a business arrangement."[5] With these Protestant understandings, employment, citizenship, morality, and gendered social roles become intertwined.

Christianity is heavily pushed on people who use drugs in these Eastern Kentucky communities, especially if they have experience with drug court or any of the regional inpatient facilities, which are all Bible-based. In areas with strong and large faith-based communities, partial privatization of some social services has equated to a Christianization of those services.[6] Christian-centered discourses present substance use treatment as a process of working on the self in order to create a new and productive community member.[7]

Kentucky drug court orientation literature explains the importance of attending self-help groups and finding the group that works for each individual, since not every group is successful for every person. While this sounds conducive to meeting individual needs, drug court participants in every county except one have a single option for group. This group is Bible-based, to which some folks take exception. The allowance of a Bible-based program that is mandated in a state program, such as drug court, reflects moral understandings of poverty and addiction among local judges and court staff.

One story demonstrates the entanglements of neoliberal capitalism, Christianity, and understandings of motherhood. The same woman who remained awake for days on end to satisfy her work and drug court obligations valued drug court for teaching her to be "normal":

> [Drug court] is a place for you not only to learn how to live without using, but it is a program to stabilize you. To teach you how to live. It teaches you the norm. Now, I work a full-time job. I work forty, sixty hours a week, I go to school, I do my [Narcotics Anonymous] meetings, I do my group, I do my individual sessions, I do my court appearances, and I do my drug screens. In drug court they teach you to find a higher power, because without that, you will never make it. For me, it was not God. I am not a Christian. My higher power was my children.

What she does not mention in this narrative is that she faces housing instability and is the primary caretaker for her ailing mother and four children, one of whom has severe developmental delays. To me, the "normal" she learned looks like an exploitative circumstance created by a factory job that pays below a living wage, intensive responsibilities to drug court, and a lack of supportive social services for single mothers and older people. She commutes one and a half hours each way to a meatpacking facility. She works twelve- to fourteen-hour flexible night shifts with two thirty-minute breaks in a room that is kept below freezing. Although suffering back pain resulting from domestic violence injuries, she is required to stay on her feet throughout the shift. This licit employment does not pay as well and lacks the flexibility of her previous job in drug trafficking. While she does find a "higher power" in her children, she rejects much of the Christian drug court talk. I spoke with her three times, and the one thing she did not do was complain.

The relationship between drug court and local pastors complicates ties with the government. A local evangelical pastor led the mandatory weekly twelve-step Bible-based group. In my observation, drug court participants barely spoke in this session. The pastor said this was customary. The textbook for the group presents addiction as a moral failure where those who use drugs have decided not to follow God and must thus seek forgiveness through Christ. In the group I attended, the pastor repeatedly equated Kentucky law with God's law, arguing that it is good that everyone in drug court has troubles with the criminal processing system. These troubles show how drug court participants are sinning against God.

Outside of this group session, the pastor said that drug court is about learning that "life is hard." I doubt any treatment clients I spoke with needed to learn this lesson. He described his role as teaching people to get over any negative life events and to work industriously without complaint, no matter how hard the conditions. Another pastor told me that this model is important because "there is only a spiritual solution to addiction." This belief makes pastors counseling people who use drugs wary of any government programs that attempt to address substance use because there is supposed to be a separation between church and state. Yet this separation is obviously absent in Adams County drug court.

I felt the preeminence of Christianity at a drug court recovery rally and graduation, held atop a decades-old mountaintop removal site. Prayers and hymn singing were amplified on the unnaturally flat and barren landscape that overlooked rolling hills and valleys. Speakers in recovery called addiction not a disease but a "sin problem." This contradicts explicit drug court goals of understanding addiction as a disease. When a pastor from an inpatient facility stood to speak, Katie and several other treatment program participants whom I had interviewed left. One woman said, "I didn't come here to get saved." I asked someone about it later, and she told me that she left because she felt uncomfortable with the heavily Christian ceremony.

In some aspects, these ways of addressing addiction that are ostensibly Christian do not fundamentally differ from other therapeutic approaches I witnessed. All are tied to outside interventions on the individual focused on personal responsibility and middle-class ideals. Yet neoconservative understandings of addiction are born from the addition of conservative Christianity to neoliberal ideology. In this neoconservatism, Christian nationalism prevails as God's law is equated to US law. Christianity is not monolithic globally or across Appalachia. The instances I describe here are coming from what I consider conservative Christian groups. Some of the most important services offered in the region are done through other types of Christian services. I have encountered numerous Catholic nuns who are formidable forces in acting against mass incarceration, pharmaceutical company maleficence, and absentee land ownership. Appalachian Christian organizations have been operating harm-reduction programs for decades. In the five-county area, the women spearheading the drive for a homeless shelter are clergy.

Only two women found the Bible-based group sessions helpful because they said it offered them hope of becoming a "good" person. While most thought the Bible study is simply boring, others were offended. To quote Alisha:

> I felt forced into religion and I have peace with my faith and I didn't think it was something people should be mandated to go to. I didn't feel like God was the cause of it so why should he be the sole fix of it?

I am not suggesting an elimination of Bible-based programs; clearly some people find them helpful. I oppose placing vulnerable people in situations in which such programs are the only ones available and are forced upon people, as is the case for Adams County drug court.

Redefining Relationships

Drug court staff are concerned with regulating what they see as another aspect of morality: relationships. Social connections become an indicator of whether participants are being productive members of their families and communities. Drug court takes a hard line when it comes to breaking past relationships, or shifting "people, places, and things," in Alcoholics Anonymous and Narcotics Anonymous terminology. Staff focus on what they call "toxic" relationships. They encourage participants to disengage from family and friends who continue to use drugs. When staff heard that a participant was associating with people who use, the participant was sanctioned and sent to jail.

Drug court participants I spoke with collectively argued that you have to sever ties with those who continue to use drugs to be successful in the program. According to this group, these cuts are no real loss because others who use are just "pill" or "drug" friends, not "real" friends. Yet the most fundamental complaint people expressed in interviews about drug court was how staff treated relationships. Clients thought staff deemed relations positive or negative based solely on drug use; people who use(d) drugs felt that their connections were more complex.

One woman had to sever connections to abide by drug court policies and mourned the loss of those she no longer saw. In some ways, she relinquished people who had supported her emotionally and helped her develop strategies to survive addiction in the fringes:

> I had to cut ties with them. And it's hard because, most of them, I have to say, are really supportive. They see me, and they'll be like, 'I'm so proud of you, I wish that I could get clean.' But then you still got the occasional one that tries to be like, 'When we going to get out and run around?'"

That last sentence reflects the harm that can come through relations that provide care in some phases. She vacillated between characterizing her associations with other people who used drugs as caring and as exploitive. When I asked her if it matters that she had to shut former friends out of her life, she said:

> It didn't really bother me because they were only around when we were using together. You know, if I had what they wanted or if they had what I wanted. I mean whenever I sat up there in jail for seven months, I didn't hear from nobody. Didn't even offer to send word with my family or nothing, "Tell her hey. Tell her I'm thinking about her." I ain't got no use for anybody like that.

Alisha nearly quit the program because of the judge's intervention in her family. She relied on her father and her son's father for emotional and financial support, both of whom continued to use while she was in drug court. The judge told Alisha he would send her to jail if she did not stop seeing them. While they continued to give her money, she did not see her father or son's father for months. Alisha labeled this time period as "almost unbearable."

At the same time, drug court can force others together. The program is run for both men and women without separation. When partners are asked to complete drug court simultaneously, the program forces partners who used together to spend all of their time together, instead of coercing them to relinquish ties. One woman was forced to complete drug court with her abusive and competitive husband. He made the program a twisted game, where he would become violent if he thought she was doing better than he was.

Star felt like she was coerced into a relationship with a sponsor.

> I just feel like when newcomers come in, they need to let them find out theirself, like not making them have to put in all their faith or trust in someone they don't even know. You have to have a mentor and you have to have a sponsor, well trust was always a big thing for me anyway. I trust my husband completely; one person on my finger that I can count. A lot of people can't just get into trust and they expect that out of you, like that's a rule. The sponsor thing, I guess it should be on your terms.

Like other participants, Star greatly valued the events drug court held outside the program to bring together current participants, alumni, their families, and community members. These included picnics, recovery rallies, and graduations. Star tried to use these voluntary gatherings to build a network outside of drug use, because she felt like she had no one outside of that network.

I attended a recovery rally and graduation ceremony. It was a space where alumni and current participants mingled, laughed, and hugged one another, along with their partners, parents, and children. They had a potluck where participants contributed to the sharing of a meal. Women felt like these were times when they could reconnect to their families and community, as well as form new relationships with others who had ceased use. These events provided a reimagined social group outside of people who were currently using. Importantly, these events that drug court formally arranged were the only times participants were supposed to see one another outside of the program. Because of the importance placed on the connections built within drug court, Star struggled with the ban on seeing other participants:

> And they tell you to change your people, places, and things. Drug court is your family now, but we're not allowed to see our family. That's not right at all. Which we done it anyway, to be honest. I mean that's all we had was each other.

Drug court took away her social network and then denied her the power to build a new network.

Drug court is a program outside of a corrections institution that uses the threat of incarceration to enforce drug disuse. Its goal is to transform people who use drugs into sober, productive, and moral citizens. The program offers the most structure of any in the area; some find it useful. Conversely, and compared to the options of either Horizons or drug court, buprenorphine programs are the most loosely tethered to state agencies.

Chapter 5
The Pharmaceutical Approach: Suboxone

B UPRENORPHINE, UNIVERSALLY KNOWN AS SUBOXONE, is one
of the more recent medication-assisted treatments (MATs)
and the most widely available in Eastern Kentucky. The medication itself is supposed to have certain effects according to the manufacturer, but bupe is experienced by individuals and communities in
ways that differ widely from pharmaceutical company claims. While
bupe programs in the five counties are for-profit, the federal government and state of Kentucky nonetheless heavily regulate them. With
Kentucky's Medicaid expansion, the government also pays for most
bupe and some affiliated services.

Kentucky has established requirements to make programs more
effective, but these have unintended consequences for providers and
clients. Programs become punitive landscapes designed to protect
providers and may offer services that clients must pay for and use,
whether they want the services or not. Law enforcement, drug court,
and DCBS are highly suspicious of bupe along with all pharmaceuticals, creating harmful gaps in which people fall as these agencies
punish people for using an evidence-based medication. People are
prevented from taking bupe, and if they do enter a program, especially while pregnant, they risk losing child custody.

Pharmaceutical Administration
The most commonly available form of bupe in rural Central Appalachia is mixed with naloxone in a sublingual strip. Every local program
I encountered provided clients take-home doses. Many women take
their full dose in the morning by dissolving it under their tongue,

which is the method providers encourage. Others took different approaches—dissolving pieces of strips sublingually throughout the day, trying to wait as many hours as they could between doses, or injecting the substance. Programs and clients approach tapering differently. Some programs and individuals try to find a dose that works and may not taper for long periods of time, expecting that the client may be on the medication long-term. Other programs taper a client in six months or so, whether the client wants to or not. On the other hand, some clients begin tapering themselves, and may or may not tell their provider, either stockpiling or selling their unused medication. When injected, naloxone is supposed to produce withdrawal symptoms. Thus, the addition of naloxone theoretically encourages individuals to swallow or dissolve bupe in their mouth rather than injecting the substance. Both health care providers and program participants question the effectiveness of naloxone as prevention from misuse because people who inject bupe with naloxone tend to feel euphoria. Bupe injection may not only produce euphoria, but also increase the risk of blood-borne pathogens if contaminated syringes are used.

Unlike methadone, bupe is supposed to be less addictive than heroin and methadone, less likely to depress the respiratory system compared to other opioids, and less likely to cause overdose.[1] Both methadone and bupe are associated with overdoses when combined with benzodiazepines or alcohol.[2] Though service providers with whom I spoke categorically defined street drugs as harmful, they viewed pharmaceuticals as healing or harmful, reflected in the concept of pharmakon.[3] The pharmacological aspects of MAT are one place where this idea of pharmakon arises.

The legality of MAT becomes tied to its intent.[4] Is it intended to be used for euphoria or therapy? Through research, development, and production, drug companies try to define the intent of MATs by making them materially different than street drugs because they are formulated to be consistent, pure, and efficient. Yet what is evidently clear to service providers in the current study, which underlies many of their concerns with MAT, is that MAT efficacy is not overdetermined. These medications may be used against indications and they do affect people differently.[5] Previous research on methadone shows that its detractors view it as just another drug that increases rates of crime and social upheaval.[6] Bupe detractors take a similar view in Central Appalachia.

Beyond pharmacology, the way the Food and Drug Administration (FDA) approves and formally distributes bupe differs from methadone. The Controlled Substances Act (1970) and the Narcotic Addiction Treatment Act (1974) heavily regulated methadone and additional MATs. In 2000, the Drug Addiction Treatment Act made it possible for bupe to be prescribed in physician offices.[7] Bupe was FDA approved to serve wealthier, primarily white clients in private clinics away from the surveillance implemented in methadone clinics, which are often located in urban neighborhoods of color.[8] In Central Appalachia as well as across the United States, methadone is only available in heavily regulated clinical spaces where clients are required to dose in front of staff on a daily basis for years before they earn privileges for take-home doses. This made methadone inaccessible to most in Eastern Kentucky, since at the time of research, there was only one methadone clinic located two hours away from Adams County. Bupe is distributed through private physicians and is immediately available to be consumed privately, offering more flexibility in provision.[9]

Increased usage of bupe in some ways parallels the rise of methadone in the 1970s, with factors both pushing and pulling people into treatment.[10] Heightened surveillance of prescribers and distributors of prescription opioids has resulted in fewer opioids being available in illicit markets. Prescription opioids' changing formulations that are increasingly difficult to manipulate for inhalation or injection has made them less popular among those who use drugs.[11] The lack of available and desirable opioids has pushed those who use drugs into bupe programs. With mental health and substance use treatment parity in Medicaid, several Medicaid insurers now cover bupe. More people also have access to Medicaid through expansion. Thus, more clients are pulled into bupe programs because they have insurance that will cover the medication and counseling sessions. Yet in these five counties, the therapeutic use of bupe has yet to garner the support from some law enforcement and policy makers that is described with methadone.[12]

In Kentucky, clients at both methadone and bupe programs are subject to random urine drug screenings to test whether they are taking the MAT and if they are consuming additional substances. Bupe's less structured method of distribution as compared to methadone has drawn criticism among the public, law enforcement, and politicians in Kentucky. In rural Appalachia, as in France and Baltimore, the diversion of bupe from formal networks where it is coded as "medicine" to informal networks where it is coded as a "dirty" commodity is the location of much of the conflict.[13] Yet informal distribution networks may help create formal networks as people who use drugs experiment with bupe on the street and then enter formal networks through clinics if they decide that it works for them.[14] Bupe's diversion is not unique considering that formal and informal networks of pharmaceutical distribution are intimately linked.

Maggie insisted that bupe saved her life, even though she was technically taking it off-label. The providers I spoke with claimed that bupe could in no way help with methamphetamine dependence and that it is not FDA-approved for this purpose, but she did take it to quit meth. Her parents drove her to go to the hospital after a particularly bad night, and hospital staff said they would not give any medication to someone coming off meth. Maggie's dad marched into a buprenorphine provider's office in River County, demanding they that take his daughter into the program; they agreed. Maggie attended the program and plans to be off bupe within a year of entering. She attributes her maintained recovery to the bupe clinic, not just bupe. She valued the additional services she obtained beyond the medication, such as counseling and case management. The case manager was helping Maggie re-enroll in college so she could finish her bachelor's degree.

Some of those who use bupe argue that the drug has stabilized their lives. For those who largely celebrate it, they focus on the ability of bupe to turn people who use drugs into "normal" citizens who can have jobs and care for their families. Katie said bupe allowed her to fulfill her social roles: "It keeps me a functioning human being in society and I can live my life and pay my bills and take care of my daughter and provide for her. I'll stay on it the rest of my life if that's what I have to do." For Katie, the drug itself helps her make it through—she found little use for the counseling and case management at the clinic.

Most of the women I spoke with do not take the full amount they are prescribed, which explains some of the diversion. This saving of bupe serves purposes beyond simple diversion. Katie was prescribed two bupe strips a day but only took half of one. The others are stored away, in anticipation of her clinic closing or bupe being criminalized. She does not want to be left without bupe in the case of either of these events, because she said she would go back to using heroin. Star is also on bupe, and she struggles with it:

> Like they put you on [bupe], saying, oh, this is going to help you, but what helps you get [off of] that? They say, taper yourself down. I taper myself down. I've tried to go without it. I don't get sick like I did with OxyContin, I don't throw up and have [the] itchy feeling, diarrhea. I feel like somebody's beating me with a baseball bat. I think my biggest fear is those bad days that you do have. As an addict, you don't have a calendar and you don't know like Monday I'm going to have a trigger or Friday I'm going to have a bad day. I don't have a fear of thinking I'm going to need it every day, my biggest fear is when I am going to need it. There's got to be a way out of all this. I'm just trying to figure out how.

She was told to take bupe daily, but she prefers to take it on an as-needed basis to help control anxiety and stress, which is exactly what she does. This gives her some control over her life, she feels; she stores some of the bupe so that she will have a supply in the event that she is unable to get it regularly. Perhaps those who favor highly controlled bupe consumption would say Star's method reduces her chances of successfully ceasing illicit drug use. Star has been removed from chaotic and harmful drug use for years at this point, so maybe not. What it does show is that people do not trust that they will have continued adequate access to MAT?

Programs

At the time of my fieldwork, it was nearly impossible to pinpoint a bupe program's structure because of constant shifts. Some programs opened and closed repeatedly without warning. Requirements at other settings changed sporadically. This chaos was caused by consistently changing reimbursement rates and government buprenorphine regulations and should be unsurprising considering bupe's relative novelty and quick uptake across the country.

Prescribers must undergo SAMHSA training and be specially licensed with a DEA number to provide buprenorphine. Providers may only have up to thirty patients at one time in their first year of prescribing. In the second and subsequent years, providers may apply to SAMHSA to qualify to have 275 patients. The DEA can audit providers at any time to ensure that they are serving only their limit and are prescribing legitimate doses. All Kentucky clinics have drug testing and a behavioral modification component as mandated by the Kentucky board of licensure. This mandate reflects federal clinical guidelines. Some clinics hold twelve-step groups to meet the behavioral modification requirement. Others provide individual therapy sessions, billing either individuals or insurance companies for these sessions.

Both of the clinics I visited required clients to attend individual counseling sessions and provided case management services, such as assistance in finding housing. Case management is limited due to fickle policies and lack of insurance reimbursement. One buprenorphine counselor spent about thirty minutes with each client from once a week to once a month, depending on how long and how successful a client has been in the program. She mainly provides cognitive behavioral therapy.

Cognitive behavioral therapy asserts that such mental health concerns as anxiety and depression result from particular negative thought and behavior patterns within the individual. These negative mental paths are disordered in that they are not changed, even when presented with contradictory information. Thus, cognitive behavioral therapy is focused on making implicit ways of thinking explicit, analyzing thought and behavioral patterns, and altering mental models to result in more positive thoughts and behaviors.[15] This type of therapy can be practiced in many types of ways; one counselor I spoke with said she focused on relaxation techniques to prevent anxiety and negative thoughts. While alterations in thinking and coping may be useful, relying on individual therapy as the only ancillary service to bupe continues the focus on the individual without altering the environment that produces individual experience.

None of the bupe clinics that participants in this study or I encountered had formal program phases like drug court and Horizons. Instead, counselors, prescribers, and clients worked together to discuss appropriate amounts of time spent in outpatient counseling and bupe dosage. There were no bupe programs in two counties. One bupe program for women was open in Adams County for a few months, but it closed because of financial difficulties that remained impossible to identify. In adjacent counties, people could receive services through three programs.

Program eligibility requirements are shifting and unclear, in part because of policy chaos and differing understandings of bupe's feasible uses. Some service providers, existing clients, and people seeking services told me that some providers adhere to FDA bupe guidelines; others alter their prescribing practices to match their own clinical experience. Some programs accept only people who are actively using opioids and nothing else; some accept people who are currently not using but fear they may begin use again. Others accept people who are using meth.

Several providers argued that Medicaid expansion has not had the full impact that it could have on substance use treatment because the managed care organizations (MCOs) that enrollees must select when signing up for expansion have limits on reimbursement for particular services. A bupe provider could get the MCOs to pay for bupe and other medications, but she and other providers have difficulty being reimbursed for physician time spent in appointments or counseling services. Programs are financially insecure because of low and uneven reimbursement rates for office services. Thus, businesses shut down frequently. Office closures leave people without prescribed bupe. If they don't want to start withdrawals, they must quickly find another source, which may be illegal, as Ashley demonstrates:

> I was going to Lexington. Dude! I go to my doctor's appointment, and there's a sign on the door that says, "Sorry, we're shut down, please call [another doctor] at this number." But that doctor charges $300 a month, and so I couldn't go there. I've been buying Suboxone off the street, but I'm in another place right now. I have to go to four counseling sessions and then they can start writing Suboxone because that's the insurance policy. So I've got two down, I've got two more, and then they'll start writing Suboxone for me.

According to Ashley, the doctor she was referred to does not accept Medicaid, which is why doctors charge $300 a month. Overall, it can be difficult to find bupe programs that accept any kind of insurance.

Women reported that bupe staff are quick to terminate services to clients because the clinics are afraid of public scrutiny. This runs contrary to understandings of ebbs and flows with drug use and to efforts by Horizons and drug court to sanction users rather than to terminate services. Three women were denied service from one program when they tested positive for cannabis. After they lost their prescription, they either began buying bupe illicitly or began using other illicit drugs, primarily meth or opioids.

Bupe Stigma

The therapeutic use of bupe is controversial. Most people I interviewed who had no experience with bupe, either personally or through close family or friends, were deeply skeptical of the drug for two main reasons. First, many hold puritanical views of drug use. They see use of all substances, ranging from alcohol to psychopharmaceuticals, as harming the body, revealing some underlying weakness in the individual, and preventing people from performing social roles. They extend their focus on the dangers of prescription opioids and benzodiazepines to all medications that can be seen as treating mental health issues, from selective serotonin reuptake inhibitors to antipsychotics. This is a gendered distrust of pharmaceuticals; the pills are seen as disrupting women's caretaking. According to a drug court staff member, women on bupe and methadone are not fulfilling their roles as protectors of their children because children might ingest these substances and overdose. Other administrators have argued that all women on bupe should be sterilized or be on long-acting reversible contraceptives to prevent pregnancies that might produce "addicted" babies.

To be fair, some who question bupe use are aware of the unsavory actions of Purdue Pharma, pharmaceutical distributors, and overprescribing physicians, and this underlies their current concerns with all pharmaceuticals, including bupe. They think bupe makers are just capitalizing on the opioid epidemic that the companies created in the first place. The pharmaceutical companies that manufacture MAT are suspect. Mallinckrodt, the primary manufacturer of methadone in the United States and worldwide, is also the maker of one of the most diverted and misused prescription opioids in rural Central Appalachia, generic instant-release oxycodone.[16] Methadone is used to treat dependence to instant-release oxycodone. As of fall 2018, Richard Sackler applied (together with a subsidiary of Purdue Pharma) for a patent for a wafer form of bupe. If approved, he will have gained a fortune from both a cause and a treatment for opioid use.

Pharmaceutical companies are part of the systematic industrial disinvestment in Appalachia. Mallinckrodt closed a plant in Appalachian South Carolina in 2012 to move 595 full-time jobs to a facility in Costa Rica.[17] Reckitt Benckiser, the primary global maker of bupe, started producing Suboxone as a sublingual dissolvable film and ceased production of Suboxone tablets because the company said the film is less likely to be accidently taken by children. Some medical providers and generic drug makers have criticized Reckitt for this move, stating that in fact the Suboxone delivery method was changed because the patent on the tablets expired in 2010 while the patent for the film does not expire until 2022.[18] In a country with already inadequate substance use treatment, Reckitt has exacerbated this lack by extending its control of the market and thus maintaining high bupe prices. Private insurers and Medicaid have been reluctant to cover bupe because of its expense.[19]

Bupe providers and clients claimed that these conflicts have led to seemingly constant law enforcement and media surveillance of clinics. This surveillance has stoked fear among providers, who pass this fear to clients, and to anthropologists. When I entered two bupe programs, staff treated me as a form of surveillance; one of my participants told me that they thought I was a "rat." Some providers have chosen to downplay that they offer bupe. The prescriber in one county was reluctant to speak to anyone, including me, about providing bupe. He couched the bupe program in the full range of services he provides from cradle to grave, which is shown in the health clinic. I spent time in the community-oriented waiting room before I interviewed the program counselor. Most patients present were seniors, with a few middle-aged patients and parents with children. Cartoons were blaring for the kids, and many folks were engaged in conversations about the community or their family.

Other providers create punitive clinical landscapes. When I attended the bupe program with Maggie, I was in the waiting room for over an hour while she saw her counselor and got her prescription.

A security guard walked through every twenty minutes. A plethora of signs were posted through the small and overcrowded room. All of the signs seemed to be yelling at you: "Don't be late; don't go anywhere while you're waiting or we will skip you; no children in appointments; you must make appointments yourself and no one can make them for you; no shoes, no service." These are strategies used by providers to protect themselves from losing their business and possibly their freedom to law enforcement and prosecutors who view bupe prescribers as dangerous. Providers also employ these techniques to dampen media critique of bupe. In this instance, state criminalization of drug use and societal stigma against bupe comes into clients' lives through their interactions with health care providers.

Clients must deal with punitive clinicians, state agencies, and health insurance MCOs. One provider argued that MCOs are trying to lessen their spending on bupe by requiring programs to administer drug tests and then stopping payment for bupe when people test positive for other drugs, even those that do not dangerously interact with bupe, such as cannabis. When MCO payment is ended, the programs end bupe treatment instantaneously if clients cannot pay out of pocket. This represents the spread of the carceral state into the private realm as MCOs are utilizing intense surveillance, examinations, and sanctions to control costs. These tensions between providers, state agencies, community members, and MCOs create clouds of misinformation that hang over people who use drugs.

Katie went into a methadone detox the day after she found out she was pregnant:

> They put me on methadone and then I was completely weaned off before I went home. It was just enough to get me off of the heroin. Not enough to get me addicted to methadone. I hadn't been out of there forty-five minutes and I had used again. I wasn't ready. But they wanted me to switch to a clinic for pregnant women who are on drugs. But now I'm glad that I didn't do that either because Subutex is ten times more dangerous for a child in the womb than heroin ever thought about being. And plus, if I would've been put

on Subutex, my child would've been took anyway. I do not understand that.

Katie's comments illustrate a lay person's knowledge and misunder-
standings of Subutex. Subutex is hardly more harmful than heroin,
but DCBS might enter a family's life whether a woman is prescribed
Subutex or illicitly taking heroin; this is important to understand
prior to entering a bupe program.

Maggie offers a good example of buprenorphine stigma. She
wanted to enroll in a clinic for a year before she was able because she
lacked transportation. She had to convince her mother of the legiti-
macy of bupe, because her mom thought bupe was "just substituting
one drug for another." When I interviewed her, Maggie kept telling
me how terribly she is treated in the community because she takes
bupe, especially by the local pharmacists:

> The stereotype of when I take my prescription to the [pharma-
> cist], they look at you like, "Oh, hi," and then they look down and
> they're like, "Oh," which I would rather see somebody on Sub-
> oxone any day than getting a prescription for Lortab or Xanax.
> Before, I stereotyped the same way. I thought if somebody's on
> Suboxone, they're just a piece a crap. They're just getting it to have
> drugs to resale, but gosh, no, for me, it levels me out.

Maggie asked me to come to the bupe clinic and the pharmacy with
her so I could see for myself.

We left Adams County in the early afternoon to drive to the bupe
clinic in the county over. After her appointment, Maggie and I drove
back to her pharmacy in Adams County. When we went in, no one
was there and the pharmacy tech was sitting behind the counter re-
stocking a display. Maggie was overly nice. She is a photographer and
brought an envelope of horse pictures for the pharmacist to give to
his daughter. She handed these pictures, along with her prescription,
to the tech. As soon as the tech looked at the bupe prescription, her
face fell. She said she did not know if she could get the prescription
ready before the pharmacy closed in three hours. Maggie was polite

but obviously infuriated. She told the tech that her doctor said they had to have the prescription for her that night because she would run out of bupe the next day. The tech said she could only get the prescription ready if no one else came in for the rest of the night.

Maggie said okay and pulled me aside. Her face was bright red and she complained that she was there first and should be served first. She was really worried because she lives thirty minutes from the pharmacy and did not have enough gas money to come back the next day for her prescription if they could not fill it that night. Another customer came to the pharmacy, and they were promptly told their prescription would be ready in twenty minutes. I thought Maggie would explode, but she sat there patiently. Almost two hours later, her prescription was ready. She texted me later that she made it back home sometime after eight in the evening. It took her almost eight hours to obtain her weekly prescription. While Maggie and some others value the counseling service available through the bupe clinic, the requirement that clients use it adds to an already long day. If we accept Sissy's definition of addiction as having your life centered around an object, then Maggie is in some ways addicted, not necessarily because of anything physical or mental, but because several days of her week every week are focused on filling her bupe prescription.

Even service providers who fundamentally support bupe agree that programs can simply be moneymaking schemes. To prevent that, they propose that programs accept insurance coverage to become legitimate and offer counseling and additional services, such as job placement. This would show that the providers care about the community, not just money. A university researcher I spoke to equated lack of counseling to a fraudulent bupe program:

> What we are seeing in many of these rural communities is doctors who come in, who understand there's a problem in the community, set up shop, and it's a moneymaking scheme. It's not altruistic in any way. They're there to make as much money as possible, which is giving Suboxone potentially a bad name. It's actually a very effective drug when used in conjunction with counseling

and all of these other services, including primary care, sometimes mental health services. But from what I'm hearing of those providers in that area, it's bring in cash, we don't take any insurance, and come and get your prescription. You may or may not even see the physician. They may or may not do any drug tests.

In one of the counties where a research project director works, some of the same physicians who faultily prescribed OxyContin are now prescribing buprenorphine. Again, as they charge people for clinic visits and in some cases own their own pharmacies, they are profiting from both misuse of opioids as well as efforts to stop using opioids.

A state substance use treatment administrator attributes the lack of counseling to diversion of bupe from licit to illicit use:

> Suboxone is an effective tool. My only concern is that the physicians are not very well regulated. The feedback that I'm getting off the street is if they typically need four to six milligrams of Suboxone, they're taking half, selling the other half to pay for treatment, so they get a free ride. And that's where the diversion is. And subsequently, if you're opiate naïve, you can get high on Suboxone. So that's an issue too.

For these gatekeepers, bupe is beneficial if it does not produce euphoria, but it becomes harmful once pleasure is introduced because pleasure is equated to addiction. I heard the story about diversion more times than I can count from community members, gatekeepers, and clients. From what women said, bupe is being diverted and injected. While this administrator is concerned about diversion, other providers see bupe diversion as indicative of a lack of access to treatment programs. People are sharing prescriptions because they do not have individual access. Yet in women's lives, diversion and illicit bupe use does not seem to be as detrimental as service providers and politicians portray. Several women, including Sissy, entered a clinic after using illicit bupe to see if the medication would work for them. Other women don't enter the clinic because they do not want a full prescription of three bupe strips a day. Instead, they buy half a strip illicitly to help with withdrawals and other physical pain.

Women's Encounters with Bupe Treatment

When women enter bupe programs, they note several positive side effects. Having bupe prescriptions keeps them from people who are selling various substances that may be more harmful and may interact dangerously. Women gain access to clinical services they want, such as counseling and drug testing. In the words of one, "I now stay at home and take care of what needs to be taken care of. Suboxone's helped me with all of that." But learning how to change old patterns and routines can be hard, as Sissy informed me:

> And that's a whole other thing, you have to learn to stay home. You get up and run after pills, every morning. That first morning when you take Suboxone and you don't have to get up and leave, it's kind of confusing. You get used to going around people and being in the middle of a crowd. The running is addictive too. You have to relearn your daily grind. I mean I can't stress enough how hard that is, to get used to not being around. And there are a lot of really good people that are on drugs, too, that you have to give up. And they will, not even meaning to, drag you into it.

This ties back to the helpfulness of structure in other programs, but it is a more self-imposed structure that occurs in the home. People must structure their lives to take bupe in the morning rather than driving to find drugs and acquaintances when they awake. Their social relationships generally change dramatically. Sissy said bupe would not have worked for her if she had not had a strong care network.

While it was difficult for her to cut ties with some people who use drugs when she was ceasing use because she thinks they are good people, Sissy was able to insert herself directly back into her family because they accepted her. This decreased any isolation she felt as she stopped spending time with people who use drugs. Sissy attributes her success with bupe to the support of her husband, who she says has never used drugs, as well as to her nonjudgmental physician and nurses:

> And [my husband's] supportive, rather than tearing me down with it, he's hold me up. Whenever I first got on the Suboxone program,

I wasn't real good at taking my medication correctly, and so I'd talk about it with my doctor, I told him, I let my husband keep it. He gives me what I'm supposed to have every day in the morning and before he leaves for work. For probably the first year that I was on it, he kept them for me and doled them out to me, which he never made it a thing, he just always put them in this little drawer in the kitchen and he never was acting like he was God or something.

For Sissy, ceasing illicit drug use is only aided, not determined, by any type of substance use treatment. For her, it is not only about the pharmaceutical or the counseling and case management available at the bupe program, but also about that life outside of treatment that enables her to remain in recovery. Without her immediate family, extended family, other women who she met through Horizons, and support provided through government agencies, she might not have ended her illicit drug use.

Being able to implement the change at home can be a more drawn out process, which may be appropriate for some. Many are in bupe programs for years, much longer than clients in Horizons or drug court. Bupe programs are helpful because they allow people to slowly change their lives, including their routines. In inpatient or outpatient programs, by contrast, people are forced to quickly change their lives for ninety days or so. After treatment, they immediately return to previous lives.

Some find bupe programs to be useful but also characterize them as moneymaking schemes. One woman contends that bupe saved her life, but nonetheless sees problems with it: "Most people trade their shit for dope, which frustrates me. It changed my life and it would change anybody's if they would take it." Those with drug court experience have the most negative connotations of bupe. I spoke with a few people who have injected bupe. Other treatment participants use that as evidence that "it is just another drug." Some find bupe to produce unacceptably harsh withdrawal symptoms. They wonder why they should not just withdraw from opioids if they are going to have to withdraw regardless. After taking bupe, four people vowed never to take the substance again because it made them extremely sick. A few offered conspiracy theories about bupe where they think the government is making vast sums of money from the drug and using the pharmaceutical to slowly kill people who use drugs through damage to kidneys, livers, and bowels. Conversations with people about these conspiracy beliefs make clear that they are obviously rooted in the very real damage Purdue Pharma did to Appalachia and in knowledge of the Central Intelligence Agency's role in distributing crack in urban US neighborhoods in the 1980s. Most of the women I spoke with are ambivalent about bupe. One was preparing to graduate from drug court when I last spoke with her, and her husband is enrolled in a bupe program. She had seen drastic improvement in his drug use and overall demeanor but was still concerned that he is "substituting one drug for another," will be on buprenorphine for life, and will lose access if buprenorphine is outlawed, which she sees as a possibility.

Bupe Stigma Experienced as Child Removal

Bupe represents the primary conflict between treatment models. The drug court administrator "hates" bupe because people still withdraw and may continue to participate in illicit economies, as they buy bupe off the street or sell their own prescription. She would not allow a drug court participant to work as a peer mentor at Horizons because they allow bupe. She perpetuated rumors about bupe at local meetings, saying that a local clinic was offering "lifetime prescriptions" and did not have a licensed clinician on staff, neither of which was accurate according to my participant observation and discussion with several service providers. Community members take her assertions seriously because she is considered an expert on all issues relating to substance use. The DCBS office's bias against bupe creates harmful fissures for women and their families. The most intense instances of unwarranted DCBS intrusion involved clinician-prescribed bupe. MAT is associated with higher rates of family reunification in Kentucky, yet MAT use is low among parents with DCBS cases, hovering at just over 9 percent in one Kentucky study.[20] This low utilization rate is understandable because DCBS violates women's rights to be mothers to their children when they take a physician-prescribed medication.

In Adams and one additional county, DCBS caseworkers remove newborn children from households upon birth if pregnant people test positive for clinician-prescribed buprenorphine without naloxone. Two Adams County Horizons staff who are in regular contact with DCBS caseworkers confirmed that DCBS is removing newborns and older children from mothers who are prescribed bupe. Although they do not think removal is right, they think it is their job to try to help women navigate DCBS, not to publicly and explicitly fight the agency's actions. This makes sense to them and to me. Conflict with DCBS could result in a refusal to send women to Horizons. At least one DCBS office has done this in the past when the local administrator did not personally like a Horizons clinician. This hurts Horizons staff because they lose clients, and it harms women because they are less likely to get their children back if they do not complete Horizons.

According to Kentucky DCBS literature and state-level administrators, DCBS ostensibly condones the use of prescribed bupe for pregnant people and parents. A DCBS regional administrator was a bit more hesitant about bupe when I spoke with her. She said that newborns who show signs of being exposed to opioids should be referred to DCBS by the hospital, but this should lead to the family becoming involved with DCBS, not necessarily removal. Yet the local-level administrator in these two counties (who openly stated her hatred of bupe) said that if a newborn is born exposed to bupe or a gestational parent tests positive for anything in addition to buprenorphine, it's an "automatic removal." Adams County DCBS caseworkers told Horizons participants that even if the parents are on prescribed bupe when they are pregnant, newborns with signs of exposure are automatically removed from the home. The determining feature appears to be signs of exposure: according to caseworkers in

their interactions with women I spoke with, newborns without exposure are not removed from the home, no matter what the parent tests
positive for (bupe or heroin).

This mother was the first and certainly not the last to have this
experience:

> Before I got pregnant, I was on [prescribed] pain medication for a
> wreck I was in. When I got pregnant they put me on, the baby doc-
> tor himself, I wasn't going to like no clinics or nothing, the baby
> doctor himself put me on Subutex. When I had [my daughter],
> they automatically removed her from my custody and nothing was
> in her but what was prescribed by the doctor himself. They told
> me to do Horizons, and as long as I stayed straight, completed it,
> I'd get her back.

Five women I spoke with lost custody of their newborns at birth because they were on prescribed bupe. All live in the Adams County
DCBS office's district. DCBS charged all with misdemeanor neglect.
A peer mentor said that the DCBS office justifies the charges by saying that women should be weaned off bupe by the time they give
birth, a claim that contradicts both state and regional DCBS policies
detailed for me by an administrator during our interview. According
to a peer mentor, this also conflicts with what women report their
physicians to be telling them. She is confused by DCBS going against
physicians' care or why physicians would be offering care that contradicts DCBS policies. When people who use drugs say they oppose
using bupe, this may not mean they are opposed to the treatment,
but the negative repercussions that come from family members, the
community, and DCBS when they do use bupe.

The state allows local offices to make decisions about newborn
removal from the home. Other offices have other policies. People living outside of this district did not have issues with DCBS when they
were on physician-prescribed bupe. When women gave birth while on
bupe, a DCBS caseworker visited them in the hospital and asked a few
questions about their living situation, but the worker did not open a

case or even contact them again. Sissy was in this situation. Throughout our conversation on the subject, she kept shaking her head and ex-
claiming that it was wrong that women were being punished for seeking help. We talked about clinicians telling people not to breastfeed
their newborn when they are on bupe. Sissy said this is ridiculous because breastfeeding is exactly what mothers should do if they want to:

> She can't even try! She can't even try to help the baby. It's not
> [DCBS] policy. So why is it happening? And it's totally wrong
> against the baby, the mother, all of it. The baby doesn't get that
> bond with the momma, you know, knowing there's somebody
> there who will always drag them back from the edge.

This level of discrimination elicits activism from and for people who
use bupe. Several women used bupe without a prescription while
pregnant so that no one in power knew they were on the treatment.
Others, like Alisha, tried to methodically explain the benefits of bupe
to everyone around them. Another woman dismissed the advice of a
DCBS caseworker who told her not to breastfeed her son while she
was prescribed bupe:

> But the stupidest thing I've ever heard is that at the hospital they
> didn't want me to breastfeed my last son because they didn't want
> me to pass along the drug to him. They tried to tell me you can't
> breastfeed if you're an addict, but bullcrap, because if you are in
> the hospital and they give you pain medicine, don't you pass that
> pain medicine?

Yet these attempts at dodging or overcoming discrimination may not
produce optimum results. When people take bupe illicitly, they are
denied the benefits that may come from a program. When clinicians
are unaware of all the medications people and their neonates are exposed to, they are unable to offer the best care.

   One bupe provider said that a large part of her job is to be a patient advocate:

> Your treatment provider needs to have a high level of understand-
> ing of the legal and the regulatory things. There are times when

someone "in charge" tries to discriminate illegally against your patient; you have to remind them of the law. I've had several issues where I've copied your rights from SAMHSA, can you be fired for taking it? I've sent that to judges. You can't say that this person can't have visitation rights to their child because they're taking buprenorphine. You have no legal grounds for that.

She argued that prescribers have to be activists so patients remain unharmed when they face a state agency or employer who discriminates against those on bupe. She saw it as part of treatment providers' jobs to educate state agencies, employers, and others on the benefits of bupe so patients do not fall into these dangerous gaps.

A Continuing Debate

This debate over bupe goes far beyond Eastern Kentucky; it has become a source of contention for state-level, national, and global organizations. Narcotics Anonymous does not consider members "sober" if they are on bupe or methadone. In the last decade, bupe has slowly gained some acceptance. More people are seeing those in their networks use bupe to make positive changes in their lives. Other programs, such as syringe services programs, are attracting more public anger than bupe use. In a state-level meeting I attended, the recently appointed secretary of the Justice and Public Safety Cabinet, John Tilly, came to introduce himself. A treatment provider asked him about MAT and he said, "it has got to be available." He affirmed that MAT is effective when combined with counseling but expressed concern about diversion.

I have my own reservations about bupe. I share the distrust of pharmaceutical companies. Bupe assumes a stable (albeit diseased) brain. The medication ignores stress that is outside of the body. This is not a novel idea. This is what counselors, providers, and community members are saying; we cannot rely on a magic pill solution. But they view education, therapy, and changing social networks as the necessary services. These are often different ways to fix the individual. What they usually ignore is the context. Bupe programs are repeating the problems with methadone clinics, failing to address socioeconomic marginalization.[21] The ideal way to approach substance use and treatment for it is confusing for women, treatment program staff, prescribers, and DCBS caseworkers. And women and their families pay the price for this confusion.

Chapter 6
Strategies for Making Do in Broken Systems

THE PEOPLE I SPOKE WITH live in a region and a nation with underfunded social services that shuffle clients through programs without necessarily meeting their basic needs for health care, housing, and employment. Some make it through these mazes; others do not. All of them develop strategies, often in conjunction with others, to make do in the everyday and to make it through state interventions. They jump through excessive hoops without saying a word, they sneer at unreasonable education campaigns, and they find ways to see value in themselves when few others do. Those who lessen drug use and all that comes with it do so with the help of family and friends.

Yet these care networks are complicated, and definitions of care differ. What one person expects from someone who offers care is not the same as others' expectations or wants. When people are wedded to specific notions of what care *should* look like, they may persecute others for demonstrating care in ways that are outside of these boundaries. As with all actions, the manner in which one person cares for another is constrained. When state agencies and treatment programs ask folks to change their patterns of care, they must find how that change can occur within the interpersonal and organizational structures in which they are embedded. Without adequate social safety nets, people can rely on only family members and friends for support. For some, cessation of drug use can equate to loss of relationships, resulting in social isolation.

Living on the edge produces radical instances of care and cooperation, but also brutality. The violence with which care intertwines at times traps people in harmful situations. Family members provide essential material and emotional support for those who have few resources. While care is necessary for navigating life, it can also be precarious and even dangerous. Care has the ability to exacerbate people's pains. Most of those I interviewed had encountered domestic or sexual violence, often at the hands of family members or intimate partners. Women connect trauma to their drug use and want trauma-informed counseling services, but programs solely focusing on victimhood may not be the answer. A centering on victimhood may prevent efforts to alter the structures of power that contextualize violence. Through encounters with violence, women show resilience. In this time and place, that resilience more often equated to making do in the household, rather than collective action.

Surviving with Limited State Support

During their treatment, most people relied on family members, partners, and friends for emotional support, childcare, housing, and food. To a lesser extent, state agencies provide some resources. Interviewees spent considerable time outlining the daily material struggles they faced as well as their methods for navigating these hardships. The only services they regularly used directly through the state were Medicaid and SNAP. Three-quarters qualified for and received SNAP, referred to as "food stamps" by all. About a third who were on food stamps said it provided enough food for their families. The other two-thirds said food stamps lasted about two to three weeks. Those who had larger numbers of people in their household were more likely to spend out-of-pocket money on groceries. Food stamps are unlikely to be enough if people lack housing, because they are forced to buy expensive individually packaged items that do not require storage and refrigeration. Not having transportation to shop for better quality and cheaper food out of the county is a common problem faced by the people I interviewed.

People struggle if they lose food stamps, even if just for a few months. Often they were disenrolled for administrative reasons when they were incarcerated or unhoused, and then they were unable to recertify with SNAP because they didn't have a valid address. One Horizons clinician was baffled that anyone could reenlist with SNAP without professional help, because the enrollment process is grueling in terms of paperwork and time spent in encounters with administrators. SNAP has instituted delays that turn a thirty-day cycle into a thirty-five-day cycle, forcing recipients to stretch these benefits even further. While state services are reduced, they are simultaneously made more difficult to use for those who still manage to qualify.

Women rarely use K-TAP, Kentucky's cash benefit Temporary Assistance for Needy Families program administered through the state's Family Self-Sufficiency Branch. Maximum monthly payment amounts ranged from $186 for an individual to $482 for a family of seven in 2016. A family is only eligible for K-TAP for sixty months in a lifetime. K-TAP provides short-term cash benefits to families with children younger than eight or children younger than nineteen who are full-time students. The vast majority of adults who receive K-TAP are required to work for the monthly benefit.[1] Only one participant I spoke to was enrolled in K-TAP, while two others owed the state for their previous enrollment. Ashley was erroneously on K-TAP after she lost child custody (and thus K-TAP eligibility), so she then owed the system four hundred dollars. When Alisha was incarcerated, her mother sued her for K-TAP to provide for Alisha's child. She owed the state $6,000. Many never attempt to enroll because they think K-TAP provides too few resources to be worth the time-consuming processes of enlistment or completing program requirements—which is exactly the point of conservative reforms.

Several community leaders and service providers, especially the administrator of the local DCBS, criticized SNAP for supposedly being heavily abused. Others said they did not care if families used food stamps "creatively"; the important thing was to get resources into people's homes. Women told me they use SNAP in unintended ways. While critics claim they trade stamps for drugs, I rarely witnessed this; it is not that easy to get cash for food stamps, at least not at a good rate. When women use stamps to buy drugs, they are more often than not purchasing cigarettes, nothing illicit. The most widespread violation of SNAP policy that I saw was the use of benefits to feed more people than actually qualified in order to prevent hunger in their social networks. When Star, her husband, and her kids were enrolled in SNAP, for example, those SNAP benefits were also used to feed Star's sister and at times her mother. Punitive state actions, such as incarceration, affect entire systems of care. State support filters through these systems in similar ways.

Those gatekeepers who scoff at SNAP or claim that food is not an issue for poor families assume that the private sector ensures that people are fed. Some folks do not have access to food banks in their county. For others, the cost of transportation to the program and the limited food given make the bank not worth going to. Ashley asked me to drive her to multiple food banks, where she had to provide a license with an in-county address, social security card, and proof of income. My notes from that day document some of the limitations of food banks.

> When the front office lady gave her the bag, Ashley looked surprised and remarked that they sure were "slimming down." The lady shrugged, smiled, and said, "Yes." Ashley said they used to give big boxes, but now it's only a small bag. She immediately started eating some chips, saying she hadn't eaten in a few days. The bag contained eight small containers of snack size food, crackers, a jar of peanut butter, two protein drinks, and a large bottle of apple juice. She couldn't believe how little it was, so she asked to go to another place. At the next food bank, she received a larger bag, but it had items neither Ashley nor I knew what to do with. How can you fix a meal from canned cranberry sauce, turkey gravy, and seafood broth?

People are only allowed to access these banks once per month. When families don't have food, they usually rely on grandparents and great-grandparents to buy them food or in the summer, to provide produce through their gardens.

Private Sector Disinvestment and Un(der)employment

As state support has dwindled, so has private investment in rural Appalachian Kentucky. Women cite lack of employment as their largest concern. The five-county area shares the "uncertain and shifting" economy characteristic of Central Appalachia, where deindustrialization coupled with increases in service-sector employment results in fewer jobs that have benefits and pay a living wage.[2] The two largest private employers in Adams County closed in the last five years: a private prison closed in 2015 that employed mostly men; and an apparel factory that employed more than one hundred people, primarily women, closed about five years ago, some of the jobs being lost to mechanization and the others to a Kentucky town closer to an interstate. As populations lessen when these jobs are lost, the local tax base suffers, resulting in poorer county-level services as well as decreased employment through the school system, health care, and service sector. According to the Adams County fiscal court judge, several large employers had considered moving to the county recently but decided against the move because there is no interstate.

Regional and national politicians seem enthralled with the idea of entrepreneurship as *the* answer to "save" Appalachia. At an Appalachian Regional Commission conference, Congressman Hal Rogers, who represents the majority of Appalachian Kentucky counties, then Kentucky governor Steve Beshear, and Earl Gohl, the commission federal cochair, exclusively championed entrepreneurship as the economic model for Appalachia.[3] The poor are expected to not rely on leaders to create policies that help the region, but to help themselves by creating their own jobs, all within the context of a history of economic, political, and environmental marginalization where infrastructure and social institutions remain eroded. Hearing the executive director of Shaping Our Appalachian Region say that we need "innovation, not investment" and Senator Mitch McConnell arguing that economic development is "not my job" is frustrating but not really surprising, because rural Appalachia has a history of governmental and industrial disinvestment.[4]

When I asked a Horizons case manager about this focus on entrepreneurship, she dramatically rolled her eyes and said, "You can't expect people on the bottom to be entrepreneurs." Yet many of the people I interviewed as well as their family members and friends are entrepreneurs within underground and noncapitalist markets. Maggie was the only person I interviewed who had started a small, licit business involving her artwork. Although she enjoyed having an income from a legal enterprise, she could not earn enough to support herself and her children. She was constantly anxious over whether she would be able to pay her monthly bills. The only way she survived financially while running this business was by relying on her parents, SNAP, and Medicaid. The women I met during my research had no college degrees and were processing through time-intensive substance use treatment; they were responsible for caretaking work, some had criminal records, they did not have access to banks, and they lived in a region without quality infrastructure. Asking them to take risks to start a small business ignores the obstacle course they must navigate daily.

A worship of entrepreneurs is part of a larger neoliberal ideology that opposes government interference in the market.[5] People in neoliberal contexts are encouraged and expected to engender economic growth by taking risks in the capitalist market, which is seen as being equally accessible to everyone.[6] At local and regional meetings, these risks are defined as investing private wealth, borrowing money via banks or investors, liquidating portions of retirement plans, and remortgaging homes to start a new business—all of which require economic stability prior to taking risks. Critiques of this model aptly note that many do not have access to the free market and certainly do not have equal opportunities.[7] People are pushed to work hard to get ahead in a neoliberal system, but when those with felony records (as one example) cannot vote and cannot attain any employment, let alone a job that pays a living wage, then it is unclear how exactly they are supposed to get ahead. Risks that are deemed "unhealthy," on the other hand, are penalized with increased surveillance from numerous state and quasi-state institutions. While capitalistic risk that requires a certain degree of wealth is encouraged, risks that poor people who use drugs must often take are criminalized. I do not argue that entrepreneurship should be excluded from postextractive Appalachian economies. Entrepreneurship can offer options in a region facing economic restructuring, but the available options through this model require long hours and low wages.[8]

Entrepreneurship can help place the power of change within a community instead of outside of it. In a capitalist society, how are communities supposed to change entire oppressive systems when they have ideas but no capital? The current focus on entrepreneurship ignores the failure rates of small businesses where most local economic developers I've spoken with in Appalachia put that failure rate at 90 percent over the past five years. It also ignores the gentrification of capital, where large sources of capital are concentrated in very few hands in specific parts of the country. The promotion of this entrepreneur model is a promotion of capitalism and thus individualistic solutions to social problems, thereby increasing the gap between the elite and non-elite. Entrepreneurship models that take into consideration the inequality produced through capitalist economies and that attempt to work outside of or against those economies would be more beneficial to those on the fringes.

When people move to more urban areas, they do have better access to some employment, but the jobs they can take are still low-paying and often temporary. This is usually because of criminal records, low education levels, gaps in employment records, and lack of connections. If people have temporary or part-time jobs, they are quickly fired if they must miss work for caretaking responsibilities, illness, or pregnancy. The working conditions are demanding. Many of the factory or service jobs that are available require standing for

hours on end. This is not possible for the several participants I spoke
with who had chronic pain or occupational injuries.

Even in urban areas, people who have felonies rarely get called
in for an interview. Child abuse, neglect, or dependency charges
through DCBS can hurt people's employment prospects as much
as or more than felonies. With DCBS charges, people are placed on
a central registry that prevents them from working in schools, day
cares, peer support, or many health-care positions. People with felonies can still work in peer support and a broader range of health-care
positions that require licensing through the state. The vast majority
of participants with some college education specialized in nursing
or early childhood education, but their course credits or degrees
are worthless if they have DCBS-related charges. Many who enter
Horizons hope to become a peer mentor after graduation, but DCBS
charges remove that possibility. Horizons touts peer support as the
best employment option for clients.

In Kentucky, misdemeanors are supposed to be removed from
one's criminal record in five years, thus not being revealed in criminal background checks for employment or additional purposes.
Yet study participants said that was not always the case. Although
charges may be deleted from their official record, they still appear on
online-based searches and on court documents other than their official record. While having a record does hurt, so do gaps in the work
record related to time spent incarcerated and in treatment. If women
can obtain employment with their records, the jobs are almost exclusively minimum-wage in fast food.

If there is little formal employment that pays a living wage, then
how do people survive? They use state services beyond SNAP and
K-TAP. Six collected Supplemental Security Income (SSI) or Social
Security and Disability Insurance disability, which provided for entire families. Two families were kept afloat by a child's disability pay-
ments. A few participants qualified for disability at one time, but had
not reenrolled since they were incarcerated and refused disability.

Enrolling for Supplemental Security Income or Social Security and Disability Insurance is often a long and arduous process. Ashley (who qualified because of her mental health conditions) had been attempting to enroll for five years.

Family members, and not social safety net services, help most people survive financially. About a third of participants relied on income from their male partners or parents, who may be informally or formally employed. This reliance results in some situations where people remain with abusive partners or partners who continue to use drugs because they control household resources. Yet most partners' incomes are unstable or are derived from seasonal work. Other people, both those with and without partners, live with extended kin in order to pool resources.

In this explanation of women receiving financial support from kin and partners, I don't want to continue the erasure of women's income-generating strategies and reproductive labor in Appalachia.[9] Women talked about "hustling," especially when they were actively using. Hustling may involve under-the-table untaxed odd jobs, like providing transportation, cleaning houses, agricultural work, home tattooing, taking care of children, or collecting and selling abandoned items and natural products, such as ginseng and geodes. Illicit forms of labor include sex work, stealing from family, shoplifting, drug trafficking, or connecting people with those who sell drugs. These ways of surviving are not new in these mountains. Moneymaking schemes may be successful because of family support, or they can be the source of familial tensions when people steal from or cheat kin. A quarter of those I spoke with had been involved in drug trafficking at some point. The majority who self-identified as a person who has substance use disorder said they would connect friends with drug suppliers and then obtain either money or drugs for making the connections.

Treatment program clients and service providers alike associate lack of access to jobs that pay a living wage with people entering into the drug economy. Stopping "the hustle" can be a hard transition for participants when ceasing drug use because they often have nothing to replace the frenetic activity in which they had been engaged. Thus, ceasing drug use is a shift in social as well as economic relationships. From the outside, this shift may appear more positive than it actually is. Prior to treatment, people survive in noncapitalist diverse economies that allow for flexibility if they have caretaking responsibilities and may not be as exploitive as factory jobs.[10] These strategies may produce solidarity in communities on the edge. But these economies might also be associated with interpersonal violence.

Ultimately, however, most of women's work is unpaid and involves caring for their children, other children in their extended family, elderly family members, and others in treatment as they lead self-help groups. While this work is crucial for families and communities during times of global economic restructuring and social disinvestment, it goes undocumented on resumes and limits women's ability to control household resources.[11] Families are a source of economic support, but women also spend much of their time supporting their families. While doing so, they are technically classified as "unemployed," but considering the time and labor they put into their families, they are working all the time.

Housing and Transit in Rural Appalachia

A primary injustice, second only to the unavailability of licit and quality employment, is the lack of affordable, stable, and safe housing. Seven out of forty women were unhoused at the time of our interviews, living in spaces not meant for human habitation, such as in cars and forests. Nine more were technically houseless, usually moving from one family member's or friend's home to another on a nightly or weekly basis. Two permanently lived with family members. Having access to a place to stay through family or friends is fundamental to survival, but some household members may be violent or using drugs. Due to an overall low housing stock in the area, extended family members or friends might rely on participants to provide shelter. Thus, if they have someone living in their house who is physically violent, kicking that person out can make them unhoused.

Lower rent apartments and trailers are available for those with poor credit, but they are hard to find and the living conditions are difficult. Several times I walked into dark, small, rodent- and insect-infested trailers and apartments without heat, air conditioning, or running water. Several trailers did not have full floors, roofs, or walls. Housing instability and poor living conditions produce stress. This stress may be manifested through anxiety and hypervigilance and additional chronic and acute health concerns, which women talked about and I witnessed through our interactions.[12]

I was able to find housing in the area after looking for a little over one month. I had several advantages in the search. I had time to look for an apartment because my partner and child were living in central Kentucky about an hour's drive from Adams County, which allowed me to commute for a short time. Since the apartment was just for me, I was able to live in a cheaper studio apartment. Most women in this study who are under DCBS supervision and want to live with their children must have a residence large enough to have one bedroom for the parent(s) and one bedroom for each child gender. For example, if a woman lived with her two daughters and son, she would have to have at least a three-bedroom residence. I would not have known about or been able to rent my studio apartment had I not had a personal connection who vouched for me and my work. My connection to the University of Kentucky and lack of a criminal record helped as well.

Each county has at least one apartment complex that supplies government-subsidized low- or no-rent housing. Yet these complexes are stigmatized by those in the larger community as having drugs and are highly surveilled by the police; they have multimonth waiting lists and do not accept anyone with felony records. Getting into the apartments is usually predicated on having child custody, and parents are evicted if they lose custody. In Adams County, applicants are required to show all of their children's birth certificates as well as their own birth certificate, which can be difficult to access if the parent or their children were born in states where people have to pay for birth certificates.

Ex-partners and others use this requirement to prevent people from accessing additional housing or to bribe people when they steal their birth certificates or identification. In Adams County, the same person has managed the one subsidized apartment complex for years, and if he decides that he does not like someone, he will evict that person or deny the application. One woman said that the only way her sister was able to sign an apartment lease at the subsidized housing in Adams County was by intensely flirting with the manager.

Although the local housing authority assists those in Adams and Douglas counties in finding housing, programs and program eligibility requirements vary over time. Their programs are determined by federal US Department of Agriculture (USDA) and Department of Housing and Urban Development funding streams. The housing authority originally focused on home ownership per specific USDA loan programs at no to low interest, which were beyond the reach of many families I spoke with. Temporary housing assistance is focused on women with child custody who have not had a drug charge in the last year. Most people wait on these federal lists for three to five years. When families finally receive a Section 8 Housing Choice Voucher for rent assistance, they cannot find landlords to accept the voucher.

One woman, who was living in her car at the time of our interview, expressed her frustration with the available programs:

> It's horrible living like this. The housing authority said they can't help me unless my children are in my home. And so they said it's not an emergency case because my children are ok. I'm like, it's not an emergency? It ain't to them but to me it is. They can't help me because I don't have my children in my custody and we're not literally sleeping outside on the ground. They said you have to be outside before they can put you in the homeless shelter.

There is no local access to a shelter in the five counties. The two closest shelters are one hour away and have fewer than ten beds. Some community members take advantage of this by charging people who are unhoused ten dollars to take a shower in their houses. Others are working to start a shelter but face resistance from local governments. One city council member compared people who are unhoused to "wild dogs" who will be drawn by the shelter and will remain in the community to steal. The owner of the local conservative newspaper joked at a city council meeting that the shelter should be put in a dilapidated house in a cemetery, because "people wouldn't stay too long."

Although women think a local shelter would be beneficial, and several went to shelters when they lived in more urban areas, the strict rules and sometimes harmful living conditions nonetheless enact another form of violence, as Ashley demonstrates:

> I lived in a homeless shelter for about nine months, me and my son did. I was pregnant with my daughter. There was no air conditioning for like three weeks. It would get to like 109 degrees in there. You had to do chores and I actually went into labor because they had me mopping the stairway. And it was a three-story shelter, so it put me into premature labor and they had to give me some kind of shot to stop it.

While those who work with homeless populations discuss how inequalities produce homelessness, shelter rules may nonetheless be directed at inspecting and disciplining individuals who are unhoused in an effort to train self-governance. These rules are supported discursively with understandings of "denial" in addiction and self-help, which individualize and explicitly ignore the social factors of homelessness and drug use.[13] This is once again an example of how characterizations of people who use drugs are employed to justify decreased or increasingly harsh social services. While the existence of programs for poor people who use drugs is vital, whether they are shelters or substance use treatment programs, the implementation of these programs may nonetheless further marginalize participants.

Women told me how their lack of transportation prevented them from going to jobs and job interviews, community college, court dates, and social gatherings. Participants may have temporary access to cars through partners and family, but these arrangements are unreliable. According to service providers, transportation has become more of an issue in the last fifteen years as county health departments and other agencies no longer have funding for mobile clinics and as community services become dispersed through counties instead of being centralized in a county seat. Five years ago, in Adams County an elementary school, the library, the health department, the extension office, and the DCBS offices were located within a few blocks of one another. People only had to acquire one ride to the county seat to access all services. Now, the elementary school, the library, the extension office, and the DCBS office are in different locations throughout the county, so people have to obtain several rides to access different services. A few programs such as Horizons help with client transportation, but this increases the amount of time women have to spend on programs by a few hours every day. At the time of my research, public transportation took people to medical appointments but only if they had Medicaid, scheduled the ride seventy-two hours in advance, had a referral if the service was out of county, and did not have a car titled in their name. The Medicaid guidelines proposed by Governor Matt Bevin would deprive people of access to even this highly regulated transportation service.

Alternative Survival Strategies

Women's stories reveal the importance of care networks in providing environments in which structural inequalities can more successfully be navigated. The care Sissy receives muddles gendered understandings of care work. While she certainly gives to others, she draws strength from her husband and brothers. Sissy made it through treatment because those around her provided emotional support, housing, food, household goods, and childcare. Her family relied on her husband's employment. Strong family support, especially from her brothers, helped Sissy navigate motherhood and withstand experiences of gendered violence:

> Anytime I've needed any kind of support, it doesn't matter what kind, with my girls, just myself, whatever, they've been there. I

mean back twelve years ago when I had a bad relationship and had to move out overnight, my brother was there to move me out. I hadn't seen him in three months maybe, but I called him and he was there.

Sissy's family supplemented her husband's income with state program assistance. She and her daughters were covered by Medicaid and qualified for food assistance through Women, Infants, and Children Nutrition Program, which she called a "lifesaver." In terms of health insurance, Medicaid is inadequate. By the last time I saw Sissy, she had all of her teeth removed after they began to break off painfully. She was embarrassed to leave her house. While Medicaid paid for the extraction, it would not cover dentures. She found a place that provided dentures at a lower cost, but driving there and back took twelve hours.

Although unemployed, Sissy provided for her family. In the summer, she grows a sizable garden to produce most of the fresh vegetables that she and her household need. She saves seeds from year to year and starts her plants as seedlings, meaning the yearly start-up costs are small. She works as the primary caretaker in her household and beyond. Sissy describes her typical day as taking care of herself and her family, which she defines as the two of her three daughters who are in her household as well as her husband.

She is also connected to several other women who formerly used drugs. I eventually spoke to two of her close friends, both of whom said that Sissy helped them cease drug use, offering reassurance whenever she could. Her care work even extended to me. About six and half months into my pregnancy, I was rushed to the hospital. I had to cancel appointments with a few people, including Sissy. I was still terrified when I called her to cancel, and I think she could tell. She talked to me for an hour about her two high-risk pregnancies, told me about her good experience with the hospital I was in, and then distracted me by talking about names. Sissy saw a difference in her care before and after ceasing substance use, but not toward others. While using, she never took care of herself. She linked this lack of self-care to childhood: "I was sexually abused as a child, so that makes it easier for me to abuse myself." Since stopping, she has adopted more regular eating and sleeping routines.

The care networks in which Sissy is embedded bind her to her home county, whether she is receiving or providing care. She is tied to this place, not by some irrational fear of leaving or bucolic independent spirit, but by a network of support that is mapped on and through the landscape. Her living relatives are all around her. She is nestled on the land bequeathed by those who have passed, teaches her children to eat purple clover just as her grandparents taught her, and has named her daughters after the strong women in her family, hoping to pass on that might. Sissy is using the resources she has, and those resources are people and land.

Ashley's history reveals how state resources can be gained and lost as relationships change. When Ashley had custody of her kids, who both have developmental delays, she received more than $1,400 a month. The funds paid for their housing, transportation, and some food. When she lost custody, her children's father began receiving the disability and she was also disenrolled from K-TAP. Her car was repossessed because she could no longer make payments. With her children, Ashley qualified for $511 in SNAP benefits, but without them she qualifies for $194, which does not quite cover her food for the month. At first, she tried to use food banks to provide for the rest. She then began a new relationship, which gave her access to another state program. The father of Ashley's new boyfriend qualifies for the USDA's Commodity Supplemental Food Program that is meant to enhance the diets of low-income persons above age sixty. His qualification for that program benefitted himself as well as his son and Ashley, with whom he shared his commodities.

Ashley did maintain Medicaid benefits as well as housing through Section 8. The new boyfriend lived with Ashley, gaining housing through her Department of Housing and Urban Development assistance. She applied for Section 8 six years before she actually received it, during which time she used a variety of strategies to remain housed. Before her children were born, she slept on friends' couches and at times could afford an apartment with her boyfriend. She spent years in and out of shelters once her children were born.

The survival strategies Alisha used are rooted in ones she learned from her father, who dealt cocaine for years. She learned how to earn an income through hustling and drug trafficking at an early age. Then she was arrested and has since attempted to remain outside of the illicit economy. Alisha lives in a larger county seat, arguably the area with the most resources in the five-county region. She had access to family housing through a treatment program and, when I first met her, a job at a restaurant that was a half-hour drive away. She disliked the job but was thankful she could find what she thought was stable employment considering the felonies on her record. Although she was employed full time during our first meeting, Alisha continued to rely on her granny for some financial support.

Alisha's job disappeared four months after I first spoke to her when corporate headquarters closed dozens of restaurants across Kentucky. Losing her job would have been hard regardless, but this blow was compounded because her son's father also worked at the restaurant. It was one of the few local places willing to hire people with felony convictions. Management told them to apply for unemployment, but Alisha only received forty-seven dollars a week. The last time I saw her, she had been looking for another job for months, without any success.

While she was married, Alisha had earned her associate's degree in early childhood education and taught preschool for a year, enjoyed it, and greatly decreased her use of anything during that time. She started using heavily after her divorce. Now with felonies on her criminal record, she can no longer be hired in the early education field. Because she has felonies but not DCBS charges, she is attempting to get the certificates needed for peer support. Yet this takes time and money.

Health-care costs are currently depleting any resources she has to pay for peer support courses. Even though she is on Medicaid, Alisha has large unpaid medical bills. She has had a series of strokes, which puts her in the hospital quite often. During her last stroke, her dad was sent to jail. She signed herself out of the hospital against medical advice to help her family contend with her father's reincarceration. Because she signed out against medical advice, she had to pay some $2,000 in fees that she would have otherwise not accrued.

Alisha spends her days volunteering at a local outpatient treatment program. She teaches court-mandated classes to parents who have open DCBS cases. In some ways, this is a contextually coerced volunteering because working for free is Alisha's only option and she struggles to provide for herself and her family. She could earn some income teaching the classes she does, but that would mean charging people money for enrolling. She doesn't want to take money from those who are having difficulties with the state and whom she thinks are less financially stable than herself. Alisha says that the care work she provides, to both family and community members, causes her stress, but also in some ways supports her decrease in drug use. "It drives me crazy but I guess it's what I need, that busyness. When I'm running, I don't have time to think about, if you took something, you'd feel better."

Like Alisha, Star lives in the same county seat, which does have more resources, but opportunities are decreasing. Star had a factory job when she graduated drug court making twenty-one dollars an hour, but the factory downsized and cut her position. Her husband earns some income selling ginseng and agate rock, but that is seasonal work and they have no income beyond that. The last time we spoke, she didn't have her driver's license back yet after being charged with driving under the influence, and she was waiting on getting her license to search for jobs. There is no available transportation unless she can drive herself. Star's SNAP benefits provide enough food for her family for about three weeks out of each month. For the fourth, she generally relies on food banks, food they buy out of pocket, or they try not to eat much at home that week, with her children receiving free breakfasts and lunches at school. They have stable housing at this time. Star said that housing was difficult to find because of her reputation in the county as a person who uses drugs. She finally found a landlord willing to rent to her because the landlord lost two children to drug overdose and is empathetic to Star's position.

What Is Care?

"These people who can see right through you never quite do you justice, because they never give you credit for the effort you're making to be better than you actually are, which is difficult and well-meant and deserving of some little notice."[14]

"What do you want from the liquor store? Something sour or something sweet? I'll buy all that your belly can hold, you can be sure you won't suffer no more. I'd swim the ocean or the deepest canal to get to you darling just to make you well."[15]

"So if you wanna burn yourself remember that I love you, and if you wanna cut yourself remember that I love you, and if you wanna kill yourself remember that I love you."[16]

I start this section with three quotes from literature and music because artists may be the most able to recreate the affect of complicated and perhaps chaotic care. Sometimes care is as simple as recognizing that another person is there and is trying to imagine as well as live a future that is better than the past or present. Taking further actions and removing sickness or withdrawal from alcohol or drugs in the short term may inadvertently prolong long-term suffering. The care that pervades these communities is limited. This is not well-resourced everyday care, but deeply constrained care that is attempting to keep people and communities from death.

Some service providers in this study question whether people who are actively using drugs can have any type of care for others. A treatment administrator claimed that people who use drugs do not have the ability to differentiate between right or wrong or to have stable relationships because of their addiction. In treatment programs, those who use drugs may not be seen as having "real" relationships, because these relationships are framed as fake and based on the acquisition of resources.[17] In this vein, a few providers exclusively focus on "toxic relationships" with others as preventing people from terminating use. Thus, faulty demonstrations of care and problematic care networks are to blame for continued use, not dependency on a substance or other issues emanating from matrices of domination.[18]

When people who use drugs are portrayed as uncaring or immoral, this justifies withholding resources, including societal care. The provision of limited resources must be framed as strict or for someone other than a person who used drugs. The following instance demonstrates this framing, as well as the gaps in what service providers and community members view as appropriate methods of care for people who use drugs. At a local antidrug coalition meeting, the fiscal court judge and a longtime treatment provider began talking about the importance of naloxone availability and training for first responders to prevent overdose deaths. A few wives of cops began grumbling that if people who use know first responders have naloxone, then they will simply increase drug use without fear of overdose. The judge and treatment provider immediately began telling stories of the harshness of receiving naloxone, where those overdosing are immediately sent into withdrawal. They justified access to health care for those who use drugs but defined this care as horrific.

As indifference is characterized as one of the primary symptoms and at times causes of addiction, changing care patterns is seen as vital to abatement of drug use. Both providers and women in Eastern Kentucky associate an end of use with a return to or novel embrace of caregiving, which aligns closely with research among Native North American women.[19] Yet the question of whether those who use drugs can provide care reveals fractures in women's understandings of care. Some contest stigmatizing portrayals of people who use drugs and argue that users of substances can provide care as moral actors. Ashley claimed her care for the community by saying that she would not and has never stolen anything. In my previous research and in discussions about active drug use in the current study, people demonstrate care for others when they provide or share drugs with close family and friends who are in withdrawal.[20] Other people eschew the idea that people actively using can be involved in care networks and categorize friends they use(d) with as "drug buddies" who do not really care about them. They see decreases in drug use as a time to begin or renew ties to individuals who do not use substances and to the community, especially by volunteering in the schools with their children and helping others with drug issues. Reduction of drug use is framed as a shift in or beginning of care.

Substance use treatment programs ask people to reimagine their past relationships and modes of care as faulty, to construct new forms of care, and to create new imaginings of future relationships that exclude people who were previously important to them if those people use substances or are abusive. Service providers emphasize the importance of having stable family and friends, but also portray interpersonal relationships as posing the most risk to people's success. If clients do not want to form new relationships and cannot imagine a future in which their modes of care change, then completion of treatment becomes a harder thing to render clear. Program aspects that help people build new communities are thus in demand.

Although people may be able to start building a new community through treatment events, they are restricted from doing this on an everyday basis because they are not allowed to see other participants outside of Horizons and drug court. Treatment participants view this rule as unreasonable because staff are asking them to relinquish social relationships with active users but then prohibiting them from finding emotional support from others who are trying not to use through a program.

When people do not see drug use as ever having conflicted with their ability to be caregivers, whether they were caring for children, siblings, other family members, or the community, their transition to treatment is less abrupt in terms of who they are connected to and how they see their roles in relation to others. People whose use prevents them from functioning in their social roles as caretakers or who do not think anyone could provide care while using face more abrupt transitions. They understand reduction in use as involving a complete reversal in their networks and caregiving strategies. Although this understanding is certainly influenced by treatment rhetoric, it is not unilaterally imposed and people talk about how being around active users triggers their desire to use. The first step people take is distancing themselves from people with whom they used drugs ("so-called friends").

Angela Garcia's work argues that drug use rarely occurs in isolation.[21] In the current setting, cessation of drug use was more often isolating. Women experienced isolation while using only when they were in abusive relationships. As they alter their "people, places, and things" when terminating use, some find themselves alone without any means of emotional or material support. This is especially the case if they do not have family members they can rely upon. They cite feelings of loneliness and desolation once they are in treatment, and while some of this could be attributed to the physical process of reducing use, it must also be attributed to the disappearance of people from their life. Alisha termed her time in drug court as "devastating" because of the loss of connections she experienced. Another woman fanaticized about suicide because she "felt so alone in the world, I couldn't tolerate it anymore." A drug court participant thought that part of her cessation was coming to terms with the idea that she may "die alone." For her, relationships with those who are using are not worth attempts to escape this possible fate because they risk pulling her into use once again.

Women who are alone may not have any living, non-using individuals in their network. They may have strained their relationships with others to the breaking point. A Horizons client spoke extensively about her connection to her husband, who has never used, but also of the pain she caused him: "I love him so much and it's so hard sometimes because I just want to be home with him. Other times I know I can't because it just don't work. I know that me and him will never find anyone we love more than each other. So much damage has been done, I don't know if it can be repaired." She claimed her husband was understanding, but her drug use had destroyed their relationship and he had separated from her. This is why it is vital for people in treatment to have service providers who seem to care about them and why they value program activities that encourage socializing outside of counseling, such as cookouts. When treatment programs do not offer these services, clients find ways to provide for themselves.

Katie discussed starting a Narcotics Anonymous (NA) group in Adams County so people who formerly used could rebuild a network.

> I would like to go to an NA meeting. Just because it gives you something to do for one. Two, it gives you an opportunity to be around people that maybe are having the same type of issues that you're having. Like if you have relapsed, you're not going to go and talk to your family members about having a relapse. I would have to be very black and white with it because either you're going to come to NA and you're going to participate and you're going to be sober when you come, or you can't come.

Having the support of the *right* people—those who understand the challenge of quitting use but do not themselves use—is critical to a former user's well-being. This is a difficult thing to achieve with the ups and downs in the mazes of addiction, inequalities, interventions, and complicated family relationships. It is unclear from my research what happens to those still using when their friends or family enter treatment. Do they become isolated? Does this harm their trajectory? Having different support systems is important, systems that address the needs of those who continue to use and those who want to cease use and must avoid people who use.

The Violence and Necessity of Care and Caregiving

I have documented throughout this book the ways in which structural violence comes into people's lives, and here I want to explore care in the context of interpersonal violence. I limit detailed descriptions to avoid voyeurism, but at the same time, I think naming brings these events to light. Over a third of the Appalachian women I spoke with had been molested or raped, generally by family members or other people they knew. This percentage matches overall Kentucky as well as national data.[22] Women face sexual violence in other ways as well, such as when they have to deal with the molestation of their children or rape of their family members or friends. These moments are not rare, as demonstrated in my interactions with Star when she was assisting her sister after a rape.

Sexual violence led to rifts in families and further physical or emotional violence:

> I had the nervous breakdown in ninth grade and the social worker came to our house. Mom went off because she said I was lying about everything. I mean here I am, I've already been raped numerous times. She made me get down on my hands and knees and crawl to this man and beg him for forgiveness for me lying. I refused to do it, so I got knocked around. She put me out of the house. I had nowhere to go.

After the trauma of prolonged sexual abuse, she became unhoused for a short time period before she could reach her grandmother to live with her. She pinpointed this moment as the root of her substance use.

Of the forty women interviewed, twenty-five had dealt with domestic violence. Women were not just beaten by their male partners, but by parents and siblings. One woman miscarried twins when her younger brother, whom she was raising, beat her. Roughly half of participants who faced domestic or sexual violence continued to experience PTSD, depression, anxiety, and suicide attempts. Women with histories of domestic violence talked about both depression and anxiety and the chronic pain associated with fractures and breaks. They consistently connected their drug use with various traumas, including the deaths of loved ones, loss of child custody, domestic violence, and sexual violence committed against themselves and their children.

Although not as extreme as rape, molestation, or domestic violence, stigma based on portrayals of women who use drugs becomes another type of embodied interpersonal violence. A drug court participant explained the pain of this judgment and the connections she made with her increasing drug use:

> People you truly love, you find out they're saying stuff about you and you're like f- [sic] it, I'll show them. After you hear that so many times, you start to really believe it in your head that I'm not good enough and I am a bad mother. I might as well do what a bad person would do. They want to sit and talk about you, but the time they're talking about you, why aren't they trying to help you? Pull you out of the dark hole you're in. In my addiction, the more I was alone, the more I wanted to use. I felt like no one cared about me. My kids did, but they didn't know what to do with me in my addiction. There were so many times I was trying to call out for help but so many people I knew the most were saying the most negative things about me.

As this quote demonstrates, judgment and lack of social support become embodied as frustration, depression, feelings of abandonment, and drug use.

The overall violence people experience is exhausting, bringing a "tiredness, an about-wore-out-ness" to families and communities.[23] This is an everyday violence that has become commonplace, but remains nonetheless unacceptable. I have heard many people who use drugs appropriate Fanny Lou Hamer's quote "I'm sick and tired of being sick and tired" to describe life in the Jim Crow South that Hamer fought against. They too are weary of the murders, overdoses, and suicides of fathers, brothers, aunts, and uncles, which have become life-defining moments. The people lost to death turn to bones or ash, but they remain fleshed in people's minds, a presence not easily lost. When living in a small community, every overdose, stabbing, shooting, and house fire in a neglected tenement is felt because the victims and perpetrators or their families are known. While I was living in very rural Adams County, in the week before Thanksgiving five people overdosed and died, two people were shot to death, one person was stabbed to death, and a major fire destroyed part of the main street. Interviews that took place after this week for the next several months often turned into hearing different people's sides of the story or how they were connected to those who died that week.

One effect of this steady violence is that people have difficulty finding care from others because many in the community are consumed in coping with their own grief. Sometimes this grief leads to use. During our initial interview, Katie told me that using again "never crossed my mind." A week later, she began using, depleted her household's savings on pharmaceuticals, and was eventually charged with driving under the influence. After she had again ceased use, she told me she had been planning it for months and was pushed over the edge when a friend fatally overdosed. Katie took a pill that night. Living with this violence can be crushing, but also gives people a sense of their own seemingly miraculous resilience. Some regard their history of drug use and survival of violence as significant in their ability to provide certain types of care, especially to people who use drugs.

Alisha viewed her physical and mental scars as attributes that allowed her to care for her community in ways that others could not. She is empathetic and has been in similar situations as those who are entangled with DCBS or the criminal processing system. She thus takes issue with programs she sees as attempting to alter her in ways other than helping her cease use. In Alisha's words, "I think I was resentful of a program to try to fix me. I think that I'm broken, but I'm not sure I can be put back together. I think it helps me more to be broken than to be fixed." When asked to explain, she said, "scars make me beautiful." Alisha found strength and a deeper understanding of humanity in her survival of violence and drug use. Further, it helps Alisha and others to provide care to people because it makes them feel like they have some success and connection with others. In these ways, drug treatment may be empowering.

Many participants want therapeutic services that address trauma. Characterizing clients as victims can be a way for program staff to gain additional resources for their clients through grants that are focused on survivors of domestic violence or sexual assault.[24] However, state agencies are assuming victimhood in targeting women for intervention. Focusing on victimhood is not important to some women. Experiences of personal violence should be understood as producing a variety of responses and not solely creating a sense of victimhood. Personal violence can be intertwined with care and is embedded within societal power structures.

When people are categorized as victims, either through their own or other's efforts, they often come under the purview of the government. People may not receive the government intervention they seek. If women are being abused and still have child custody, then they can lose custody for not leaving a situation in which a child may witness domestic violence or become a victim of violence. DCBS required several women to complete Horizons because their husbands, boyfriends, or sons abused them. The husbands and boyfriends generally did not have to do anything through DCBS. Yet when women wanted the state to intervene because they were being beaten, they feared calling law enforcement because they thought DCBS would also step in. The agency was known to remove children from the home when the mothers were experiencing domestic violence.

The fear about calling law enforcement can be on more personal terms. One woman's husband was beating her, but she knew her husband's family was friends with the sheriff. She thus called the state police instead of the sheriff, but the state police and sheriff communicate, so the state police brought the sheriff to her home. When the sheriff arrived, he told her he was going to call DCBS and have her drug tested. She tested positive for cannabis. DCBS asked the husband to get drug tested, he refused, and DCBS accepted that refusal.

She presumed their leniency was due to her husband's connection to the sheriff. DCBS removed her children and placed them with her mother and then her husband's mother. She was able to live with her children the entire time they were removed from her custody, because the grandmothers allowed her to do so without the DCBS caseworker's knowledge. She told me she would never again call the police for domestic violence. She was charged with misdemeanor neglect and had to complete Horizons as part of her DCBS case plan. Her husband received probation for domestic violence.

Gatekeepers often blamed geography and supposed isolation for violence and drug use in Appalachia, viewing violence against women as intrinsic to the place. A treatment provider originally from non-Appalachian Kentucky said that a high level of gendered violence is unique to Appalachia and causes much of women's drug use in the region. A research assistant from Eastern Kentucky viewed rural Appalachia as particularly harmful for poor women: "I wish that they could see that there's so much more than staying here and marrying the boy up the road." This assumed intrinsic violence in Appalachia, along with other stereotypes, creates discourses in which leaving Appalachia becomes *the* answer for mitigating all types of violence women face. Yet people often do leave, but they don't necessarily leave the violence behind.

Overall, DCBS and treatment programs focus on women as victims of interpersonal violence who need to learn appropriate coping skills and to remove themselves from violent situations where their children may be at risk. They do not view women as part of families and care networks who all consistently navigate domination. Shallow examinations of interpersonal violence that do not consider the broader contexts in which violence takes place risk depoliticizing and pathologizing poverty as something that happens among violent "others" because of criminal personalities or cultures.[25]

Eastern Kentucky programs often stereotype Appalachian culture in ways that echo culture of poverty arguments of Appalachia as an inherently violent and isolationist place.[26] By ignoring the effects of structural violence on interpersonal violence, those who benefit from a hierarchical social organization are absolved from responsibility. The context in which women experience violence is ignored and the barriers they face in cooperating with the government to reduce domestic violence are made invisible.[27] Society, family, and community members may then blame women for continuing to endure the abuse.[28]

Substance use treatment programs may dismiss both the webs of power in which people find themselves as well as people's actions. Staff, administrators, and policy makers seem to think that people who use drugs have agency only as perpetrators. Treatment program and DCBS staff view women as actors only when they harm their children or are unsuccessful in treatment. Staff's positive evaluations of women who use drugs are grounded in these women's constructed roles as victims of sexual or domestic violence, where they are regarded as having no agency. When women were doing well in treatment, staff generally owed this to the treatment program or women's stable and strong family. Ultimately, female clients are seen as incapable of making good decisions for themselves.

Women do take action, but the strategies they develop to survive remain unsupported and unacknowledged within programs. The inability of program staff to speak to women about certain types of violence because of their duty to report to DCBS hinders the possibility of assisting clients in surviving these types of violence or understanding how these necessary strategies may be harmful. Women withstand violence. Sometimes women perpetrate crime, the most common being drug use and trafficking, stealing in order to buy drugs, and neglect of children due to drug use.

Sometimes women remained in abusive relationships because they needed the material resources or feared abandoning their children. More often, women left these situations of their own volition. Few women I spoke with said they were currently in violent relationships. DCBS told a few women that they would close their DCBS case as long as they did not reunite with their abusive male partner. Although these actions by DCBS may be seen as reducing violence against women and children, they are paternalistic and pit women's interests against their children's. This abusive ex may be the person providing housing, clothing, and food. From women's narratives, DCBS never offered alternative resources.

Women develop protective strategies against assault, including extra vigilance. The first woman I interviewed whom I had not previously met demonstrated this protectiveness in a way not unknown to most women. She told me that she saw a flyer about my research in her uncle's truck and decided to call me. I do not know how the flyer made it to the truck. We met at her house and drove to a park for the interview. As I was driving her back home, we discussed how we were both a little anxious about meeting one another. She thought I was probably with the police. After having talked for a few hours and become comfortable, we were laughing about this.

Then we started sharing ways we keep ourselves safe. I told her that on days when I was going to unfamiliar places, I let my partner track my cell phone. She regularly checks in with a cousin and an aunt, so they know everyone is okay. She amiably pulled out a pocketknife: "Yeah, I always pack one of these. I usually like the box cutter knives better because they let you cut people just a little. It lets them know they're alive and they usually stop." I admitted that I have carried a pocketknife for years as well. My father gave me my first knife as a coming-of-age gift he would have given any child as a useful tool. A high-school boyfriend threw a much larger second knife in my lap one day, telling me I needed to have something for protection, while he ominously nodded at a group of men outside his car; this is the knife I still carry nearly twenty years later. These methods reflect strategies, but also the prevalence of gendered violence in our society. The woman I spoke to with the knife had her own personal brutal experiences. She was assaulted in two different episodes. In one situation, both she and her female cousin were unknowingly drugged at a party and raped by two men. At another time, her male cousin brought her to a drug trafficking deal. The two men they met raped her and severely beat her male cousin.

Some models for understanding this cruelty against women take into account political and socioeconomic contexts. Anthropologists and feminist theorists connect gendered violence in the United States to racism, xenophobia, poverty, and neoliberal policies that eliminate safety net services.[29] As some men perpetrate brutality, they may be drawing on violence to exert their dominance in a world where they are limited by poverty, addiction, and marginalization.[30] In connecting interpersonal with structural violence, I am not trying to apologize for interpersonal cruelty.[31] Instead, I am advocating for an understanding of how systems of domination bleed into the home and familial relationships through interpersonal violence and of the overall context in which assault takes shape. Recognizing interpersonal violence as situated in multiple systems of power (including those based on gender, class, race, and location) limits reliance on a biased criminal processing system to protect women. This recognition moves beyond criminalization to changes that can be made in hierarchical systems to lessen instances of abuse, as well as women's vulnerability to abuse.[32]

These models are reflected in women's understandings of violence. Ashley connected her partner's brutality to their financial situation, their drug use, and his history:

> He really wasn't a bad guy; he just couldn't control his temper. His dad beat up on his mom and grandpa beat up on his grandma and he came from a family that beat up on women. That's the type of people he was raised up with, so he kind of was taught it. Then when we had kids, everything changed. I told him, I said, "I'll leave you."

She sees the cruelty she experienced as complicated, bleeding through familial generations but not in and of itself defining her children's father as a "bad guy."

What are gatekeepers' proposed solutions to domestic violence and women's drug use? State administrators, politicians, and service providers from outside the region particularly argue that individuals must leave Appalachia in order to change their lives. Drawing on stereotypes of Appalachia, most make two assumptions: that Appalachians never leave their home community and that leaving will solve people's problems. This subset of gatekeepers often foreclosed the possibility of anyone in Appalachia changing. A university-based researcher stated:

> We knew people weren't leaving the community to get treatment and to make, if you will, better lives for themselves. That's when something like a drug epidemic can more easily take hold because we've got a constant. People in recovery in rural areas have to leave because it's such a small insular community that it's hard for them to change their behaviors because there's so many negative influences on them.

The women I interviewed developed their own strategies, and they pushed against these ideas of leaving in several ways. First, over half had moved to different areas, leaving their home county for another county or state for months or years at a time, primarily to search for employment. Other women wanted to leave but felt like they could not because they would be leaving their children as well, for whom they did not have custody. Ashley wanted to go to an inpatient treatment program, especially since her children were already living with their father in another state. She did not go because she would have lost her stable housing. Although Maggie had custody, her family provided childcare while she worked. She was not going to move when she would have had to pay for childcare she did not trust. Others were attempting to save enough money to leave, but they had to save thousands of dollars for rent and transportation. This seemed like an insurmountable goal.

When women did leave their home counties, it didn't change their marginalized positions. Whether they moved to urban central Kentucky, Texas, Ohio, or Alaska, they were nonetheless ensnared in similar mazes of homelessness, unemployment, incarceration, and drug use. Leaving did not change the stigma they felt. People may be stigmatized because of their reputation and former drug use in their hometown. When they left, they were stigmatized for their drug use and birthplace in rural Appalachia. They reasoned that if they were going to be treated "like dogs" regardless of place, then perhaps being in the place where they have some support is more advantageous. When people moved to different areas several times and did not find better conditions, they saw no point in leaving again. Star and her family moved to another county with better jobs, but her children were miserable in the school system that has poorer outcomes than the one in her home county. She quickly returned home and vowed not to attempt to leave again until her youngest child had graduated high school.

Katie relocated to urban areas where she found low-wage employment, expensive and substandard living conditions, and heroin. Heroin's cheapness compared to prescription opioids allowed her to increase use. Katie gave birth to a daughter in central Kentucky about a year before we met. She decided to come back to her parents' home in Adams County in hopes of receiving support as a new mother who also had an open DCBS case. Instead, she became entwined in conflicted familial relations. Her father has abstained from alcohol and the violence related to its use for decades, but then her mother became abusive. The week before our first interview, her mother had broken Katie's nose, but Katie did not report it because this would bring unwanted attention from DCBS or law enforcement. Despite this turmoil, she had strong family support in her grandparents and aunts, who watched her daughter regularly.

This moving away and returning reflects the ambivalence most of the people I spoke with have for the region. When people leave, they may lose a piece of their identity and access to their survival strategies. But home places should not be over sentimentalized—these are the places where most abuse occurs. People love the beauty and their community, but they feel like they cannot move out of their marginalized positions. One of the character's observations from *Strange as This Weather Has Been* exemplifies this feeling: "Because for a long time, I'd known the tightness of these hills, the way they penned. But now, I also felt their comfort. . . . I understood how when I left, I lost part of myself, but when I stayed, I couldn't stretch myself full."[33]

A few women truly embraced this ambivalence as reflecting society's mixed feelings toward them as beloved but flawed Appalachians. Pancake successfully displays how the pain and hope of this place can live through its residents: "This place not pure, and how that somehow makes him more tender for it, makes him love it deeper, for its vulnerability, for its weariness and its endurance. This place so subtly beautiful and so overlaid with doom. . . . Killed again and again, and each time, the place rising back on its haunches, diminished, but once more alive."[34] I do not take these words to be as disheartened as they might seem. I connect this to Alisha's understanding of her scars as painful but beautiful aspects of herself that give her tenacity and empathy.

These regions, including Appalachia, that are stereotyped as having high rates of drug use and overdose deaths are intimately tied to exploitive global capitalism.[35] Women's placement in a marginalized region materially constricts their lives, yet these limitations do not disappear when they relocate. Leaving Appalachia does not provide an escape from gendered inequalities, punitive discourses and policies regarding people who use drugs, or state surveillance. Further, leaving threatens systems of care that are vital for people's survival. Some of the women in this study are arguably the most marginalized county residents in an area with poor economic and health indicators. Yet they find ways to make do among people as they fight for each other's survival.

Women's resilience against inequalities has a long history in Appalachia. They have been fundamental in labor disputes. This was most popularly displayed in the 1976 documentary *Harlan County U.S.A.*, which highlighted women's support of the United Mine Workers of America strikers through the Brookside Women's Club.[36] Women, including Maria Gunnoe and the late Judy Bonds, have been at the forefront of protests against mountaintop removal and the negative consequences of the coal industry.[37] Women of color have demanded inclusion in an Appalachian region that is stereotyped as all white.[38] Appalachian communities have come together to respond to opioid use and overdose deaths.[39] In the five counties in this study, women have organized antidrug coalitions. Yet a select few gatekeepers attend these meetings. When I asked women in recovery if they would attend, none said they would feel comfortable going because of their status as former drug users. Activism does not mean that everyone's interests are included.

The resilience I describe among these women going through treatment more often takes place in the home or the family, rather than collectively in the community. Maybe this is why people who have only a cursory or elite view of communities miss the resistance. Only five women took part in collective action. Alisha joined a statewide social justice organization. Star worked with other drug court participants to advocate for a court drug screening site that was located in their home county, as opposed to a neighboring county. Katie and Maggie came together with another Horizons client to start a community-led substance use support group. I think women's struggles with addiction, other health issues, caregiving work, and material deprivation limit the energy available to organize. Resilience takes its own tolls, often robbing energy and space that could be directed elsewhere if it were not required. Women's discomfort with attending antidrug coalition and additional community meetings indicates they may be prevented from organizing in the public sphere through the shaming of people who are poor or use drugs. A next step I am taking in my current setting in East Tennessee is thinking through the ways to support the efforts of women like Alisha, Star, Katie, and Maggie.

Most actions I witnessed did not occur on a public stage. Yet surviving on the edge is a political act in and of itself. Women's strategies for navigating inequalities and gendered violence are constrained and may represent the best choice out of several poor options. But

these strategies represent creative ways of generating a life primarily
based on care networks that are undetermined by a capitalist labor
market.[40] In areas with uncertain or wavering economies, care networks may provide more predictable assistance than labor economies.[41] Building onto understandings of care may be a starting place
for treatment programs to support people's navigations. This may
be a more helpful and less isolating path as opposed to sanctioning
people for how they engage with care or encouraging clients to enter
low-wage and exploitive employment. Yet any investigation of how
to build upon care networks should avoid reinforcing gendered cat-
egories of who can provide care and gendered burdens of care work,
especially when it comes to parenting.

Chapter 7
Moving Forward

"THESE HILLS ARE JIST DIRT WAVES, washing through eternity . . . they hain't a valley so low but what hit'll rise agin. They hain't a hill standing so proud but hit'll sink to the low ground o' sorrow."[1]

This quote describes my frame of mind as I conducted much of my research. Despite the pain I document, there is hope. The energy in people and places is humbling. But there are innumerable battles to fight and brutality permeates almost every aspect of some people's lives. So many of my days resembled this: driving through the flattened mountains in Eastern Kentucky mourning what we have done to this place, and then speaking to an awe-inspiring woman who has spent decades working on social justice, succeeding in ways that seemed impossible. My intention throughout has been to show the cruelty and the inequalities as well as the work against these forces in ways that do not romanticize, but reveal the complicated strategies that individuals, families, and communities must create as they make their way through this life. These navigations do not happen alone, but with others, living and dead. Sissy, Katie, and Maggie continue to find stability through their own work as well as through family and community support.

I conclude by summarizing what my research has to say about representation, marginalization, and encounters with the state. These encounters can be confusing, as in the case with buprenorphine and its various treatments by state actors. The lives people lead are situated within care networks, which offer their own complicated webs of love and hostility, resources and desperation. The women, communities, and colleagues I encountered provide ideas of how to move forward. I see these as starting points that can be built upon as people engage with their own communities and with the people living in the gaps within these places.

Negative representations are hurtful, slowly cutting away at people. The women I spoke with face a host of stereotypes, based on their class, drug use, and location in Appalachia, that create tensions as they attempt to live their lives within families and communities. Stereotypes are most detrimental when they become part of policies. Harmful policies diminish resources to already marginalized populations and create institutions in which individuals are filtered through chaotic and punitive programs.

For me, this persistent overdose catastrophe reflects the very definition of a neoliberal capitalist state that values deregulation of corporations and overregulation of individuals. For families and communities, that translates into slashed or heavily underfunded social services. The family or community becomes the only source of care, survival, and resistance. Yet the care that can be offered is stifled, because all are dealing with injustices. People are left to suffer and die. We must make demands on the state to provide needed services, but obviously we cannot wait on the state. Communities, families, and individuals have to take steps. While we advocate for social change, we must come together to take care of one another.

Representation

Using stories is a precarious strategy. People often listen to stories better than numbers, but individual stories may be easily dismissed as aberrations in a distant land. The intent of this ethnography is to place narratives within larger contexts to create something that can be heard and not as easily dismissed because these stories expand on themes. I situated women's stories within analyses of large-scale political, economic, and social forces to humanize women who use drugs as well as move understandings of their experiences beyond explanations that focus on individual or cultural differences or dysfunctions.[2] The last time I had contact with Star and Alisha, both were still looking for employment. To be fully understood, these searches must be contextualized within understandings of disinvestment in Appalachia as well as stigma against those with felony and misdemeanor records.

Though discussing his fictional book that takes place in Central Appalachia, Robert Gipe captures some of the intricacies of written representation: "I try to write stories that help people identify with and love people with too-complicated lives. I don't want anybody feeling sorry for them. I want people to see what it's like, and realize maybe hard-luck people are actually pretty smart and creative and have a lot of grit."[3] I am writing against portrayals of women processing through treatment as perpetual victims, unable to take action on their own behalf. They take actions every day. Sometimes these actions are undoubtedly harmful to themselves and those close to them. At other times, their actions are deemed harmful from the outside, but are more nuanced. People's lives are bound by the cultural, political, and economic environments in which they live. Some people face inflexible constraints that feel like they are forever bound in handcuffs; others occasionally face a slight tug that may be shrugged off. Most of the women I spoke with narrated lives of being restrained, but nonetheless charging forward, even if into a wall. Some were abused and some have abused. Most cited feelings of being treated at some point as though they were useless because they use drugs. This shunning is dangerous for women, their families, and their communities.

Some gatekeepers viewed women who use drugs and come into contact with state programs as "unworthy" poor. They classified treatment clients as irresponsible women who chose to be mothers, chose to use drugs, chose to be poor, and chose not to leave their home area to obtain a better life. Women were only characterized as valuable within this view if they were able to participate in legal economies while performing unpaid caretaking work.

Some gatekeepers and community members frame the women in this study as the "worthy" poor because of their roles as mothers as well as their victimhood within an Appalachian culture that is construed as especially harmful. At state-level meetings especially, Appalachian and rural women were incorrectly pictured as all white, which lends further support for their categorization as worthy recipients of social entitlements. Yet I argue that women are primarily considered worthy because of their white children, not only because of their own whiteness. People considered adults who use drugs to be already lost, but their children perhaps could be saved. To be fair, two service providers refuted these simple categorizations. They argued that all social safety net services should be expanded and they understood their work as being part of a larger social justice movement.

Populations that are marginalized discursively as well as materially experience increased state surveillance as compared to the privileged. State intervention can be based on what women's bodies look like, whether they are white, appear pregnant, or have scars. A deep blue or black puncture mark on the arm indicating injection drug use can result in child removal or incarceration. Yet state surveillance among and between populations on the fringes differs. The women in this research qualify for and at times are coerced to use particular state services because of their gender, race, class, and motherhood status.

With society's deeply flawed understandings of addiction, mental health, and homelessness, we are delivered aspects of programs that are ineffective and wasteful. Both clients and staff are forced to jump through pointless hoops that require reserves of already constrained energies. The relationships between therapeutic as well as rehabilitative services and punitive agencies make program environments tense and perhaps adverse to successful therapeutic practice. Through its mission, Horizons is inextricably linked to DCBS. Drug court is embedded in the criminal processing system. The public, media, and law enforcement have largely viewed buprenorphine treatment as illegitimate and harmful. Bupe providers become punitive toward clients in attempts to legitimize their businesses and to protect themselves legally. Women face the consequences of these conflicts over bupe and may lose child custody as a result.

Stigma affects women's maintenance of child custody, emotional state, and talk about themselves and others in similar positions. Stigma is embodied as another aspect of domination. For these women, physical pain and the emotional stress caused by brutality are manifested as depression, anxiety, and drug use. To cope with stress and pain, the only available forms of self-care may be detrimental and inadvertently lead to further harm. Health and pharmaceutical industry policies shape the availability of self-care options, where pain and poverty are addressed through medication. Ashley's use of prescribed and illicit substances is a primary example of this form of self-care—a self-care that lead to cycles of further harm as she increased medication because she did not have child custody, which lead to missed court dates and continued child removal, which turned into further anxiety, depression, and medication. I unfortunately could not get into contact with Ashley after leaving the area and am unsure where she ended up.

The participants in this research live on the margins in an area that has poor economic indicators and is stereotyped because it is located within Appalachia. The negative assumptions that often accompanied the mid-twentieth-century War on Poverty and its culture of poverty models persist to this day. At times, culture is used as a weapon to blame those in subordinate positions. Exploitation is hidden through processes that remove political and economic considerations. People in power see the site of intervention as the individual or family, and this is a political act because it places the site of intervention in these private spaces instead of in the public sphere.

Women must navigate these discursive representations. Women, all of whom are construed as mothers, have a series of impossible identities they may be forced to accept when interacting with government programs. Some go into programs having lived for years with the stigmatized identity of a mother who uses drugs; others must suddenly switch from considering themselves "normal" to identifying as a mother who uses drugs, at least when presenting themselves to program staff. Local understandings of drug use include individualistic ideas of addiction as a chronic neurological disorder that is, at the same time, attributed to moral failings. Some people subscribe to a culture of addiction model where women are framed as bad mothers and citizens who assault children and perpetuate drug use through reproduction of damaged children.

Material Realities in a Neoliberal State

Stigma limits material resources. Characterizations of poor mothers justify decreases in government spending. Just as spending is reduced, portrayals of Appalachians as being overly dependent on government dollars and addicted to drugs propagate new arguments for entrepreneurial innovations as the savior of the area rather than private or public investments. Criminalization of people who use drugs constricts their access to entitlement programs when incarcerated and once they have felony records. Community members and families at times deny employment and housing to women based on their class, surname, and past drug use. Businesses and individuals prey on those on the margins by charging exorbitant prices for basic services, such as showers and single-serving food items, or trading SNAP benefits for cents on the dollar. In the midst of these inequalities, women are swept into government programs that may be more about surveillance than services.

People also rely on the privileges they have. Whiteness largely goes unmarked across the United States, and it is often unexamined. The participants in this research may be heavily surveilled for many reasons, but for thirty-seven of the forty women I interviewed, it is not because of the color of their skin. While their families and communities may be economically distressed, they have not faced the systemic racism experienced by communities of color. These women may thus have access to care networks that have socially and economically benefitted from white supremacist policies privileging whites in terms of housing, education, employment, and power.

Women's access to entitlement programs and involvement in coercive regimes of state care are predicated on their social locations.

At times women's gender, class, or drug use status place them in programs that they otherwise would not have access to. This study focuses on their placement in forms of drug treatment that are not universally available in the five counties. Yet these same social positions open them to DCBS intervention and incarceration. Their involvement with one state entity may undermine their ability to utilize another service. Women's placement in drug court prevents them from enrolling in bupe programs and in some counties at certain times, they are prevented from entering Horizons. This reveals the multiple and at times contradictory conditions that flow through state agencies.

People differentially find particular aspects of state punitive, rehabilitative, and therapeutic programs helpful and harmful. Structural violence constrains these programs. I outline how systems of governance, which are implemented by both state and nonstate actors, intrude in people's lives. Cuts in funding for social services do not mean the state is any further out of their lives. Underfunded programs may be more chaotic, as exemplified with DCBS caseworkers who do not have cell phones and the consistent turnover of Horizons staff. This makes the state difficult to navigate because rules are unclear, but people can also find gaps to exploit within and between programs.

Survival and Resistance within Care Networks

The vast majority of people agree that these treatment programs, although needed, do not adequately address substance use or gendered inequalities. People find therapeutic and rehabilitative services helpful, but they also value material support through case management. In terms of economic resources, most rely on SNAP and those few who have housing subsidies see these as preventing homelessness. Medicaid expansion and to a lesser extent additional ACA provisions have given some people or their family members unprecedented access to health care, including substance use treatment. Yet people want access to more individual counseling sessions as well as to quality health care across the spectrum of mental and physical health.

These services may not be available because there are no local providers. Poor quality care, whether health care or familial care, can in some cases be worse than no care at all.

Drug use involves more than the individual. Structural forces frame entry into and maintenance of use as well as illicit economies. Networks of people, places, and things bind people to others in ways that hurt and strengthen. Yet use is also tied to inner worlds. Pain and love, desires to leave and to stay, isolation and connection are all bound up in the self. Both drugs and relationships are taken within, entangled in the sense of self, and only let go with anguish. People's care networks represent the localized place where drug use and treatment occur.

The stories I presented in the preceding chapters show that care and care networks defy easy categorization. A definition of care that focuses on positive outcomes leaves out particular relationships and the unevenness of relationships. Just as state programs represent mazes, relations are equally labyrinthine. Even when care is intended to be supportive, it may not be. Program staff are limited in what they can offer. Families are taken to the brink of letting people go, and sometimes they must do that for their own survival. Women at times feel unable to take care of themselves, let alone anyone else. Kinship is how people make it through, and family members or intimate partners are the most likely to harm or kill women. Care networks and even the same relationship can support abatement of drug use.

Program staff ask people to treat their drug using lives as unproductive and pernicious. In this vein, staff ask clients to change their "people, places, and things." For those few women who are removed from drug using networks and who do not think their use ever defined or transformed their social roles, they may have to change very little about their social world. For those who are suddenly asked to remove themselves from all friends and family members and even neighborhoods and communities, this break is materially and emotionally jarring. The complexities of care presented here are within systems of domination. Interpersonal relationships may turn destructive not because the people involved are inherently evil, but because they are in a system that fosters cruelty. Thus interpersonal and structural violence must be addressed simultaneously.[4] Health education or anti-violence campaigns that focus on personal responsibility, cultural difference, and lack of individual knowledge ignore injustices and thereby support continued cruelty.[5] Further, structural violence is systemic and thus cannot be abolished by removing an individual who holds power. The system itself must be dismantled.[6]

Some people successfully navigate programs, policies, and kin. Sissy, Katie, and Maggie seem to have found peace. Without taking away from their own actions, they have strong family members upon whom they can rely, have found camaraderie with others who used drugs, and have found acceptance in their community through their caretaking work and in Maggie's case, her art. Even though Katie experienced a devastating loss in the death of her partner after I moved, she made it through with this support.

Most of those I interviewed do not take part in explicit political action because they are consumed with daily survival, but many attempt to regain political rights. They are fighting for their rights to be parents by struggling for child custody. Some of those who have been incarcerated fight to restore their voting rights. Every single person with whom I spoke is attempting to cease harmful drug use. Some were caught in the state system for testing positive for cannabis once, and they cited little problem in stopping use. For the people who identified as addicted, some had been former users for years and others relayed stories of recent relapse, but all are fighting to decrease use. People who formerly used have taken it upon themselves to care for one another and to try to help others find a way to end chaotic use. Sometimes this means volunteering or working for an existing organization, like Horizons. At times, this means seeing a need in the community and filling it.

People contest negative labels. They attempt to redefine what it means to be a parent and build cases to support their redefinition.

People find ways that are constrained and at times unsuccessful to avoid DCBS, to ignore caseworker recommendations, and to regain child custody. Some treatment clients contest programmatic aspects that solely focus on a motherhood identity. Inadequately resourced treatment programs and state agencies structure people's strategies. These strategies become potentially more harmful when there are gaps between these service providers, as in the case of bupe treatment. Community members and program staff are often informed in ways that negatively portray Appalachian women and people who use drugs, creating spaces where negative characterizations are normalized.

Staff and administrators within treatment programs also attempt to make changes. They offer services that are unavailable elsewhere. Some regional and state administrators, particularly those affiliated with Horizons, support the retention of Medicaid expansion and provisions of the ACA as well as destigmatizing bupe. They make this support clear at state and regional meetings and publicly through Facebook and local newspaper editorials. While people who use drugs are stigmatized and work to fight against this stigma, so do some providers. They are acutely aware of stigma and see it as part of their mission to lessen the harm to clients. Although it may be important for people to understand their structural limitations so they map a navigable path, it is equally important to construe structures as changeable. Even those structures that seem immutable were created and can be undone with a series of (often hard-won) decisions.

Recommendations

There is need for greater access to better quality treatment. People did not agree over which treatment models are best or worst, but they wanted a variety of treatment models to be made available. While Maggie wanted a buprenorphine program that could help her get back into school and find employment, Star wanted a Bible-based program that included childcare and opportunities to congregate with other participants. At the same time, it is unlikely that any substance use treatment program could, on its own, address the gendered and economic inequalities in Central Appalachia.

Some program staff have a deep knowledge of the structural inequalities with which people contend and do what they can to help people cope with these circumstances by offering various kinds of support. Yet some staff's propagation of negative stereotypes of Appalachians and women who use drugs results in harsh interactions with program participants. Staff demonize people's relationships, causing difficult to overcome rifts in people's considerations of themselves and those they hold dear. Community members and politicians ostracize people who use drugs as causing poverty in Appalachia, instead of understanding poverty and substance use as resulting from the same fundamental dysfunction of unequal power relations in a neoliberal capitalist economy. In the same breath, folks will criticize use of terms like "hillbilly" and "hick," while using the equally inaccurate and degrading terms "drug babies" or "addicted babies."

People feel this stigma. Treatment programs and community places must be safe spaces for those who need them. Clients will not return to programs where they feel they are treated like "dogs" (a comparison communicated to me many times). People are not getting services they want, and communities are left with residents who are frustrated with lack of support from the entities to which they turn. Tying services to vulnerabilities objectifies and highlights these vulnerabilities for all to see. Focusing on people's overall health and context within the political economic framework would likely be more effective and less marginalizing than pinpointing substance use as *the* problem. While Alisha said she wanted to end her use when she entered treatment, housing, employment, and additional health conditions were larger concerns.

The daily expression of stigma seems more like micro-aggressions to be endured—frustrating, but people usually make it through. Fixing negative attitudes toward poor people, women who use drugs, or Appalachians is necessary but not sufficient for real change. If every biased service provider altered their attitude, they would still be working in underfunded programs with problematic policies serving populations marginalized by exploitive economic and political processes. This is where stigma devastates, when it leads to further material marginalization or child removal. Lack of resources and losing children is felt as a Promethean pain.

Appalachian communities need public investment. Overall, there is limited public investment in substance use treatment as well as education-based prevention, but the dollars are really not there for harm-reduction or wraparound services to make recovery more attainable. Kentucky is an anomaly for harm reduction in Appalachia where syringe services programs are run through local health departments, but this is not the case for other states in the central and southern region. While prevention focuses on education, the money for building economically sustainable and equitable communities is minimal, might be further reduced, or is simply nonexistent. Following the 2017 Tax Cuts and Jobs Act, we will see further inequalities as the ultra-wealthy reap the most benefits from tax reform.[7] Federal and Kentucky state politicians have promised even deeper cuts to government programs in years to come.

Further state support is important, but it is not a cure for the system. Many in this ethnography rely heavily on SNAP and may go hungry when that resource is taken. Only one woman I talked to, Ashley, was focused on enrolling in SSI. Most others just want anything to do that will help them live what they describe as normal lives. Employment opportunities are not available in the area. For change to occur, efforts must be made across state and federal governments and communities to create livable options. Perhaps the call centers that are opening in rural Eastern Kentucky are one minor avenue, but communities need more options that offer stable employment with desirable wages and benefits. There are many diverse economic ventures across the region, from organic mushroom farmers to documentary filmmakers to permaculture experts. But despite the grand hopes and true importance of entrepreneurism, the belief that entrepreneurship will save the region seems naïve. Maggie was the only person who had her own business and her household needed government and familial assistance, especially when she was getting started. I do not think that placing the burden of a full economic shift on already distressed communities and families will be successful.

A rethinking of the economy and government is in order for the nation, and especially for Appalachia. Most of these women are classified as unemployed, but that does not describe their lives. They find ways to make do in formal and informal economies. They provide unpaid care to children, to older and chronically ill kin, and to the community. We must support care work that often falls on women in this patriarchal society.

If we can support diverse economies, we have a chance to transform the structures of power that place people on the edge. All levels of government currently throw money at national or multinational corporations that promise dozens or hundreds of "good paying" jobs, but communities often end up with few positions that have stagnant wages and limited benefits. When a cheaper alternative presents itself, the companies move out, leaving hundreds unemployed, as they did in Adams County. I agree that some of this funding would be better invested in entrepreneurs. Worker-owned cooperatives represent another option to avoid reliance on capitalist enterprises. In retooling the economy, a host of issues arise that must be grappled with, such as infrastructure concerns, environmental degradation, land ownership patterns that privilege elite whites, and unequal education systems funded through local property taxes.

It is time to rethink the relationship between the government and the people. In many instances, government policies must be altered to address these issues. While marginalized populations rely on state protections and resources, the US government consistently bolsters elite power by violating people's civil and reproductive rights. Yes, most women I spoke to relied on SNAP and Medicaid, but the carceral state was far more pervasive in their lives and communities than any other aspect of the state. Several questions arise here: What level of power do we want the government to have and over whom? What do we want the relationship between government, industry, and people to look like? How do we save ourselves and our communities when the government refuses to act?

Treatment clients are showing up, and so can communities and families. Materially and emotionally supporting those struggling with addiction is fundamental. Many kin are already doing this. I see communities working extensively on prevention, but many are largely missing when it comes to harm-reduction and treatment efforts. Normalizing these efforts may be a next step. No matter what efforts are made, listening to what those on the fringes say they need is essential. The most effective harm-reduction models I have seen are rooted in communities of people who use drugs, not in the ideas of people who rarely speak to people who use drugs. The strongest ask I have heard is for affordable and safe housing. Other actions discussed include syringe services programs, foot and wound care clinics, safer consumption sites, financial and organizational support for people who use(d) drugs to start their own programs, and employers who are willing to hire people with legal records. Paternalistic policies and programs that attempt to shape communities and individuals according to idealized notions of what women, the rural, or care *should* be will falter or fail because they often operate outside of what actually is and what individuals and communities want.

Beyond substance use treatment programs, state agencies, and economic policies, health and drug policies should be shifted. If drug use patterns are to be changed, the policies around pharmaceuticals and other health technologies must be reexamined and enforced. When the cost of corporate lying is minimal, especially in comparison to exorbitant profits, the lying will not stop. Policies involving illicit drug use continue the mass incarceration of poor people and people of color. This harms individuals, families, and communities. When people are incarcerated, they are removed from care networks and may be permanently disenfranchised from the economic as well as political system. Communities are left decimated when people are removed and tax dollars are spent on incarceration.

Policies that support the tenets of reproductive justice are also paramount to these women. Those who have the ability to reproduce need full access to reproductive health care, including the spectrum of contraceptive methods. Having access to contraceptive and abortive care gives some control over whom people provide for. More important, we must have an environment where parenthood is supported through the adequate provision of resources. People who have uteruses are reproductive laborers, and all caregivers are socializing laborers; they should be recognized as such. Policies that separate parents' health from children's health and disproportionality separate children from their parents in low-income communities and communities of color are unjust and should be opposed. Voting is a minimal commitment; next steps include showing up to community meetings, contacting politicians, writing editorials, and documenting injustices.

When this research came to an end, I felt I had to take a step back from focuses on substance use. Women's stories about employment and housing lead me to focus on sustainable and equitable community change. I could not stay away from service provision though, as I currently work at an organization that abides by a harm-reduction framework, having the only syringe services program in the East Tennessee area. I am certainly not opposed to "sinking this capitalist system to the darkest bits of hell," in the lyrics of Sarah Ogan Gunning,[8] writing in support of striking coal miners. But as we work in the current everyday, it is vital to find ways of fighting the exploitive system while using it to work toward justices we seek, whether that is through harm-reduction models, international social justice movements, or diverse economies. Those who provide services while simultaneously dismantling domination are models for us all, and I aspire to be of some use in both the everyday and in larger struggles.

As we travel forward, the more harm-reduction services we have, including naloxone distribution, syringe services programs, and safer consumption spaces, the fewer people will die. Harm-reduction programs can also serve as sources of social support and community action. As we repeatedly learn, whether in terms of substance use treatment or actions done in the name of human rights, the road to hell, or at least a realm of it, is paved with good intentions. Yet careful attention to the details of the lives of people who programs intend to serve may limit these negative consequences. We cannot expect programs or their clients to succeed if we continue to socially and economically ostracize both.

Appendix
A Few Relevant Advocacy Organizations

Appalachia

Appalshop (www.appalshop.org): Documents the lives and voices the concerns of Appalachians through place-based arts and media.

Highlander Research and Education Center (www.highlandercenter .org): Provides education and engages in participatory research to create spaces where organizing can occur to produce cultural change based on social and economic justice.

Queer Appalachia (www.queerappalachia.com): Uses popular media and art to celebrate queer voices and to advance cultural change to make rural and Appalachian spaces safer for communities of color, for people who identify as queer and trans, and for people who use drugs.

The Stay Project (www.thestayproject.com): The Stay Together Appalachian Youth Project is a diverse regional youth network that collaborates to imagine and create a sustainable, justice-oriented Appalachian future.

Young Appalachian Leaders and Learners (Y'ALL; www.instagram .com/yall4asa): A committee with the Appalachian Studies Association that seeks to foster relationships between emerging scholars and leaders to encourage lifelong regional engagement and activism.

Harm Reduction

Drug Policy Alliance (www.drugpolicy.org): A national and international advocacy organization based in the United States focused on reforming regressive drug and criminal policies.

Harm Reduction Coalition (harmreduction.org): A United States national organization providing education, resources, and leadership on harm reduction and drug policy reform.

Harm Reduction International (www.hri.global): An international organization providing education, research, and advocacy for harm reduction.

Insite Supervised Consumption Site (www.vch.ca/public-health/harm-reduction): Opened North America's first supervised consumption site in 2003 where people are able to use drugs in a space that is made safer by the provision of unused consumption supplies and access to trained medical personnel.

Choice Health Network Harm Reduction (www.instagram.com/chnharmreduction): Advocates for harm reduction and delivers harm-reduction services at multiple sites in Knoxville, Tennessee.

North Carolina Harm Reduction Coalition (www.nchrc.org): Advocates for harm reduction in North Carolina and supports a network of harm-reduction programs across the state.

Steady Collective (www.thesteadycollective.org): Advocates for harm reduction and delivers harm-reduction services at multiple sites in Asheville, North Carolina.

North Carolina Urban Survivor's Union (https://ncurbansurvivorunion.org): A program based in North Carolina aimed at empowering people who use drugs to advocate for their rights and engage in harm-reduction programming.

Reproductive Justice

National Advocates for Pregnant Women (www.advocatesfor-pregnantwomen.org): A United States national reproductive justice organization that provides legal services and research to advocate for drug policies that do not violate reproductive rights.

SisterSong (www.sistersong.net): A United States national women of color reproductive justice organization that uses arts and cultural programs as well as additional direct services to center Black women's leadership and issues.

All Access EKY (www.allaccesseky.org): Supports policies, programs, and services that provide the full range of contraceptive methods to young people in Eastern Kentucky.

Kentucky Health Justice Network (www.kentuckyhealthjustice-network.org): Advocates for reproductive justice and supports an abortion fund in Kentucky.

Healthy and Free Tennessee (www.healthyandfreetn.org): A reproductive justice organization based in Nashville, Tennessee, that works on a breadth of issues, including defeating policies and programs that criminalize people who are pregnant and use drugs.

SisterReach (sisterreach.org): A reproductive justice organization based in Memphis, Tennessee, that provides education, policy advocacy, and cultural shift to support the reproductive needs of people of color, LGBTQ+, and poor and rural people. Provides research on policies that criminalize people who are pregnant and use drugs.

WV Free (www.wvfree.org): Advocates for and provides education on reproductive justice in West Virginia.

Acknowledgments

I WISH TO THANK THE PARTICIPANTS who spoke with me. All took risks in sharing their stories, as all are bound by systems that work to oppress. May those processing through treatment, as well as service providers, continue to "Pray for the dead, and fight like hell for the living," in the apt words of Mother Jones. I sincerely hope all are able to find some sort of peace in this life.

While it is an individual work, this book benefited from the insights and direction of many people. My dissertation chair, Mary Anglin, exemplifies the high-quality scholarship to which I aspire. I wish to thank the complete dissertation committee: Ann Kingsolver, Erin Koch, Carl Leukefeld, Carol Mason, and Shaunna Scott. Each individual provided insights that guided and challenged my thinking throughout the process. In addition, Heather Worne gave instructive comments on my proposal. I thank the University of Kentucky Appalachian Center for providing partial funding for this dissertation through research grants.

This book is built on the foundations of a long tradition of radical actions. Reproductive justice is rooted in women of color's activism. The work of Loretta Ross, Patricia Hill Collins, Kimberle Crenshaw, Dána-Ain Davis, Dorothy Roberts, and Gloria Anzaldúa, among many others, has challenged me to analyze my social position and the white privilege that has been bestowed upon me, my body, and many of those with whom I spent time. Their analyses of neoliberalism and the state are also key, as are analyses by Jeff Maskovsky, Sandra Morgen, James C. Scott, and Loïc Wacquant. I am incredibly lucky in that many of the Appalachian scholars I admire the most were on my committee, or I was able to take classes with people like Dwight

Billings during graduate school. I drove to Berea several times to attend talks by bell hooks and Silas House. The Appalachian Studies Association (ASA) provides a space to learn from others, often not in official forums, but in tucked away nooks and behind the scenes meetings. If not for ASA, I would not have met Jordan Laney, Skye McFarland, Lou Murrey, Emily Satterwhite, Helen Lewis, Barbara Ellen Smith . . . Just looking at the might on that shortened list makes me tear up, because I know there are comrades not too far away.

 Bless all the friends and colleagues from the University of Kentucky; the University of Colorado, Denver; the Tennessee Department of Health; and numerous national and regional social justice organizations who attentively listened to what I was doing and provided constructive feedback, helping me grow into a more thoughtful scholar, activist, and resident. Late night talks and common graduate student discussions with Brittney Howell, Barry and Sarah Kidder, Dan Ball, Kathryn Engle, Henry Bundy, Tammy Clemons, Emily Chasco, and Mary Beth Schmid helped me get through a heap of issues. I am thankful for the opportunities I had to share my work in progress at conferences, but also at universities in the Appalachian region, where I always received quality feedback. National Advocates for Pregnant Women and Healthy and Free Tennessee have assisted me in bridging the gap between an academic and activist life. As I have moved from academia to more applied work, I thank those who have made the move before me and have offered good advice, including Bayla Ostrach and Elizabeth Catte. To be clear, none of these people or organizations radicalized me, I owe that all to communities and people who must remain unnamed here. And, of course, to a lot of running around the woods as a kid.

 I received equally important assistance from family and friends. My partner, Arie Buer, supported me throughout the dissertation and successfully prevented our family and home from falling into chaos when I was in the field. My family, especially the strong women, inspired me to continue my education, seemingly without end at some points. I have a group of friends from East Tennessee who invaluably keep me grounded in our roots. I am truly blessed to have such a fine arrangement of folks who I have been connected to for decades and who share a similar sense of caring. I could not have completed this dissertation without the women (and Grandpa) who provided my family with safe and stable childcare. Thank you.

References

Abu-Lughod, Lila. "The Romance of Resistance: Tracing Transformations of Power through Bedouin Women." *American Ethnologist* 17, no. 1 (1990): 41–55.

Agar, Michael and Heather Schacht Reisinger. "A Tale of Two Policies: The French Connection, Methadone, and Heroin Epidemics." *Culture, Medicine, and Psychiatry* 26, no. 3 (2002): 371–96.

Allbee, Allison, Rebecca Johnson, and Jeffrey Lubell. *Preserving, Protecting, and Expanding Affordable Housing: A Policy Toolkit for Public Health.* Oakland, CA: ChangeLab Solutions, 2015.

Amason, J. Hope. "Uncertain Lives: Neoliberalism and the Shaping of Home among Service Workers in Gatlinburg." *North American Dialogue* 18, no. 1 (2015): 1–14.

Anderson, Warwick. *Colonial Pathologies: American Tropical Medicine, Race, and Hygiene in the Philippines.* Durham, NC: Duke University Press, 2006.

Anglin, Mary K. "Erasures of the Past: Culture, Power, and Heterogeneity in Appalachia." *Journal of Appalachian Studies* 10, no. 1/2 (2004): 73–84.

———. "Lessons from Appalachia in the 20th Century: Power, Poverty, and the Grassroots." *American Anthropologist* 104, no. 3 (2002): 565–82.

———. "Moving Forward: Gender and Globalization in/of Appalachian Studies." *Appalachian Journal* 37, no. 3/4 (2010): 286–300.

Anzaldúa, Gloria. *Borderlands: La Frontera.* San Francisco: Spinsters/Aunt Lute, 1987.

Appalachian Land Ownership Task Force. *Who Owns Appalachia? Landownership and Its Impact.* Lexington: University Press of Kentucky, 1983.

Appalachian Regional Commission. "Appalachian Apps: Transforming the Region's Economy Conference." Somerset, KY, October 14–15, 2015.

———. "County Economic Status in Appalachia, FY 2017." 2016, www.Arc.Gov/Research/Mapsofappalachia.Asp?Map_Id=116.

———. "Data Reports: Socioeconomic Data Profile by County." 2017, www.arc.gov/data.

Aretxaga, Begona. "Maddening States." *Annual Review of Anthropology* 32 (2003): 393–410.

Baker, Phyllis L. and Amy Carson. "'I Take Care of My Kids': Mothering

Practices of Substance-Abusing Women." *Gender and Society* 13, no. 3 (1999): 347–63.

Bandstra, Emmalee S., Connie E. Morrow, Elana Mansoor, and Veronic H. Accornero. "Prenatal Drug Exposure: Infant and Toddler Outcomes." *Journal of Addictive Diseases* 29, no. 2 (2010): 245–58.

Banks, Pat, Stephanie McSpirit, Jessica Pulliam, and Alan Banks. "Building Alliances to Conserve and Protect the Kentucky River." *Journal of Appalachian Studies* 19, no. 1/2 (2013): 133–50.

Barney, Sandra Lee. *Authorized to Heal: Gender, Class, and the Transformation of Medicine in Appalachia, 1880–1930*. Chapel Hill: University of North Carolina Press, 2000.

Beck, Judith S. *Cognitive Behavioral Therapy: Basics and Beyond*. 2nd ed. New York: Guilford Press, 2011.

Becker, Gay. "The Uninsured and the Politics of Containment in US Health Care." *Medical Anthropology* 26, no. 4 (2007): 299–321.

Becker, Jane S. *Selling Tradition: Appalachia and the Construction of an American Folk 1930–1940*. Chapel Hill: University of North Carolina Press, 1998.

Beckett, Katherine and Bruce Western. "Governing Social Marginality: Welfare, Incarceration, and the Transformation of State Policy." *Punishment & Society* 3, no. 1 (2001): 43–59.

Behnke, Marylou and Vincent C. Smith. "Prenatal Substance Abuse: Short- and Long-Term Effects on the Exposed Fetus." *Pediatrics* 131, no. 3 (2013): 1009–24.

Bell, Hannah S., Anna C. Matínez-Hume, Allison M. Baker, Kristan Elwell, Isabel Montemayor, and Linda M. Hunt. "Medicaid Reform, Responsibilization Policies, and the Synergism of Barriers to Low-Income Health Seeking." *Human Organization* 76, no. 3 (2017): 275–86.

Bell, Shannon Elizabeth. *Our Roots Run Deep as Ironweed: Appalachian Women and the Fight for Environmental Justice*. Urbana: University of Illinois Press, 2013.

Bell, Susan E. and Anne E. Figert. "Medicalization and Pharmaceuticalizaton at the Intersections: Looking Backward, Sideways, and Forward." *Social Science & Medicine* 75, no. 5 (2012): 775–83.

Bevin, Matt. "State of the Commonwealth." Frankfort, KY, January 16, 2018.

Biehl, João. "The Judicialization of Biopolitics: Claiming the Right to Pharmaceuticals in Brazilian Courts." *American Ethnologist* 40, no. 3 (2013): 419–36.

———. "'Medication Is Me Now': Human Values and Political Life in the Wake of Global Aids Treatment." In *In the Name of Humanity: The*

Government of Threat and Care, edited by Ilana Feldman and Miriam
Ticktin, 151–89. Durham, NC: Duke University Press, 2010.

———. "Pharmaceutical Governance." In *Global Pharmaceuticals: Ethics,
Markets, and Practices,* edited by Andrew Lakoff, Adriana Petryna, and
Arthur Kleinman, 206–38. Durham, NC: Duke University Press, 2006.

Billings, Dwight B. "Appalachian Studies and the Sociology of Appalachia." In
21st Century Sociology: A Reference Handbook, edited by Clifford D. Bryant
and Dennis L. Peck, 390–96. Thousand Oaks, CA: Sage, 2007.

Billings, Dwight B. and Kathleen Blee. *The Road to Poverty: The Making of
Wealth and Hardship in Appalachia.* New York: Cambridge University
Press, 2000.

Billings, Dwight B., Gurney Norman, and Katherine Ledford. *Back Talk
from Appalachia: Confronting Stereotypes.* Lexington: University Press of
Kentucky, 1999.

Bourgois, Philippe. "Disciplining Addictions: The Bio-Politics of Methadone
and Heroin in the United States." *Culture, Medicine, and Psychiatry* 24, no.
2 (2000): 165–95.

———. "The Moral Economies of Homeless Heroin Addicts: Confronting
Ethnography, HIV Risk, and Everyday Violence in San Francisco
Shooting Encampments." *Substance Use and Misuse* 33, no. 11 (1998):
2323–51.

Bourgois, Philippe and Jeff Schonberg. *Righteous Dopefiend.* Berkeley:
University of California Press, 2009.

Briggs, Charles L. and Clara Mantini-Briggs. *Stories in the Time of Cholera:
Racial Profiling During a Medical Nightmare.* Berkeley: University of
California Press, 2003.

Broaddus, Matt, Peggy Bailey, and Aviva Aron-Dine. *Medicaid Expansion
Dramatically Increased Coverage for People with Opioid-Use Disorders, Latest
Data Show.* Washington, DC: Center on Budget and Policy Priorities, 2018.

Buer, Lesly-Marie, Jennifer R. Havens, and Carl G. Leukefeld. "Does the
New Formulation of OxyContin Deter Misuse? A Qualitative Analysis."
Substance Use and Misuse 49, no. 6 (2014): 770–74.

Buer, Lesly-Marie, Carl G. Leukefeld, and Jennifer R. Havens. "'I'm Stuck':
Women's Navigations of Social Networks and Prescription Drug Misuse
in Central Appalachia." *North American Dialogue* 19, no. 2 (2016): 70–84.

Butler, Judith. *Bodies That Matter: On the Discursive Limits of "Sex."* New York:
Routledge, 1993.

Cain, Carole. "Personal Stories: Identity Acquisition and Self-Understanding in
Alcoholics Anonymous." *Ethos* 19, no. 2 (1991): 210–53.

Campbell, Howard. "Female Drug Smugglers on the U.S.–Mexico Border: Gender, Crime, and Empowerment." *Anthropological Quarterly* 81, no. 1 (2008): 233–67.

Carr, E. Summerson. *Scripting Addiction: The Politics of Therapeutic Talk and American Sobriety.* Princeton, NJ: Princeton University Press, 2011.

Carsten, Janet. *After Kinship.* New York: Cambridge University Press, 2004.

Catte, Elizabeth. *What You Are Getting Wrong about Appalachia.* Cleveland, OH: Belt Publishing, 2018.

Chavkin, Wendy and Vicki Breitbart. "Substance Abuse and Maternity: The United States as a Case Study." *Addiction* 92, no. 9 (1997): 1201–5.

Chiplis, Kathryn D. "Alternative Programs for Drug Offenders: An Evaluation of a Rural Drug Court." MA thesis, Northern Illinois University, 2010.

Chubinski, Jennifer, Sarah Walsh, Toby Sallee, and Eric Rademacher. "Painkiller Misuse among Appalachians and in Appalachian Counties in Kentucky." *Journal of Appalachian Studies* 20, no. 2 (2014): 154–69.

Cicero, Theodore J., James A. Inciardi, and Alvaro Muñoz. "Trends in Abuse of OxyContin® and Other Opioid Analgesics in the United States: 2002–2004." *Journal of Pain* 6, no. 10 (2005): 662–72.

Clarke, Adele E., Janet K. Shim, Laura Mamo, Jennifer Ruth Fosket, and Jennifer R. Fishman. "Biomedicalization: Technoscientific Transformations of Health, Illness, and U.S. Biomedicine." *American Sociological Review* 68, no. 2 (2003): 161–94.

Collins, Patricia Hill. *Black Feminist Thought: Knowledge, Consciousness, and the Politics of Empowerment.* 2nd ed. New York: Routledge, 2000.

Conwill, William L. "Neoliberal Policy as Structural Violence: Its Links to Domestic Violence in Black Communities in the United States." In *The Gender of Globalization: Women Navigating Cultural and Economic Marginalities,* edited by Nandini Gunewardena and Ann Kingsolver, 127–46. Santa Fe, NM: School for Advanced Research Press, 2007.

Covidien. "About Covidien." April 28, 2013, www.covidien.com/covidien /pages.aspx?page=AboutUs.

Craven, Christa. "Claiming Respectable American Motherhood: Homebirth Mothers, Medical Officials, and the State." *Medical Anthropology Quarterly* 19, no. 3 (2005): 194–215.

Craven, Christa and Dána-Ain Davis. "Introduction: Feminist Activist Ethnography." In *Feminist Activist Ethnography: Counterpoints to Neoliberalism in North America,* edited by Christa Craven and Dána-Ain Davis, 1–22. New York: Lexington Books, 2013.

Crenshaw, Kimberle. "From Private Violence to Mass Incarceration: Thinking

Intersectionally About Women, Race, and Social Control." *UCLA Law Review* 59 (2012): 1418–72.

———. "Mapping the Margins: Intersectionality, Identity Politics, and Violence against Women of Color." *Stanford Law Review* 43, no. 6 (1991): 1241–99.

Dahl, Ulrika. "Progressive Women, Traditional Men: Globalization, Migration, and Equality in the Northern Periphery of the European Union." In *The Gender of Globalization: Women Navigating Cultural and Economic Marginalities*, edited by Nandini Gunewardena and Ann Kingsolver, 105–26. Santa Fe, NM: School for Advanced Research Press, 2007.

Daniels, Jessie and Amy J. Schulz "Constructing Whiteness in Health Disparities Research." In *Gender, Race, Class, and Health: Intersectional Approaches*, edited by Amy J. Schulz and Leith Mullings, 89–127. San Francisco: Jossey-Bass, 2006.

Das, Veena. "Violence, Gender, and Subjectivity." *Annual Review of Anthropology* 37 (2008): 283–99.

Das, Veena and Ranendra K. Das. "Pharmaceuticals in Urban Ecologies: The Register of the Local." In *Global Pharmaceuticals: Ethics, Markets, and Practices*, edited by Andrew Lakoff, Adriana Petryna, and Arthur Kleinman, 171–204. Durham, NC: Duke University Press, 2006.

Das, Veena and Deborah Poole. "State and Its Margins: Comparative Ethnographies." In *Anthropology at the Margins of the State*, edited by Veena Das and Deborah Poole, 3–33. Santa Fe, NM: School of Advanced Research Press, 2004.

Davis, Dána-Ain. "Manufacturing Mammies: The Burdens of Service Work and Welfare Reform among Battered Black Women." *Anthropologica* 46, no. 2 (2004): 273–88.

Dawson, Kimya. "Loose Lips." *Remember That I Love You*. Olympia, WA: K Records, 2006.

Dean, Meredith, Edna Gulley, and Linda McKinney. "Organizing Appalachian Women: Hope Lies in the Struggle." In *Transforming Places: Lessons from Appalachia*, edited by Stephen L. Fisher and Barbara Ellen Smith, 109–21. Urbana: University of Illinois Press, 2012.

Dickinson, Maggie. "Working for Food Stamps: Economic Citizenship and the Post-Fordist Welfare State in New York City." *American Ethnologist* 43, no. 2 (2016): 270–81.

Drew, Elaine M. and Nancy E. Schoenberg. "Deconstructing Fatalism: Ethnographic Perspectives on Women's Decision Making about Cancer Prevention and Treatment." *Medical Anthropology Quarterly* 25, no. 2 (2011): 164–182.

Dumit, Joseph. *Drugs for Life: How Pharmaceutical Companies Define Our Health.* Durham, NC: Duke University Press, 2012.

Dunaway, Wilma A. "Speculators and Settler Capitalists: Unthinking the Mythology About Appalachian Landholding, 1790–1860." In *Appalachia in the Making: The Mountain South in the Nineteenth Century,* edited by Dwight B. Billings, Mary Beth Pudup, and Altina L. Waller, 50–75. Chapel Hill: University of North Carolina Press, 1995.

———. *Women, Work, and Family in the Antebellum Mountain South.* New York: Cambridge University Press, 2008.

Engelhardt, Elizabeth S. D. *Tangled Roots of Feminism, Environmentalism, and Appalachian Literature.* Columbus: Ohio University Press, 2003.

Epele, María Esther. "Gender, Violence and HIV: Women's Survival in the Streets." *Culture, Medicine, and Psychiatry* 26, no. 1 (2002): 33–54.

Etkin, Nina L. "'Side Effects': Cultural Construction and Reinterpretations of Western Pharmaceuticals." *Medical Anthropology Quarterly* 6, no. 2 (1992): 99–113.

Farmer, Paul. *Aids and Accusation: Haiti and the Geography of Blame.* Berkeley: University of California Press, 1992.

———. *Infections and Inequalities: The Modern Plagues.* Berkeley: University of California Press, 1999.

———. *Pathologies of Power: Health, Human Rights, and the New War on the Poor.* Berkeley: University of California Press, 2005.

Farmer, Paul, Bruce Nizeye, Sara Stulac, and Salmaan Keshavjee. "Structural Violence and Clinical Medicine." *PLOS Medicine* 3, no. 10 (2006): 1686–91.

Fassin, Didier. "Inequality of Lives, Hierarchies of Humanity: Moral Commitments and Ethical Dilemmas of Humanitarianism." In *In the Name of Humanity: The Government of Threat and Care,* edited by Ilana Feldman and Miriam Ticktin, 238–55. Durham, NC: Duke University Press, 2010.

Federal Bureau of Investigation and Drug Enforcement Agency. *Chasing the Dragon: The Life of an Opiate Addict.* Washington, DC: FBI and DEA, 2018.

Feldman, Ilana and Miriam Ticktin. "Introduction: Government and Humanity." In *In the Name of Humanity: The Government of Threat and Care,* edited by Ilana Feldman and Miriam Ticktin, 1–26. Durham, NC: Duke University Press, 2010.

Fickey, Amanda. "Speaking a New Economic Language in Central Appalachia." *Social & Cultural Geography* 15, no. 8 (2014): 973–74.

Fisher, Stephen L. and Barbara Ellen Smith. "Introduction: Placing

Appalachia." In *Transforming Places: Lessons from Appalachia*, edited by Stephen L. Fisher and Barbara Ellen Smith, 1–15. Urbana: University of Illinois Press, 2012.

Flavin, Jeanne. *Our Bodies, Our Crimes: The Policing of Women's Reproduction in America*. New York: New York University Press, 2009.

Flavin, Jeanne and Lynn M. Paltrow. "Punishing Pregnant Drug-Using Women: Defying Law, Medicine, and Common Sense." *Journal of Addictive Diseases* 29, no. 2 (2010): 231–44.

Fletcher, Rebecca Adkins. "Keeping up with the Cadillacs: What Health Insurance Disparities, Moral Hazard, and the Cadillac Tax Mean to the Patient Protection and Affordable Care Act." *Medical Anthropology Quarterly* 30, no. 1 (2014): 18–36.

Frankel, Barbara. *Transforming Identities: Context, Power, and Ideology in a Therapeutic Community*. New York: Peter Lang, 1989.

Fuentes, Catherine Mitchell. "Nobody's Child: The Role of Trauma and Interpersonal Violence in Women's Pathways to Incarceration and Resultant Service Needs." *Medical Anthropology Quarterly* 28, no. 1 (2014): 85–104.

Galtung, Johan. "Cultural Violence." *Journal of Peace Research* 27, no. 3 (1990): 291–305.

———. "Violence, Peace, and Peace Research." *Journal of Peace Research* 6, no. 3 (1969): 167–91.

Garcia, Angela. *The Pastoral Clinic: Addiction and Dispossession Along the Rio Grande*. Berkeley: University of California Press, 2010.

Garriott, William and Eugene Raikhel. "Addiction in the Making." *Annual Review of Anthropology* 44, (2015): 477–91.

Geronimus, Arline T. "Deep Integration: Letting the Epigenome out of the Bottle without Losing Sight of the Structural Origins of Population Health." *American Journal of Public Health* 103, no. S1 (2013): 56–63.

———. "Understanding and Eliminating Racial Inequalities in Women's Health in the United States: The Role of the Weathering Conceptual Framework." *Journal of American Medical Women's Association* 56, no. 4 (2001): 133–36.

Gibson-Graham, J. K. "Building Community Economies: Women and the Politics of Place." In *Women and the Politics of Place*, edited by Wendy Harcourt and Arturo Escobar, 130–157. Bloomfield, CT: Kumarian Press, 2005.

———. "Rethinking the Economy with Thick Description and Weak Theory." *Current Anthropology* 55, no. S9 (2014): 147–53.

Gillmore, Ruth Wilson. "Globalization and US Prison Growth: From Military

Keynesianism to Post-Keynesian Militarism." *Race and Class* 40, no. 2/3 (1999): 171–88.

Gipe, Robert. "In the Place I Live: Welcome to Rural Kentucky and 'Weedeater.'" *BookPage* Behind the Book, March 19, 2018, http://bookpage.com/behind-the-book/22490-place-i-live-welcome-to-rural-kentucky-weedeater#.WrKqbLpFyM_.

———. *Trampoline: An Illustrated Novel.* Athens: Ohio University Press, 2015.

Givens, Marjory, Keith Gennuso, Amanda Jovagg, and Julie Willems Van Dijk. *County Health Rankings 2017.* Madison: University of Wisconsin Population Health Institute, 2017.

Goan, Melanie Beals. *Mary Breckinridge: The Frontier Nursing Service and Rural Health in Appalachia.* Chapel Hill: University of North Carolina Press, 2008.

Goodwin, Michele Bratcher. "Precarious Moorings: Tying Fetal Drug Law Policy to Social Profiling." *Rutgers Law Journal* 42 (2011): 659–94.

Gordon, Avery F. "Globalism and the Prison Industrial Complex: An Interview with Angela Davis." *Race and Class* 40, no. 2/3 (1999): 145–57.

Gunewardena, Nandini and Ann Kingsolver. "Introduction." In *The Gender of Globalization: Women Navigating Cultural and Economic Marginalities,* edited by Nandini Gunewardena and Ann Kingsolver, 3–22. Santa Fe, NM: School for Advanced Research Press, 2007.

Gunning, Sarah Ogan. "Come All You Coal Miners." New York: Alan Lomax, 1937.

Guy, Gery P., Kun Zhang, Michele K. Bohm, Jan Losby, Brian Lewis, Randall Young, Louise B. Murphy, and Deborah Dowell. "Vital Signs: Changes in Opioid Prescribing in the United States, 2006–2015." *Morbidity and Mortality Weekly Report* 66, no. 26 (2017): 697–704.

Hall, Elizabeth A., Dana M. Baldwin, and Michael L. Prendergast. "Women on Parole: Barriers to Success after Substance Abuse Treatment." *Human Organization* 60, no. 3 (2001): 225–33.

Hall, Martin T., Jordan Wilfong, Ruth A. Huebner, Lynn Posze, and Tina Willauer. "Medication-Assisted Treatment Improves Child Permanency Outcomes for Opioid-Using Families in the Child Welfare System." *Journal of Substance Abuse Treatment* 71 (2016): 63–67.

Han, Clara. *Life in Debt: Times of Care and Violence in Neoliberal Chile.* Berkeley: University of California Press, 2012.

Hansen, Helena and Julie Netherland. "Is the Prescription Opioid Epidemic a White Problem?" *American Journal of Public Health* 106, no. 12 (2016): 2127–29.

Harris, Angela. "Race and Essentialism in Feminist Legal Theory." *Stanford Law*

Review 42, no. 3 (1990): 581–616.

Harris, Shana. "The Social Practice of Harm Reduction in Argentina: A 'Latin' Kind of Intervention." *Human Organization* 75, no. 1 (2016): 1–9.

———. "To Be Free and Normal: Addiction, Governance, and the Therapeutics of Buprenorphine." *Medical Anthropology Quarterly* 29, no. 4 (2015): 512–30.

Hartigan, John Jr. "Whiteness and Appalachian Studies: What's the Connection?" *Journal of Appalachian Studies* 10, no. 1/2 (2004): 58–72.

Hartman, Ian C. "Appalachian Anxiety: Race, Gender, and the Paradox of 'Purity' in an Age of Empire, 1873–1901." *American Nineteenth Century History* 13, no. 2 (2012): 229–55.

Harvey, David. *A Brief History of Neoliberalism*. New York: Oxford University Press, 2007.

Hautzinger, Sarah J. *Violence in the City of Women: Police and Batterers in Bahia, Brazil*. Berkeley: University of California Press, 2007.

Hawkins, Ted. "Sorry You're Sick." *Watch Your Step*. Nashville, TN: Rounder, 1982.

Hayden, Wilburn Jr. "In Search of Justice: White Privilege in Appalachia." *Journal of Appalachian Studies* 8, no. 1 (2002): 120–31.:

Hayes, Lauren A. "Notes from the Field: Navigating the Role of Researcher at a Factory Fieldsite in Appalachian Kentucky." *Arizona Anthropologist* 24 (2015): 42–50.

Hedges, Kristin. "Teens in the Grey Zone: The Structural Violence of Substance-Using Youth Being Raised in the System." *Human Organization* 71, no. 3 (2015): 317–25.

Hedwig, Travis H. "The Cultural Politics of Fetal Alcohol Spectrum Disorders and the Diagnosis of Difference." PhD diss., University of Kentucky, 2013.

Higham, Scott and Lenny Bernstein. "Cherokee Nation Sues Drug Firms, Retailers for Flooding Communities with Opioids." *Washington Post*, April 20, 2017.

hooks, bell. *Belonging: A Culture of Place*. New York: Taylor and Francis, 2009.

House, Silas and Jason Howard, eds. *Something's Rising: Appalachians Fighting Mountaintop Removal*. Lexington: University Press of Kentucky, 2009.

Howard, Grace. "The Limits of Pure White: Raced Reproduction in the Methamphetamine Crisis." *Women's Rights Law Reporter* 35, no. 3/4 (2014): 373–405.

Huling, Tracy. "Building a Prison Economy in Rural America." In *Invisible Punishment: The Collateral Consequences of Mass Imprisonment*, edited by Marc Mauer and Meda Chesney-Lind, 197–213. New York: New Press, 2002.

Hutton, T. R. C. *Bloody Breathitt: Politics and Violence in the Appalachian South.* Lexington: University Press of Kentucky, 2013.

Hyde, Sandra Teresa. "Migrations in Humanistic Therapy: Turning Drug Users into Patients and Patients into Healthy Citizens in Southwest China." *Body and Society* 17, no. 2/3 (2011): 183–204.

Inciardi, James A. and Jennifer L. Goode. "Miracle Medicine or Problem Drug: OxyContin and Prescription Drug Abuse." *Consumers' Research* (July 2003): 17–21.

Institute for Health Metrics. "Life Expectancy at Birth, Both Sexes, 2014." 2016, vizhub.healthdata.org/subnational/usa.

Jacobsen, Carol and Lora Bex Lempert. "Institutional Disparities: Considerations of Gender in the Commutation Process for Incarcerated Women." *Signs* 39, no. 1 (2013): 265–89.

Jaffe, Rivke. "The Hybrid State: Crime and Citizenship in Urban Jamaica." *American Ethnologist* 40, no. 4 (2013): 734–48.

Jain, S. Lochlann. "The Mortality Effect: Counting the Dead in the Cancer Trial." In *In the Name of Humanity: The Government of Threat and Care*, edited by Ilana Feldman and Miriam Ticktin, 218–37. Durham, NC: Duke University Press, 2010.

The Kaiser Commission on Medicaid and the Uninsured. "Proposed Changes to Medicaid Expansion in Kentucky." 2016, kff.org/medicaid/fact-sheet/proposed-changes-to-medicaid-expansion-in-kentucky/.

Kalofonos, Ippolytos. "'All They Do Is Pray': Community Labour and the Narrowing of 'Care' During Mozambique's HIV Scale-Up." *Global Public Health* 9, no. 1/2 (2014): 7–24.

Kaltenbach, Karol, Kevin E. O'Grady, Sarah H. Heil, Amy L. Salisbury, Mara G. Coyle, Gabriele Fischer, Peter R. Martin, Susan Stine, and Hendrée E. Jones. "Prenatal Exposure to Methadone and Buprenorphine: Early Childhood Developmental Outcomes." *Drug and Alcohol Dependence* 185 (2018): 40–49.

Karandinos, George, Laurie Kain Hart, Fernando Montero Castrillo, and Philippe Bourgois. "The Moral Economy of Violence in the US Inner City." *Current Anthropology* 55, no. 1 (2014): 1–22.

Karch, Steven B. "Is It Time to Reformulate Racemic Methadone?" *Journal of Addiction Medicine* 5, no. 3 (2011): 229–31.

Kentuckians for the Commonwealth. *Right to Vote.* London, KY: Kentucky for the Commonwealth, 2019.

Kentucky Department for Community Based Services. "Division of Family Support." 2017. https://chfs.ky.gov/agencies/dcbs/dfs/Pages/default.aspx.

Kingfisher, Catherine and Michael Goldsmith. "Reforming Women in the United States and Aotearoa, New Zealand: A Comparative Ethnography of Welfare Reform in Global Context." *American Anthropologist* 103, no. 3 (2001): 714–32.

Kingsolver, Ann E. "Farmers and Farmworkers: Two Centuries of Strategic Alterity in Kentucky's Tobacco Fields." *Critique of Anthropology* 27, no. 1 (2007): 87–102.

———. "Five Women Negotiating the Meaning of Negotiation." *Anthropological Quarterly* 65, no. 3 (1992): 101–4.

———. "Neoliberal Governance and Faith-Based Initiatives: Agentive Cracks in the Logic Informing Homeless Sheltering in South Carolina's Capital." *Rethinking Marxism: A Journal of Economics, Culture, & Society* 24, no. 2 (2012): 202–14.

———. *Tobacco Town Futures.* Long Grove, IL: Waveland Press, 2011.

Knight, Kelly Ray. *addicted.pregnant.poor.* Durham, NC: Duke University Press, 2015.

Knight, Kelly R., Margot Kushel, Jamie S. Change, Kara Zamora, Rachel Ceasar, Emily Hurstak, and Christine Miaskowski. "Opioid Pharmacovigilance: A Clinical–Social History of the Changes in the Opioid Prescribing for Patients with Co-Occuring Chronic Non-Cancer Pain and Substance Use." *Social Science & Medicine* 186 (2017): 87–95.

Kobak, Sue Ella. "OxyContin Flood in the Coalfields: 'Searching for Higher Ground.'" In *Transforming Places: Lessons from Appalachia*, edited by Stephen L. Fisher and Barbara Ellen Smith, 198–209. Urbana: University of Illinois Press, 2012.

Koch, Erin. *Free Market Tuberculosis: Managing Epidemics in Post-Soviet Georgia.* Nashville, TN: Vanderbilt University Press, 2013.

Krause, Elizabeth L. and Silvia De Zordo. "Introduction. Enthnography and Biopolitics: Tracing 'Rationalities' of Reproduction across the North–South Divide." *Anthropology & Medicine* 19, no. 2 (2012): 137–51.

LaGasse, Linda L., Chris Derauf, Lynne M. Smith, Elana Newman, Rizwan Shah, Charles Neal, Amelia Arria, Marilyn A. Huestis, Sheri Della Grotta, Hai Lin, Lynne M. Dansereau, and Barry M. Lester. "Prenatal Methamphetamine Exposure and Childhood Behavior Problems at 3 and 5 Years of Age." *Pediatrics* 129, no. 4 (2012): 681–88.

Lakoff, Andrew. *Pharmaceutical Reason.* New York: Cambridge University Press, 2005.

Leahy, Robert L. *Cognitive Therapy Techniques: A Practitioner's Guide.* 2nd ed. New York: Guilford Press, 2017.

LeBaron, Genevieve and Adrienne Roberts. "Toward a Feminist Political Economy of Capitalism and Carcerality." *Signs* 36, no. 1 (2010): 19–44.

L'Estoile, Benoît de. "'Money Is Good, but a Friend Is Better': Uncertainty, Orientation to the Future, and 'the Economy.'" *Current Anthropology* 55, no. S9 (2014): 62–73.

Leukefeld, Carl, Robert Walker, Jennifer Havens, Cynthia A. Leedham, and Valarie Tolbert. "What Does the Community Say: Key Informant Perceptions of Rural Prescription Drug Use." *Journal of Drug Issues* 37, no. 3 (2007): 503–24.

Lock, Margaret. "Comprehending the Body in the Era of the Epigenome." *Current Anthropology* 56, no. 2 (2015): 151–77.

López, Iris. "Negotiating Different Worlds: An Integral Ethnography of Reproductive Freedom and Social Justice." In *Feminist Activist Ethnography: Counterpoints to Neoliberalism in North America*, edited by Christa Craven and Dána-Ain Davis, 145–64. New York: Lexington Books, 2013.

Lovell, Anne M. "Addiction Markets: The Case of High-Dose Buprenorphine in France." In *Global Pharmaceuticals: Ethics, Markets, and Practices*, edited by Andrew Lakoff, Adriana Petryna, and Arthur Kleinman, 136–69. Durham, NC: Duke University Press, 2006.

Lyon-Callo, Vincent. *Inequality, Poverty, and Neoliberal Governance: Activist Ethnography in the Homeless Sheltering Industry*. Toronto, ON: University of Toronto Press, 2004.

MacLean, Nancy. *Democracy in Chains: The Deep History of the Radical Right's Stealth Plan for America*. New York: Penguin Books, 2017.

Malkki, Liisa. "When Humanity Sits in Judgement: Crimes against Humanity and the Conundrum of Race and Ethnicity at the International Criminal Tribunal for Rwanda." In *In the Name of Humanity: The Government of Threat and Care*, edited by Ilana Feldman and Miriam Ticktin, 27–57. Durham, NC: Duke University Press, 2010.

Martin, Emily. "The Pharmaceutical Person." *BioSocieties* 1, no. 3 (2006): 273–87.

Maskovsky, Jeff. "The Other War at Home: The Geopolitics of US Poverty." *Urban Anthropology* 30, no. 2/3 (2001): 215–38.

Mason, Carol. "The Hillbilly Defense: Culturally Mediating US Terror at Home and Abroad." *NWSA Journal* 17, no. 3 (2005): 39–63.

Mason, Carol. *Reading Appalachia from Left to Right: Conservatives and the 1974 Kanawha County Textbook Controversy*. Ithaca, NY: Cornell University Press, 2009.

Massey, Carissa. "Appalachian Stereotypes: Cultural History, Gender, and Sexual Rhetoric." *Journal of Appalachian Studies* 13, no. 1/2 (2007): 124–36.

McKenna, Stacey A. "Reproducing Hegemony: The Culture of Enhancement and Discourses on Amphetamines in Popular Fiction." *Culture, Medicine, and Psychiatry* 35, no. 1 (2011):90–97.

McKim, Allison. "'Getting Gut-Level': Punishment, Gender, and Therapeutic Governance." *Gender & Society* 22, no. 3 (2008): 303–23.

McKinney, Gordon B. "The Civil War and Reconstruction." In *High Mountains Rising: Appalachia in Time and Place*, edited by Richard A. Straw and H. Tyler Blethen, 46–58. Chicago: University of Illinois Press, 2004.

Meier, Barry. *Painkiller: A "Wonder" Drug's Trail of Addiction and Death.* Emmaus, PA: Rodale, 2003.

Meloni, Maurizio. "Comments to: Comprehending the Body in the Era of the Epigenome." *Current Anthropology* 56, no. 2 (2015): 168.

Mental Health Parity and Addiction Equity Act, H.R. 6983 (2008).

Meyers, Todd. *The Clinic and Elsewhere: Addiction, Adolescents, and the Afterlife of Therapy.* Seattle: University of Washington Press, 2013.

———. "Promise and Deceit: Pharmakos, Drug Replacement Therapy, and the Perils of Experience." *Culture, Medicine, and Psychiatry* 38, no. 2 (2014): 182–96.

Morgan, Lynn M. and Elizabeth F. S. Roberts. "Reproductive Governance in Latin America." *Anthropology & Medicine* 19, no. 2 (2012): 241–54.

Morgen, Sandra and Jeff Maskovsky. "The Anthropology of Welfare 'Reform': New Perspectives on US Urban Poverty in the Post-Welfare Era." *Annual Review of Anthropology* 32 (2003): 315–38.

Mullinax, Maureen. "Resistance through Community-Based Arts." In *Transforming Places: Lessons from Appalachia*, edited by Stephen L. Fisher and Barbara Ellen Smith, 92–106. Urbana: University of Illinois Press, 2012.

Mullings, Leith. "Losing Ground: Harlem, the War on Drugs, and the Prison Industrial Complex." *Souls: A Critical Journal of Black Politics, Culture, and Society* 5, no. 2 (2003): 1–21.

———. "Resistance and Resilience: The Sojourner Syndrome and the Social Context of Reproduction in Central Harlem." In *Gender, Race, Class, and Health: Intersectional Approaches*, edited by Amy J. Schulz and Leith Mullings, 345–70. San Francisco: Jossey-Bass, 2006.

Mullings, Leith and Amy J. Schulz. "Intersectionality and Health: An Introduction." In *Gender, Race, Class, and Health: Intersectional Approaches*, edited by Amy J. Schulz and Leith Mullings, 3–20. San Francisco: Jossey-Bass, 2006.

Musumeci, MaryBeth, Robin Rudowitz, and Elizabeth Hinton. *Approved Changes to Medicaid in Kentucky.* Menlo Park, CA: Henry J. Kaiser Family Foundation, 2018.

Netherland, Julie and Helena Hansen. "White Opioids: Pharmaceutical Race and the War on Drugs that Wasn't." *Biosocieties* 12, no. 2 (2017): 217–38.

Oaks, Laury. "Smoke-Filled Wombs and Fragile Fetuses: The Social Politics of Fetal Representation." *Signs* 26, no. 1 (2000): 63–108.

Oberhauser, Ann M. "Relocating Gender and Rural Economic Strategies." *Environment and Planning A: Economy and Space* 34, no. 7 (2002): 1221–37.

Office of Policy Planning and Research. *The Negro Family: The Case for National Action.* Washington, DC: United States Department of Labor, 1965.

O'Hare, Brian J. "Book Review: Merrill Singer and J. Bryan Page. The Social Value of Drug Addicts: Uses of the Useless." *North American Dialogue* 18, no. 1 (2015): 26–28.

Oldani, Michael J. "Thick Prescriptions: Toward an Interpretation of Pharmaceutical Sales Practices." *Medical Anthropology Quarterly* 18, no. 3 (2004): 325–56.

Ornstein, Charles. "Drug Distributors Penalized for Turning Blind Eye in Opioid Epidemic." *ProPublica*, January 27, 2017.

Oro, Amy S. and Suzanne D. Dixon. "Perinatal Cocaine and Methamphetamine Exposure: Maternal and Neonatal Correlates." *Journal of Pediatrics* 111, no. 4 (1987): 571–78.

Paltrow, Lynn M. and Jeanne Flavin. "Arrests of and Forced Interventions on Pregnant Women in the United States, 1973–2005: Implications for Women's Legal Status and Public Health." *Journal of Health Politics, Policy, and Law* 38, no. 2 (2013): 299–343.

Pancake, Ann. *Strange as This Weather Has Been.* Berkeley: Counterpoint, 2007.

Passik, Steven D. "Same as It Ever Was? Life after the OxyContin® Media Frenzy." *Journal of Pain and Symptom Management* 25, no. 3 (2003): 199–201.

Patient Protection and Affordable Care Act, 42 U.S.C. § 18001 (2010).

Petryna, Adriana. "The Politics of Experimentality." In *In the Name of Humanity: The Government of Threat and Care*, edited by Ilana Feldman and Miriam Ticktin, 256–89. Durham, NC: Duke University Press, 2010.

Petryna, Adriana and Arthur Kleinman. "The Pharmaceutical Nexus." In *Global Pharmaceuticals: Ethics, Markets, and Practices*, 1–32. Durham, NC: Duke University Press, 2006.

Pine, Jason. "Economy of Speed: The New Narco-Capitalism." *Public Culture* 19, no. 2 (2007): 357–66.

Powell, Douglas Reichert. *Critical Regionalism: Connecting Politics and Culture in the American Landscape.* Chapel Hill: University of North Carolina Press, 2007.

Prussing, Erica. "Reconfiguring the Empty Center: Drinking, Sobriety, and Identity in Native American Women's Narratives." *Culture, Medicine, and Psychiatry* 31, no. 4 (2007): 499–526.

———. "Sobriety and Its Cultural Politics: An Ethnographer's Perspective on 'Culturally Appropriate' Addiction Services in Native North America." *Ethos* 36, no. 3 (2008): 354–75.

Pudup, Mary Beth, Dwight B. Billings, and Altina L. Waller, eds. *Appalachia in the Making: The Mountain South in the Nineteenth Century.* Chapel Hill: University of North Carolina Press, 1995.

Quinones, Sam. *Dreamland: The True Tale of America's Opiate Epidemic.* New York: Bloomsbury Press, 2015.

Radcliffe, Polly and Alex Stevens. "Are Drug Treatment Services Only for 'Thieving Junkie Scumbags'? Drug Users and the Management of Stigmatised Identities." *Social Science & Medicine* 67, no. 7 (2008): 1065–73.

Raffaetà, Roberta and Mark Nichter. "Negotiating Care in Uncertain Settings and Looking beneath the Surface of Health Governance Projects." *Anthropology in Action* 22, no. 1 (2015): 1–6.

Rai, Shirin M. *The Gender Politics of Development.* New York: Zed Books, 2008.

Reagan, Leslie J. *Dangerous Pregnancies: Mothers, Disabilities, and Abortion in Modern America.* Berkeley: University of California Press, 2010.

Rhodes, Lorna A. "Toward an Anthropology of Prisons." *Annual Review of Anthropology* 30 (2001): 65–83.

Rice, James and Hanna Björg Sigurjónsdóttir. "Notifying Neglect: Child Protection as an Application of Bureaucratic Power against Marginalized Parents." *Human Organization* 77, no. 2 (2018): 112–21.

Roberts, Dorothy. "Prison, Foster Care, and the Systemic Punishment of Black Mothers." *UCLA Law Review* 59 (2012): 1474–1500.

Robinson, Marilynne. *Gilead: A Novel.* New York: Picador, 2006.

Rockoff, Jonathan D. "Gilead Gets U.S. Approval to Sell New Hepatitis C Drug." *Wall Street Journal,* October 10, 2014

Rose, Nikolas. *The Politics of Life Itself: Biomedicine, Power, and Subjectivity in the Twenty-First Century.* Princeton, NJ: Princeton University Press, 2007.

Ross, Loretta J. "Reproductive Justice as Intersectional Feminist Activism."

Souls: A Critical Journal of Black Politics, Culture, and Society 19, no. 3 (2017): 286–314.

Saris, A. Jamie. "An Uncertain Dominion: Irish Psychiatry, Methadone, and the Treatment of Opiate Abuse." *Culture, Medicine, and Psychiatry* 32, no. 2 (2008): 259–77.

Sarpatwari, Ameet, Michael S. Sinha, and Aaron S. Kesselheim. "The Opioid Epidemic: Fixing a Broken Pharmaceutical Market." *Harvard Law and Policy Review* 11, no. 2 (2017): 463–84.

Scheper-Hughes, Nancy. *Death without Weeping: The Violence of Everyday Life in Brazil.* Berkeley: University of California Press, 1992.

Scherz, China. "Protecting Children, Preserving Families: Moral Conflict and Actuarial Science in a Problem of Contemporary Governance." *Political and Legal Anthropology Review* 34, no. 1 (2011): 33–50.

Schneider, David M. "What Is Kinship All About?" In *Kinship Studies in the Morgan Centennial Year,* edited by Priscilla Reining, 32–63. Washington, DC: Anthropological Society of Washington, 1972.

Schneider, Jane and Peter Schneider. "The Anthropology of Crime and Criminalization." *Annual Review of Anthropology* 37 (2008): 351–73.

Scott, James. *Domination and the Arts of Resistance: Hidden Transcripts.* New Haven, CT: Yale University Press, 1990.

Scott, Rebecca R. *Removing Mountains: Extracting Nature and Identity in the Appalachian Coalfields.* Minneapolis: University of Minnesota Press, 2010.

Scott, Shaunna L., Stephanie McSpirit, Sharon Hardesty, and Robert Welch. "Post Disaster Interviews with Martin County Citizens: 'Gray Clouds' of Blame and Distrust." *Journal of Appalachian Studies* 11, no. 1/2 (2005): 7–29.

Shah, Rizwan, Sabrina D. Diaz, Amelia Arria, Linda L. LaGasse, Chris Derauf, Elana Newman, Lynne M. Smith, Marilyn A. Huestis, William Haning, Arthur Strauss, Sheri Della Grotta, Lynne M. Dansereau, Mary B. Roberts, Charles Neal, and Barry M. Lester. "Prenatal Methamphetamine Exposure and Short-Term Maternal and Infant Medical Outcomes." *American Journal of Perinatology* 29, no. 5 (2012): 391–400.

Siddiqui, Zeba. "Covidien to Shutter South Carolina Plant, Lay Off 595." *Reuters,* September 13, 2012. www.reuters.com/article/2012/09/13 /us-covidien-plantclosure-idUSBRE88C1ES20120913.

Silverman, Ed. "Reckitt's Suboxone Strategy Is Really About Patients or Profits." *Forbes,* October 12, 2012. https://www.forbes.com/sites /edsilverman/2012/10/12/reckitts-suboxone-strategy-is-really -about-patients-or-profits/#60db23466c3f.

Singer, Elyse Ona. "From Reproductive Rights to Reponsibilization:

Fashioning Liberal Subjects in Mexico City's New Public Sector Abortion Program." *Medical Anthropology Quarterly* 31, no. 4 (2017): 445–63.

Singer, Merrill and J. Bryan Page. *The Social Value of Drug Addicts: Uses of the Useless.* Walnut Creek, CA: Left Coast Press, 2013.

Skoll, Geoffrey R. *Walk the Walk and Talk the Talk: An Ethnography of Drug Abuse Treatment Facility.* Philadelphia, PA: Temple University Press, 1992.

Smith, Barbara Ellen. "Another Place Is Possible? Labor Geography, Spatial Dispossession, and Gendered Resistance in Central Appalachia." *Annals of the Association of American Geographers* 105, no. 3 (2015): 567–82.

———. "'Beyond the Mountains': The Paradox of Women's Place in Appalachian History." *NWSA Journal* 11, no. 3 (1999): 1–17.

Smith, Lynne M., Linda L. LaGasse, Chris Derauf, Penny Grant, Rizwan Shah, Amelia Arria, Marilyn Huestis, William Haning, Arthur Strauss, Sheri Della Grotta, Jing Liu, and Barry M. Lester. "The Infant Development, Environment, and Lifestyle Study: Effects of Prenatal Methamphetamine Exposure, Polydrug Exposure, and Poverty on Intrauterine Growth." *Pediatrics* 118, no. 3 (2006): 1149–56.

Smith, Lynne M., Linda L. LaGasse, Chris Derauf, Elana Newman, Rizwan Shah, William Haning, Amelia Arria, Marilyn Huestis, Arthur Strauss, Sheri Della Grotta, Hai Lin, Lynne M. Dansereau, and Barry M. Lester. "Motor and Cognitive Outcomes through Three Years of Age in Children Exposed to Prenatal Methamphetamine." *Neurobiology and Teratology* 33, no. 1 (2011): 176–84.

Smith, Lynne M., Lynn Yonekura, Toni Wallace, Nancy Berman, Jennifer Kuo, and Carol Berkowitz. "Effects of Prenatal Methamphetamine Exposure on Fetal Growth and Drug Withdrawal Symptoms in Infants Born at Term." *Journal of Developmental and Behavioral Pediatrics* 24, no. 1 (2003): 17–23.

Smith, Sharon G., Jieru Chen, Kathleen C. Basile, Leah K. Gilbert, Melissa T. Merrick, Nimesh Patel, Margie Walling, and Anurag Jain. *The National Intimate Partner and Sexual Violence Survey (NISVS): 2010–2012 State Report.* Atlanta, GA: National Center for Injury Prevention and Control, Centers for Disease Control and Prevention, 2017.

Smith-Nonini, Sandy. "Neoliberal Infections and the Politics of Health: Resurgent Tuberculosis Epidemics in New York City and Lima, Peru." In *Anthropology and Public Health: Bridging Differences in Culture and Society,* edited by Robert A. Hahn and Marcia C. Inhorn, 588–622. New York: Oxford University Press, 2009.

Steager, Tabitha. "Women, Food, and Activism: Rediscovering Collectivist

Action in an Individualized World." In *Feminist Activist Ethnography: Counterpoints to Neoliberalism in North America*, edited by Christa Craven and Dána-Ain Davis, 165–80. New York: Lexington Books, 2013.

Stevenson, Lisa. *Life Beside Itself: Imagining Care in the Canadian Artic.* Berkeley: University of California Press, 2014.

Stewart, Michelle. "Fictions of Prevention: Fetal Alcohol Spectrum Disorder and Narratives of Responsibility." *North American Dialogue* 19, no. 1 (2016): 55–66.

Still, James. *River of Earth.* Lexington: University Press of Kentucky, 1978.

Substance Abuse and Mental Health Services Administration. *National Survey on Drug Use and Health, 2015 and 2016.* Rockville, MD: Center for Behavioral Health Statistics and Quality, 2017.

Sun, An-Pyng. "Relapse among Substance-Abusing Women: Components and Processes." *Substance Use and Misuse* 42, no. 1 (2007): 1–21.

Susser, Ida. "The Construction of Poverty and Homelessness in US Cities." *Annual Review of Anthropology* 25 (1996): 411–35.

Tax Cuts and Jobs Act of 2017, Pub. L. No. 115-97, 131 Stat. 2054 (2017).

Thomas, Katie and Charles Ornstein. "Amid Opioid Crisis, Insurers Restrict Pricey, Less Addictive Painkillers." *New York Times* and *ProPublica*, September 17, 2017.

Tice, Karen W. "School–Work and Mother–Work: The Interplay of Maternalism and Cultural Politics in the Educational Narratives of Kentucky Settlement Workers, 1910–1930." *Journal of Appalachian Studies* 4, no. 2 (1998): 191–224.

Tronto, Joan C. "Beyond Gender Difference to a Theory of Care." *Signs* 12, no. 4 (1987): 644–63.

———. "Care as a Basis for Radical Political Judgements." *Hypatia* 10, no. 2 (1995): 141–49.

Trostle, James A. *Epidemiology and Culture.* New York: Cambridge University Press, 2005.

Trotter, Joe William, Jr. "The Formation of Black Community in Southern West Virginia Coalfields." In *Appalachians and Race: The Mountain South from Slavery to Segregation*, edited by John C. Inscoe, 284–301. Lexington: University Press of Kentucky, 2001.

Trundle, Catherine. "Biopolitical Endpoints: Diagnosing a Deserving British Nuclear Test Veteran." *Social Science & Medicine* 73, no. 6 (2011): 882–88.

Unger, Annemarie, Erika Jung, Bernadette Winklbaur, and Gabriele Fischer. "Gender Issues in the Pharmacotherapy of Opioid-Addicted Women: Buprenorphine." *Journal of Addictive Diseases* 29, no. 2 (2010): 217–30.

United States Census Bureau. *2011–2015 American Community Survey 5-Year Estimates.* Washington, DC: American Community Survey Office, 2015.

United States Department of Health and Human Services. "Major Provisions of the Welfare Law." 1996. www.acf.hhs.gov/ofa/resource /law-reg/finalrule/aspesum.

United States General Accounting Office. *Prescription Drugs: OxyContin Abuse and Diversion and Efforts to Address the Problem.* Washington, DC: USGAO, 2003.

Vance, J. D. *Hillbilly Elegy: A Memoir of a Family and Culture in Crisis.* London: William Collins, 2016.

Van Zee, Art. "The Promotion and Marketing of OxyContin: Commercial Triumph, Public Health Tragedy." *American Journal of Public Health* 99, no. 2 (2009): 221–27.

Vera Institute. "Incarceration Trends." 2018. trends.vera.org/incarceration-rates.

Wacquant, Loïc. *Punishing the Poor: The Neoliberal Government of Social Insecurity.* Durham, NC: Duke University Press, 2009.

Wagner, Peter and Wendy Sawyer. *State of Incarceration: The Global Context 2018.* Prison Policy Initiative, 2018. www.prisonpolicy.org/global/2018.html.

Wailoo, Keith. "The New Politics of Old Differences." In *How Cancer Crossed the Color Line,* 148–73. New York: Oxford University Press, 2011.

Ward Maggard, Sally. "Coalfield Women Making History." In *Back Talk from Appalachia: Confronting Stereotypes,* edited by Dwight B. Billings, Gurney Norman, and Katherine Ledford, 228–50. Lexington: University Press of Kentucky, 1999.

Weber, Lynn. "Reconstructing the Landscape of Health Disparities Research: Promoting Dialogue and Collaboration between Feminist Intersectional and Biomedical Paradigms." In *Gender, Race, Class, and Health: Intersectional Approaches,* edited by Amy J. Schulz and Leith Mullings, 21–59. San Francisco: Jossey-Bass, 2006.

Weber, Max. *The Protestant Ethic and the "Spirit" of Capitalism and Other Writings.* New York: Penguin Books, 2002.

Websdale, Neil. "Rural Woman Abuse: The Voices of Kentucky Women." *Violence Against Women* 1, no. 4 (1995): 309–38.

Wenzel, Michael, Tyler G. Okimoto, Norman T. Feather, and Michael J. Platow. "Retributive and Restorative Justice." *Law and Human Behavior* 32, no. 5 (2008): 375–89.

Whiteford, Linda M. and Judi Vitucci. "Pregnancy and Addiction: Translating Research into Practice." *Social Science & Medicine* 44, no. 9 (1997): 1371–80.

Whyte, Susan Reynolds, Sjaak van der Geest, and Anita Hardon. *Social Lives of Medicines*. New York: Cambridge University Press, 2002.

Wies, Jennifer R. "Feminist Ethnography with Domestic Violence Shelter Advocates: Negotiating the Neoliberal Era." In *Feminist Activist Ethnography: Counterpoints to Neoliberalism in North America*, edited by Christa Craven and Dána-Ain Davis, 53–68. New York: Lexington Books, 2013.

Wilkinson, Crystal E. "On Being 'Country': One Affrilachian Woman's Return Home." In *Back Talk from Appalachia: Confronting Stereotypes*, edited by Dwight B. Billings, Gurney Norman, and Katherine Ledford, 184–86. Lexington: University Press of Kentucky, 1999.

Wilson, Robert A. "Kinship Past, Kinship Present: Bio-Essentialism in the Study of Kinship." *American Anthropologist* 118, no. 3 (2016): 570–84.

Wolf, Eric. *Enivisioning Power: Ideologies of Dominance and Crisis*. Berkeley: University of California Press, 1999.

Yang, Lawrence H., Fang-pei Chen, Kathleen Janel Sia, Jonathan Lam, Katherine Lam, Hong Ngo, Sing Lee, Arthur Kleinman, and Byron Good. "'What Matters Most': A Cultural Mechanism Moderating Structural Vulnerability and Moral Experience of Mental Illness Stigma." *Social Science & Medicine* 103 (2014): 84–93.

Zigon, Jarrett. *"HIV Is God's Blessing": Rehabilitating Morality in Neoliberal Russia*. Berkeley: University of California Press, 2011.

Notes

Introduction: An Ethnography of Intervention

1. Patricia Hill Collins, *Black Feminist Thought: Knowledge, Consciousness, and the Politics of Empowerment*, 2nd ed. (New York: Routledge, 2000); James C. Scott, *Domination and the Arts of Resistance: Hidden Transcripts* (New Haven, CT: Yale University Press, 1990); Eric Wolf, *Envisioning Power: Ideologies of Dominance and Crisis* (Berkeley: University of California Press, 1999).

2. Lila Abu-Lughod, "The Romance of Resistance: Tracing Transformations of Power Through Bedouin Women," *American Ethnologist* 17, no. 1 (1990): 41–55; Judith Butler, *Bodies That Matter: On the Discursive Limits of "Sex"* (New York: Routledge, 1993); Collins, *Black Feminist Thought*; Kimberle Crenshaw, "Mapping the Margins: Intersectionality, Identity Politics, and Violence against Women of Color," *Stanford Law Review* 43, no. 6 (1991): 1241–99; Kimberle Crenshaw, "From Private Violence to Mass Incarceration: Thinking Intersectionally About Women, Race, and Social Control," *UCLA Law Review* 59 (2012): 1418–72; Angela Harris, "Race and Essentialism in Feminist Legal Theory," *Stanford Law Review* 42, no. 3 (1990): 581–616; Lynn Weber, *Understanding Race, Class, Gender, and Sexuality: A Conceptual Framework* (New York: Oxford University Press, 2010).

3. Collins, *Black Feminist Thought*; Nandini Gunewardena and Ann Kingsolver, "Introduction," in *The Gender of Globalization: Women Navigating Cultural and Economic Marginalities*, ed. Nandini Gunewardena and Ann Kingsolver (Santa Fe, NM: School for Advanced Research Press, 2007), 3–22; Jeff Maskovsky, "The Other War at Home: The Geopolitics of US Poverty," *Urban Anthropology* 30, no. 2/3 (2001): 215–38; Leith Mullings, "Resistance and Resilience: The Sojourner Syndrome and the Social Context of Reproduction in Central Harlem," in *Gender, Race, Class, and Health: Intersectional Approaches*, ed. Amy J. Schulz and Leith Mullings (San Francisco: Jossey-Bass, 2006), 345–70.

4. Philippe Bourgois, "The Moral Economies of Homeless Heroin Addicts:

Confronting Ethnography, HIV Risk, and Everyday Violence in San Francisco Shooting Encampments," *Substance Use and Misuse* 33, no. 11 (1998): 2323–51; Paul Farmer, *Infections and Inequalities: The Modern Plagues* (Berkeley: University of California Press, 1999).

5. Scott, *Domination and the Arts of Resistance.*

6. Helena Hansen and Julie Netherland, "Is the Prescription Opioid Epidemic a White Problem?" *American Journal of Public Health* 106, no. 12 (2016): 2127–29.

7. Grace Howard, "The Limits of Pure White: Raced Reproduction in the Methamphetamine Crisis," *Women's Rights Law Reporter* 35, no. 3/4 (2014): 373–405.

8. Ann Pancake, *Strange as This Weather Has Been* (Berkeley: Counterpoint, 2007).

9. William Garriott and Eugene Raikhel, "Addiction in the Making," *Annual Review of Anthropology* 44 (2015): 477–91; Kelly Ray Knight, *addicted. pregnant.poor* (Durham, NC: Duke University Press, 2015).

10. Christa Craven and Dána-Ain Davis, "Introduction: Feminist Activist Ethnography," in *Feminist Activist Ethnography: Counterpoints to Neoliberalism in North America*, ed. Christa Craven and Dána-Ain Davis (New York: Lexington Books, 2013), 1–22; Tabitha Steager, "Women, Food, and Activism: Rediscovering Collectivist Action in an Individualized World," in *Feminist Activist Ethnography*, 165–80.

11. Allison McKim, "'Getting Gut-Level': Punishment, Gender, and Therapeutic Governance," *Gender and Society* 22, no. 3 (2008): 303–23.

12. Carol Jacobsen and Lora Bex Lempert, "Institutional Disparities: Considerations of Gender in the Commutation Process for Incarcerated Women," *Signs* 39, no. 1 (2013): 265–89.

13. Iris López, "Negotiating Different Worlds: An Integral Ethnography of Reproductive Freedom and Social Justice," in *Feminist Activist Ethnography*, 145–64.

14. Barbara Frankel, *Transforming Identities: Context, Power, and Ideology in a Therapeutic Community* (New York: Peter Lang, 1989); Erica Prussing, "Reconfiguring the Empty Center: Drinking, Sobriety, and Identity in Native American Women's Narratives," *Culture, Medicine, and Psychiatry* 31, no. 4 (2007): 499–526; Geoffrey R. Skoll, *Walk the Walk and Talk the Talk: An Ethnography of a Drug Abuse Treatment Facility* (Philadelphia: Temple University Press, 1992).

15. Begona Aretxaga, "Maddening States," *Annual Review of Anthropology* 32 (2003): 393–410; Crenshaw, "From Private Violence to Mass

Incarceration"; Veena Das and Deborah Poole, "State and Its Margins: Comparative Ethnographies," in *Anthropology at the Margins of the State*, ed. Veena Das and Deborah Poole (Santa Fe, NM: School of Advanced Research Press, 2004), 3–33; Dána-Ain Davis, "Manufacturing Mammies: The Burdens of Service Work and Welfare Reform among Battered Black Women," *Anthropologica* 46, no. 2 (2004): 273–88; Vincent Lyon-Callo, *Inequality, Poverty, and Neoliberal Governance: Activist Ethnography in the Homeless Sheltering Industry* (Toronto, Canada: University of Toronto Press, 2004); Roberta Raffaetà and Mark Nichter, "Negotiating Care in Uncertain Settings and Looking beneath the Surface of Health Governance Projects," *Anthropology in Action* 22, no. 1 (2015): 1–6; Lynn Weber, "Reconstructing the Landscape of Health Disparities Research: Promoting Dialogue and Collaboration between Feminist Intersectional and Biomedical Paradigms," in *Gender, Race, Class, and Health*, 21–59.

16. Jessie Daniels and Amy J. Schulz, "Constructing Whiteness in Health Disparities Research," in *Gender, Race, Class, and Health*, 89–127; Paul Farmer, *Aids and Accusation: Haiti and the Geography of Blame* (Berkeley: University of California Press, 1992); Kristin Hedges, "Teens in the Grey Zone: The Structural Violence of Substance-Using Youth Being Raised in the System," *Human Organization* 71, no. 3 (2015): 317–25; Leith Mullings and Amy J. Schulz, "Intersectionality and Health: An Introduction," in *Gender, Race, Class, and Health*, 3–20.

17. Ruth Wilson Gillmore, "Globalization and US Prison Growth: From Military Keynesianism to Post-Keynesian Militarism," *Race and Class* 40, no. 2/3 (1999): 171–88; Avery F. Gordon, "Globalism and the Prison Industrial Complex: An Interview with Angela Davis," *Race and Class* 40, no. 2/3 (1999): 145–57; Tracy Huling, "Building a Prison Economy in Rural America," in *Invisible Punishment: The Collateral Consequences of Mass Imprisonment*, ed. Marc Mauer and Meda Chesney-Lind (New York: The New Press, 2002), 197–213; Maskovsky, "Other War at Home"; Leith Mullings, "Losing Ground: Harlem, the War on Drugs, and the Prison Industrial Complex," *Souls: A Critical Journal of Black Politics, Culture, and Society* 5, no. 2 (2003): 1–21; Dorothy Roberts, "Prison, Foster Care, and the Systemic Punishment of Black Mothers," *UCLA Law Review* 59 (2012): 1474–500; Jane Schneider and Peter Schneider, "The Anthropology of Crime and Criminalization," *Annual Review of Anthropology* 37 (2008): 351–73; Loïc Wacquant, *Punishing the Poor: The Neoliberal Government of Social Insecurity* (Durham, NC: Duke University Press, 2009).

18. Ulrika Dahl, "Progressive Women, Traditional Men: Globalization, Migration, and Equality in the Northern Periphery of the European Union," in *The Gender of Globalization*, 105–26; Shirin M. Rai, *The Gender Politics of Development* (New York: Zed Books, 2008).

19. Aretxaga, "Maddening States."

20. João Biehl, "Pharmaceutical Governance," in *Global Pharmaceuticals: Ethics, Markets, and Practices*, ed. Andrew Lakoff, Adriana Petryna, and Arthur Kleinman (Durham, NC: Duke University Press, 2006), 206–38; Erin Koch, *Free Market Tuberculosis: Managing Epidemics in Post-Soviet Georgia* (Nashville, TN: Vanderbilt University Press, 2013); Catherine Trundle, "Biopolitical Endpoints: Diagnosing a Deserving British Nuclear Test Veteran," *Social Science & Medicine* 73, no. 6 (2011): 882–88.

21. Jeanne Flavin, *Our Bodies, Our Crimes: The Policing of Women's Reproduction in America* (New York: New York University Press, 2009); Laury Oaks, "Smoke-Filled Wombs and Fragile Fetuses: The Social Politics of Fetal Representation," *Signs* 26, no. 1 (2000): 63–108.

22. Christa Craven, "Claiming Respectable American Motherhood: Homebirth Mothers, Medical Officials, and the State," *Medical Anthropology Quarterly* 19, no. 3 (2005): 194–215; Veena Das, "Violence, Gender, and Subjectivity," *Annual Review of Anthropology* 37 (2008): 283–99; Michele Bratcher Goodwin, "Precarious Moorings: Tying Fetal Drug Law Policy to Social Profiling," *Rutgers Law Journal* 42 (2011): 659–94; Elizabeth L. Krause and Silvia De Zordo, "Introduction. Ethnography and Biopolitics: Tracing 'Rationalities' of Reproduction across the North–South Divide," *Anthropology and Medicine* 19, no. 2 (2012): 137–51; Nikolas Rose, *The Politics of Life Itself: Biomedicine, Power, and Subjectivity in the Twenty-First Century* (Princeton, NJ: Princeton University Press, 2007); Loretta J. Ross, "Reproductive Justice as Intersectional Feminist Activism," *Souls: A Critical Journal of Black Politics, Culture, and Society* 19, no. 3 (2017): 286–314; Elyse Ona Singer, "From Reproductive Rights to Responsibilization: Fashioning Liberal Subjects in Mexico City's New Public Sector Abortion Program," *Medical Anthropology Quarterly* 31, no. 4 (2017): 445–63; Linda M. Whiteford and Judi Vitucci, "Pregnancy and Addiction: Translating Research into Practice," *Social Science and Medicine* 44, no. 9 (1997): 1371–80.

23. Carl Leukefeld et al., "What Does the Community Say: Key Informant Perceptions of Rural Prescription Drug Use," *Journal of Drug Issues* 37, no. 3 (2007): 503–24.

24. Gay Becker, "The Uninsured and the Politics of Containment in US

Health Care," *Medical Anthropology* 26, no. 4 (2007): 299–321; Crenshaw, "From Private Violence"; Rivke Jaffe, "The Hybrid State: Crime and Citizenship in Urban Jamaica," *American Ethnologist* 40, no. 4 (2013): 734–48; Ippolytos Kalofonos, "'All They Do Is Pray': Community Labour and the Narrowing of 'Care' During Mozambique's HIV Scale-Up," *Global Public Health* 9, no. 1/2 (2014): 7–24; Genevieve LeBaron and Adrienne Roberts, "Toward a Feminist Political Economy of Capitalism and Carcerality," *Signs* 36, no. 1 (2010): 19; Raffaetà and Nichter, "Negotiating Care"; Roberts, "Prison, Foster Care"; Wacquant, *Punishing the Poor*.

25. Shana Harris, "To Be Free and Normal: Addiction, Governance, and the Therapeutics of Buprenorphine," *Medical Anthropology Quarterly* 29, no. 4 (2015): 512–30.

26. Michael Agar and Heather Schacht Reisinger, "A Tale of Two Policies: The French Connection, Methadone, and Heroin Epidemics," *Culture, Medicine, and Psychiatry* 26, no. 3 (2002): 371–96; E. Summerson Carr, *Scripting Addiction: The Politics of Therapeutic Talk and American Sobriety* (Princeton, NJ: Princeton University Press, 2011); Erica Prussing, "Sobriety and Its Cultural Politics: An Ethnographer's Perspective on 'Culturally Appropriate' Addiction Services in Native North America," *Ethos* 36, no. 3 (2008): 354–75; A. Jamie Saris, "An Uncertain Dominion: Irish Psychiatry, Methadone, and the Treatment of Opiate Abuse," *Culture, Medicine, and Psychiatry* 32, no. 2 (2008): 259–77; Jarrett Zigon, *"HIV Is God's Blessing": Rehabilitating Morality in Neoliberal Russia* (Berkeley: University of California Press, 2011).

27. João Biehl, "'Medication Is Me Now': Human Values and Political Life in the Wake of Global Aids Treatment," in *In the Name of Humanity: The Government of Threat and Care*, ed. Ilana Feldman and Miriam Ticktin (Durham, NC: Duke University Press, 2010), 151–89; Wendy Chavkin and Vicki Breitbart, "Substance Abuse and Maternity: The United States as a Case Study," *Addiction* 92, no. 9 (1997): 1201–5; Skoll, *Walk the Walk*; Singer, "From Reproductive Rights to Responsibilization"; An-Pyng Sun, "Relapse among Substance-Abusing Women: Components and Processes," *Substance Use and Misuse* 42, no. 1 (2007): 1–21; Zigon, *"HIV is God's Blessing."*

28. Carr, *Scripting Addiction*; Lyon-Callo, *Inequality, Poverty and Neoliberal Governance*; McKim, "'Getting Gut-Level.'"

29. Krause and De Zordo, "Ethnography and Biopolitics"; Sandy Smith-Nonini, "Neoliberal Infections and the Politics of Health: Resurgent Tuberculosis Epidemics in New York City and Lima, Peru," in

Anthropology and Public Health: Bridging Differences in Culture and Society, ed. Robert A. Hahn and Marcia C. Inhorn (New York: Oxford University Press, 2009), 588–622; Susan Reynolds Whyte, Sjaak van der Geest, and Anita Hardon, *Social Lives of Medicines* (New York: Cambridge University Press, 2002).

30. Bourgois, "Moral Economies"; María Esther Epele, "Gender, Violence and HIV: Women's Survival in the Streets," *Culture, Medicine, and Psychiatry* 26, no. 1 (2002): 33–54.

31. Veena Das and Ranendra K. Das, "Pharmaceuticals in Urban Ecologies: The Register of the Local," in *Global Pharmaceuticals,* 171.

32. Johan Galtung, "Violence, Peace, and Peace Research," *Journal of Peace Research* 6, no. 3 (1969): 167–91; Johan Galtung, "Cultural Violence," *Journal of Peace Research* 27, no. 3 (1990): 291–305.

33. Paul Farmer et al., "Structural Violence and Clinical Medicine," *PLOS Medicine* 3, no. 10 (2006): 1686–91.

34. Farmer, *Infections and Inequalities*; Nancy Scheper-Hughes, *Death without Weeping: The Violence of Everyday Life in Brazil* (Berkeley: University of California Press, 1992).

35. Paul Farmer, *Pathologies of Power: Health, Human Rights, and the New War on the Poor* (Berkeley: University of California Press, 2005).

36. Kalofonos, "'All They Do Is Pray'"; Ann Kingsolver, "Neoliberal Governance and Faith-Based Initiatives: Agentive Cracks in the Logic Informing Homeless Sheltering in South Carolina's Capital," *Rethinking Marxism: A Journal of Economics, Culture, and Society* 24, no. 2 (2012): 202–14.

37. Galtung, "Violence, Peace, and Peace Research."

38. Ilana Feldman and Miriam Ticktin, "Introduction: Government and Humanity," in *In the Name of Humanity,* 1–26; Sandra Morgen and Jeff Maskovsky, "The Anthropology of Welfare 'Reform': New Perspectives on US Urban Poverty in the Post-Welfare Era," *Annual Review of Anthropology* 32 (2003): 315–38; Ida Susser, "The Construction of Poverty and Homelessness in US Cities," *Annual Review of Anthropology* 25 (1996): 411–35.

39. Keith Wailoo, "The New Politics of Old Differences," in *How Cancer Crossed the Color Line* (New York: Oxford University Press, 2011), 148–73.

40. Catherine Kingfisher and Michael Goldsmith, "Reforming Women in the United States and Aotearoa, New Zealand: A Comparative Ethnography of Welfare Reform in Global Context," *American Anthropologist* 103, no. 3 (2001): 714–32.

41. Scheper-Hughes, *Death without Weeping*.
42. Maggie Dickinson, "Working for Food Stamps: Economic Citizenship and the Post-Fordist Welfare State in New York City," *American Ethnologist* 43, no. 2 (2016): 270–81; LeBaron and Roberts, "Toward a Feminist Political Economy."
43. Kathryn D. Chiplis, *Alternative Programs for Drug Offenders: An Evaluation of a Rural Drug Court* (DeKalb: Northern Illinois University Press, 2010).
44. Joan C. Tronto, "Beyond Gender Difference to a Theory of Care," *Signs* 12, no. 4 (1987): 644–63; Joan C. Tronto, "Care as a Basis for Radical Political Judgements," *Hypatia* 10, no. 2 (1995): 141–49.
45. Lisa Stevenson, *Life Beside Itself: Imagining Care in the Canadian Artic* (Berkeley: University of California Press, 2014); Tronto, "Beyond Gender Difference."

Chapter 1: How Did We Get Here?

1. J. D. Vance, *Hillbilly Elegy: A Memoir of a Family and Culture in Crisis* (London: William Collins, 2016).
2. Dwight B. Billings, Gurney Norman, and Katherine Ledford, *Back Talk from Appalachia: Confronting Stereotypes* (Lexington: University Press of Kentucky, 1999); Carol Mason, "The Hillbilly Defense: Culturally Mediating US Terror at Home and Abroad," *NWSA Journal* 17, no. 3 (2005): 39–63; Carissa Massey, "Appalachian Stereotypes: Cultural History, Gender, and Sexual Rhetoric," *Journal of Appalachian Studies* 13, no. 1/2 (2007): 124–36; Rebecca R. Scott, *Removing Mountains: Extracting Nature and Identity in the Appalachian Coalfields* (Minneapolis: University of Minnesota Press, 2010).
3. Patricia Hill Collins, *Black Feminist Thought: Knowledge, Consciousness, and the Politics of Empowerment*, 2nd ed. (New York: Routledge, 2000); Office of Policy Planning and Research, *The Negro Family: The Case for National Action* (Washington, DC: United States Department of Labor, 1965).
4. See Vance, *Hillbilly Elegy*.
5. Charles L. Briggs and Clara Mantini-Briggs, *Stories in the Time of Cholera: Racial Profiling During a Medical Nightmare* (Berkeley: University of California Press, 2003); Paul Farmer, *Aids and Accusation: Haiti and the Geography of Blame* (Berkeley: University of California Press, 1992).
6. J. Hope Amason, "Uncertain Lives: Neoliberalism and the Shaping of Home among Service Workers in Gatlinburg," *North American Dialogue* 18, no. 1 (2015): 1–14; Mary K. Anglin, "Erasures of the Past: Culture, Power, and Heterogeneity in Appalachia," *Journal of Appalachian Studies*

10, no. 1/2 (2004): 73–84; Elizabeth Catte, *What You Are Getting Wrong about Appalachia* (Cleveland: Belt Publishing, 2018); Carol Mason, *Reading Appalachia from Left to Right: Conservatives and the 1974 Kanawha County Textbook Controversy* (Ithaca: Cornell University Press, 2009); Scott, *Removing Mountains;* Joe William Trotter Jr., "The Formation of Black Community in Southern West Virginia Coalfields," in *Appalachians and Race: The Mountain South from Slavery to Segregation,* ed. John C. Inscoe (Lexington: University Press of Kentucky, 2001), 284–301.

7. John Hartigan, Jr., "Whiteness and Appalachian Studies: What's the Connection?" *Journal of Appalachian Studies* 10, no. 1/2 (2004): 58–72; Ian C. Hartman, "Appalachian Anxiety: Race, Gender, and the Paradox of 'Purity' in an Age of Empire, 1873–1901," *American Nineteenth Century History* 13, no. 2 (2012): 229–55; Massey, "Appalachian Stereotypes"; Douglas Reichert Powell, *Critical Regionalism: Connecting Politics and Culture in the American Landscape* (Chapel Hill: The University of North Carolina Press, 2007); Scott, *Removing Mountains.*

8. Sandra Lee Barney, *Authorized to Heal: Gender, Class, and the Transformation of Medicine in Appalachia, 1880–1930* (Chapel Hill: University of North Carolina Press, 2000); Jane S. Becker, *Selling Tradition: Appalachia and the Construction of an American Folk 1930–1940* (Chapel Hill: University of North Carolina Press, 1998); Wilma A. Dunaway, *Women, Work, and Family in the Antebellum Mountain South* (New York: Cambridge University Press, 2008); Elizabeth S. D. Engelhardt, *Tangled Roots of Feminism, Environmentalism, and Appalachian Literature* (Columbus: Ohio University Press, 2003); Melanie Beals Goan, *Mary Breckinridge: The Frontier Nursing Service and Rural Health in Appalachia* (Chapel Hill: University of North Carolina Press, 2008); Karen W. Tice, "School-Work and Mother-Work: The Interplay of Maternalism and Cultural Politics in the Educational Narratives of Kentucky Settlement Workers, 1910–1930," *Journal of Appalachian Studies* 4, no. 2 (1998): 191–224.

9. Grace Howard, "The Limits of Pure White: Raced Reproduction in the Methamphetamine Crisis," *Women's Rights Law Reporter* 35, no. 3/4 (2014): 373–405.

10. Elaine M. Drew and Nancy E. Schoenberg, "Deconstructing Fatalism: Ethnographic Perspectives on Women's Decision Making about Cancer Prevention and Treatment," *Medical Anthropology Quarterly* 25, no. 2 (2011): 164–182.

11. Amason, "Uncertain Lives"; Appalachian Land Ownership Task Force,

Who Owns Appalachia? Landownership and Its Impact (Lexington: University Press of Kentucky, 1983).

12. Mary K. Anglin, "Lessons from Appalachia in the 20th Century: Power, Poverty, and the Grassroots," *American Anthropologist* 104, no. 3 (2002): 565–82; Pat Banks et al., "Building Alliances to Conserve and Protect the Kentucky River," *Journal of Appalachian Studies* 19, no. 1/2 (2013): 133–50; Shannon Elizabeth Bell, *Our Roots Run Deep as Ironweed: Appalachian Women and the Fight for Environmental Justice* (Urbana: University of Illinois Press, 2013); Meredith Dean, Edna Gulley, and Linda McKinney, "Organizing Appalachian Women: Hope Lies in the Struggle," in *Transforming Places: Lessons from Appalachia*, ed. Stephen L. Fisher and Barbara Ellen Smith (Urbana: University of Illinois Press, 2012), 109–21; Stephen L. Fisher and Barbara Ellen Smith, "Introduction: Placing Appalachia," in *Transforming Places*, 1–15; Silas House and Jason Howard, eds. *Something's Rising: Appalachians Fighting Mountaintop Removal* (Lexington: University Press of Kentucky, 2009); Ann E. Kingsolver, "Five Women Negotiating the Meaning of Negotiation," *Anthropological Quarterly* 65, no. 3 (1992): 101–4; Scott, *Removing Mountains*; Shaunna L. Scott et al. "Post Disaster Interviews with Martin County Citizens: 'Gray Clouds' of Blame and Distrust," *Journal of Appalachian Studies* 11, no. 1/2 (2005): 7–29.

13. Dwight B. Billings and Kathleen Blee, *The Road to Poverty: The Making of Wealth and Hardship in Appalachia* (New York: Cambridge University Press, 2000); T. R. C. Hutton, *Bloody Breathitt: Politics and Violence in the Appalachian South* (Lexington: University Press of Kentucky, 2013); Powell, *Critical Regionalism*.

14. Appalachian Regional Commission, "County Economic Status in Appalachia, FY 2017," 2016, www.Arc.Gov/Research/Mapsofappalachia. Asp?Map_Id=116.

15. Ida Susser, "The Construction of Poverty and Homelessness in US Cities," *Annual Review of Anthropology* 25 (1996): 411–35.

16. Amason, "Uncertain Lives"; Mary K. Anglin, "Moving Forward: Gender and Globalization in/of Appalachian Studies," *Appalachian Journal* 37, no. 3/4 (2010): 286–300; Amanda Fickey, "Speaking a New Economic Language in Central Appalachia," *Social & Cultural Geography* 15, no. 8 (2014): 973–74; Rebecca Adkins Fletcher, "Keeping up with the Cadillacs: What Health Insurance Disparities, Moral Hazard, and the Cadillac Tax Mean to the Patient Protection and Affordable Care Act," *Medical Anthropology Quarterly* 30, no. 1 (2014): 18–36; Ann E.

Kingsolver, *Tobacco Town Futures* (Long Grove: Waveland Press, 2011).

17. Lauren A. Hayes, "Notes from the Field: Navigating the Role of Researcher at a Factory Fieldsite in Appalachian Kentucky," *Arizona Anthropologist* 24 (2015): 42–50.

18. Hutton, *Bloody Breathitt*; Barbara Ellen Smith, "Another Place Is Possible? Labor Geography, Spatial Dispossession, and Gendered Resistance in Central Appalachia," *Annals of the Association of American Geographers* 105, no. 3 (2015): 567–82.

19. Wilma A. Dunaway, "Speculators and Settler Capitalists: Unthinking the Mythology About Appalachian Landholding, 1790–1860," in *Appalachia in the Making: The Mountain South in the Nineteenth Century*, ed. Dwight B. Billings, Mary Beth Pudup, and Altina L. Waller (Chapel Hill: University of North Carolina Press, 1995), 50–75; Hutton, *Bloody Breathitt*; Mary Beth Pudup, Dwight B. Billings, and Altina L. Waller, eds., *Appalachia in the Making: The Mountain South in the Nineteenth Century* (Chapel Hill: University of North Carolina Press, 1995).

20. Appalachian Land Ownership Task Force, *Who Owns Appalachia?*; Billings and Blee, *The Road to Poverty*; Dunaway, "Speculators and Settler Capitalists"; Pudup et al., *Appalachia in the Making*.

21. Appalachian Land Ownership Task Force, *Who Owns Appalachia?*; Billings and Blee, *The Road to Poverty*.

22. Barney, *Authorized to Heal*; Goan, *Mary Breckinridge*.

23. Becker, *Selling Tradition*; Hutton, *Bloody Breathitt*.

24. Catte, *What You Are Getting Wrong about Appalachia*.

25. Ann Pancake, *Strange as This Weather Has Been* (Berkeley: Counterpoint, 2007), 256.

26. United States Census Bureau, *2011–2015 American Community Survey 5-Year Estimates* (Washington, DC: US Census Bureau's American Community Survey Office, 2015).

27. US Census Bureau, *2011–2015 American Community Survey*.

28. Wilburn Hayden, Jr., "In Search of Justice: White Privilege in Appalachia," *Journal of Appalachian Studies* 8, no. 1 (2002): 120–31.

29. Appalachian Regional Commission, "Data Reports: Socioeconomic Data Profile by County," 2017, www.arc.gov/data.

30. US Census Bureau, *2011–2015 American Community Survey*.

31. Peter Wagner and Wendy Sawyer, "State of Incarceration: The Global Context 2018," Prison Policy Initiative, 2018, www.prisonpolicy.org /global/2018.html.

32. US Census Bureau, *2011–2015 American Community Survey*.

33. US Census Bureau, *2011–2015 American Community Survey.*
34. Marjory Givens et al., *County Health Rankings 2017* (Madison: University of Wisconsin Population Health Institute, 2017).
35. Institute for Health Metrics, "Life Expectancy at Birth, Both Sexes, 2014," 2016, vizhub.healthdata.org/subnational/usa.
36. Patient Protection and Affordable Care Act, 42 U.S.C. § 18001 (2010); Mental Health Parity and Addiction Equity Act, H.R. 6983 (2008).
37. Matt Broaddus, Peggy Bailey, and Aviva Aron-Dine, *Medicaid Expansion Dramatically Increased Coverage for People with Opioid-Use Disorders, Latest Data Show* (Washington, DC: Center on Budget and Policy Priorities, 2018).
38. The Kaiser Commission on Medicaid and the Uninsured, "Proposed Changes to Medicaid Expansion in Kentucky," 2016, kff.org/medicaid/fact-sheet/proposed-changes-to-medicaid-expansion-in-kentucky/; MaryBeth Musumeci, Robin Rudowitz, and Elizabeth Hinton, *Approved Changes to Medicaid in Kentucky* (Menlo Park, CA: The Henry J. Kaiser Family Foundation, 2018).
39. Hannah S. Bell et al., "Medicaid Reform, Responsibilization Policies, and the Synergism of Barriers to Low-Income Health Seeking," *Human Organization* 76, no. 3 (2017): 275–86.
40. Jonathan D. Rockoff, "Gilead Gets U.S. Approval to Sell New Hepatitis C Drug," *Wall Street Journal*, October 10, 2014.
41. Kelly R. Knight et al., "Opioid Pharmacovigilance: A Clinical-Social History of the Changes in the Opioid Prescribing for Patients with Co-Occuring Chronic Non-Cancer Pain and Substance Use," *Social Science & Medicine* 186 (2017): 87–95; Sam Quinones, *Dreamland: The True Tale of America's Opiate Epidemic* (New York: Bloomsbury Press, 2015); Ameet Sarpatwari, Michael S. Sinha, and Aaron S. Kesselheim, "The Opioid Epidemic: Fixing a Broken Pharmaceutical Market," *Harvard Law and Policy Review* 11 (2017): 463–84; Katie Thomas and Charles Ornstein, "Amid Opioid Crisis, Insurers Restrict Pricey, Less Addictive Painkillers," *New York Times* and *ProPublica*, September 17, 2017.
42. Gery P. Guy et al., "Vital Signs: Changes in Opioid Prescribing in the United States, 2006–2015," *Morbidity and Mortality Weekly Report* 66, no. 26 (2017): 697–704.
43. Sarpatwari et al., "Opioid Epidemic."
44. Joseph Dumit, *Drugs for Life: How Pharmaceutical Companies Define Our Health* (Durham, NC: Duke University Press, 2012); Andrew Lakoff, *Pharmaceutical Reason* (New York: Cambridge University Press, 2005); Michael J. Oldani, "Thick Prescriptions: Toward an Interpretation of

Pharmaceutical Sales Practices," *Medical Anthropology Quarterly* 18, no. 3 (2004): 325–56.

45. Dumit, *Drugs for Life*; S. Lochlann Jain, "The Mortality Effect: Counting the Dead in the Cancer Trial," in *In the Name of Humanity: The Government of Threat and Care*, ed. Ilana Feldman and Miriam Ticktin (Durham, NC: Duke University Press, 2010), 218–37; Adriana Petryna and Arthur Kleinman, "The Pharmaceutical Nexus," in *Global Pharmaceuticals: Ethics, Markets, and Practices* (Durham, NC: Duke University Press, 2006), 1–32.

46. Nina L. Etkin, "'Side Effects': Cultural Construction and Reinterpretations of Western Pharmaceuticals," *Medical Anthropology Quarterly* 6, no. 2 (1992): 99–113; Emily Martin, "The Pharmaceutical Person," *BioSocieties* 1 (2006): 273–87; Oldani, "Thick Prescriptions"; Petryna and Kleinman, "Pharmaceutical Nexus."

47. Adriana Petryna, "The Politics of Experimentality," in *In the Name of Humanity*, 256–89.

48. Adele E. Clark et al., "Biomedicalization: Technoscientific Transformations of Health, Illness, and U.S. Biomedicine," *American Sociological Review* 68, no. 2 (2003): 161–94.

49. Sarpatwari et al., "Opioid Epidemic."

50. Barry Meier, *Painkiller: A "Wonder" Drug's Trail of Addiction and Death* (Emmaus: Rodale, 2003); Art Van Zee, "The Promotion and Marketing of Oxycontin: Commercial Triumph, Public Health Tragedy," *American Journal of Public Health* 99, no. 2 (2009): 221–27.

51. Sarpatwari et al., "Opioid Epidemic."

52. Theodore J. Cicero, James A. Inciardi, and Alvaro Muñoz, "Trends in Abuse of OxyContin® and Other Opioid Analgesics in the United States: 2002–2004," *Journal of Pain* 6, no. 10 (2005): 662–72.

53. Jennifer Chubinski et al., "Painkiller Misuse among Appalachians and in Appalachian Counties in Kentucky," *Journal of Appalachian Studies* 20, no. 2 (2014): 154–69; Cicero et al., "Trends in Abuse"; Sue Ella Kobak, "Oxycontin Flood in the Coalfields: 'Searching for Higher Ground,'" in *Transforming Places*, 198–209; Steven D. Passik, "Same as It Ever Was? Life after the OxyContin® Media Frenzy," *Journal of Pain and Symptom Management* 25, no. 3 (2003): 199–201; US General Accounting Office, *Prescription Drugs: OxyContin Abuse and Diversion and Efforts to Address the Problem* (Washington, DC: United States General Accounting Office, 2003); Van Zee, "Promotion and Marketing of OxyContin."

54. Substance Abuse and Mental Health Services Administration, *National

Survey on Drug Use and Health, 2015 and 2016 (Rockville, MD: Center for Behavioral Health Statistics and Quality, 2017).

55. Guy et al., "Vital Signs."

56. Centers for Disease Control and Prevention, *Compressed Mortality File (CMF) on CDC WONDER Online Database* (Atlanta: National Center for Health Statistics, 2016).

57. João Biehl, "The Judicialization of Biopolitics: Claiming the Right to Pharmaceuticals in Brazilian Courts," *American Ethnologist* 40, no. 3 (2013): 419–36; Dumit, *Drugs for Life.*

58. Susan E. Bell and Anne E. Figert, "Medicalization and Pharmaceuticalizaton at the Intersections: Looking Backward, Sideways, and Forward," *Social Science & Medicine* 75, no. 5 (2012): 775–83.

59. Helena Hansen and Julie Netherland, "Is the Prescription Opioid Epidemic a White Problem?" *American Journal of Public Health* 106, no. 12 (2016): 2127–29.

60. Julie Netherland and Helena Hansen, "White Opioid: Pharmaceutical Race and the War on Drugs that Wasn't," *Biosocieties* 12, no. 2: 217–38.

61. James A. Inciardi and Jennifer L. Goode, "Miracle Medicine or Problem Drug: OxyContin and Prescription Drug Abuse," *Consumers' Research* (July 2003): 17–21; US General Accounting Office, *Prescription Drugs;* Passik, "Same as It Ever Was?"; Van Zee, "Promotion and Marketing of OxyContin"; Sarpatwari et al., "Opioid Epidemic."

62. Sarpatwari et al., "Opioid Epidemic."

63. Lenny Berstein and Scott Higham, "Purdue Pharma in Talks over Multibillion-Dollar Deal to Settle More than 2,000 Opioid Lawsuits," *Washington Post,* August 27, 2019.

64. Charles Ornstein, "Drug Distributors Penalized for Turning Blind Eye in Opioid Epidemic," *ProPublica,* January 27, 2017.

65. Berstein and Higham, "Purdue Pharma in Talks."

66. Scott Higham and Lenny Bernstein, "Cherokee Nation Sues Drug Firms, Retailers for Flooding Communities with Opioids," *Washington Post,* April 20, 2017.

67. Knight et al., "Opioid Pharmacovigilance."

68. Katherine Beckett and Bruce Western, "Governing Social Marginality: Welfare, Incarceration, and the Transformation of State Policy," *Punishment & Society* 3, no. 1 (2001): 43–59; Lorna A. Rhodes, "Toward an Anthropology of Prisons," *Annual Review of Anthropology* 30 (2001): 65–83; Loïc Wacquant, *Punishing the Poor: The Neoliberal Government of Social Insecurity* (Durham, NC: Duke University Press, 2009).

69. Kimberle Crenshaw, "From Private Violence to Mass Incarceration: Thinking Intersectionally About Women, Race, and Social Control," *UCLA Law Review* 59 (2012): 1418–72.

70. Genevieve LeBaron and Adrienne Roberts, "Toward a Feminist Political Economy of Capitalism and Carcerality," *Signs* 36, no. 1 (2010): 19–44.

71. Howard Becker, cited in Merrill Singer and J. Bryan Page, *The Social Value of Drug Addicts: Uses of the Useless* (Walnut Creek, CA: Left Coast Press, 2013).

72. Brian J. O'Hare, "Book Review: Merrill Singer and J. Bryan Page. The Social Value of Drug Addicts: Uses of the Useless," *North American Dialogue* 18, no. 1 (2015): 26–28.

73. Yang et al., "'What Matters Most': A Cultural Mechanism Moderating Structural Vulnerability and Moral Experience of Mental Illness Stigma," *Social Science & Medicine* 103 (2014): 84–93.

74. Polly Radcliffe and Alex Stevens, "Are Drug Treatment Services Only for 'Thieving Junkie Scumbags'? Drug Users and the Management of Stigmatised Identities," *Social Science & Medicine* 67, no. 7 (2008): 1065–73.

75. Philippe Bourgois, "Disciplining Addictions: The Bio-Politics of Methadone and Heroin in the United States," *Culture, Medicine, and Psychiatry* 24, no. 2 (2000): 165–95; E. Summerson Carr, *Scripting Addiction: The Politics of Therapeutic Talk and American Sobriety* (Princeton, NJ: Princeton University Press, 2011).

76. Todd Meyers, "Promise and Deceit: Pharmakos, Drug Replacement Therapy, and the Perils of Experience," *Culture, Medicine, and Psychiatry* 38, no. 2 (2014): 182–96.

77. Stacey A. McKenna, "Reproducing Hegemony: The Culture of Enhancement and Discourses on Amphetamines in Popular Fiction," *Culture, Medicine, and Psychiatry* 35, no. 1 (2011): 90–97; Jason Pine, "Economy of Speed: The New Narco-Capitalism," *Public Culture* 19, no. 2 (2007): 357–66.

78. Phyllis L. Baker and Amy Carson, "'I Take Care of My Kids': Mothering Practices of Substance-Abusing Women," *Gender and Society* 13, no. 3 (1999): 347–63; Angela Garcia, *The Pastoral Clinic: Addiction and Dispossession Along the Rio Grande* (Berkeley: University of California Press, 2010); Michele Bratcher Goodwin, "Precarious Moorings: Tying Fetal Drug Law Policy to Social Profiling," *Rutgers Law Journal* 42 (2011): 659–94; Kelly Ray Knight, *addicted.pregnant.poor* (Durham, NC: Duke University Press, 2015); Linda M. Whiteford and Judi Vitucci, "Pregnancy and Addiction: Translating Research into Practice," *Social*

Science & Medicine 44, no. 9 (1997): 1371–80; Stacey A. McKenna, "Reproducing Hegemony: The Culture of Enhancement and Discourses on Amphetamines in Popular Fiction," *Culture, Medicine, and Psychiatry* 35, no. 1 (2011); 90–97; Jason Pine, "Economy of Speed: The New Narco-Capitalism," *Public Culture* 19, no. 2 (2007): 357–66.

79. Jeanne Flavin and Lynn M. Paltrow, "Punishing Pregnant Drug-Using Women: Defying Law, Medicine, and Common Sense," *Journal of Addictive Diseases* 29, no. 2 (2010): 231–44.

80. Howard Campbell, "Female Drug Smugglers on the U.S.–Mexico Border: Gender, Crime, and Empowerment," *Anthropological Quarterly* 81, no. 1 (2008): 233–67; Carr, *Scripting Addiction*; María Esther Epele, "Gender, Violence and HIV: Women's Survival in the Streets," *Culture, Medicine, and Psychiatry* 26, no. 1 (2002): 33–54.

81. Crenshaw, "From Private Violence to Mass Incarceration"; Catherine Mitchell Fuentes, "Nobody's Child: The Role of Trauma and Interpersonal Violence in Women's Pathways to Incarceration and Resultant Service Needs," *Medical Anthropology Quarterly* 28, no. 1 (2014): 85–104.

82. Dorothy Roberts, "Prison, Foster Care, and the Systemic Punishment of Black Mothers," *UCLA Law Review* 59 (2012): 1474–500.

83. Tracy Huling, "Building a Prison Economy in Rural America," in *Invisible Punishment: The Collateral Consequences of Mass Imprisonment*, ed. Marc Mauer and Meda Chesney-Lind (New York: The New Press, 2002).

84. Dwight B. Billings, "Appalachian Studies and the Sociology of Appalachia," in *21st Century Sociology: A Reference Handbook*, ed. Clifford D. Bryant and Dennis L. Peck (Thousand Oaks, CA: Sage, 2007), 390–96.

85. Warwick Anderson, *Colonial Pathologies: American Tropical Medicine, Race, and Hygiene in the Philippines* (Durham, NC: Duke University Press, 2006); Barney, *Authorized to Heal*; James A. Trostle, *Epidemiology and Culture* (New York: Cambridge University Press, 2005).

86. Vera Institute, "Incarceration Trends," 2018, trends.vera.org/incarceration-rates.

87. Kentuckians for the Commonwealth, *Right to Vote* (London, KY: Kentuckians for the Commonwealth, 2019).

Chapter 2: Facing the State

1. Federal Bureau of Investigation and Drug Enforcement Agency, *Chasing the Dragon: The Life of an Opiate Addict* (Washington, DC: FBI and DEA, 2018).

2. Janet Carsten, *After Kinship* (New York: Cambridge University Press, 2004); David M. Schneider, "What Is Kinship All About?" in *Kinship Studies in the Morgan Centennial Year*, ed. Priscilla Reining (Washington, DC: Anthropological Society of Washington, 1972), 32–63; Robert A. Wilson, "Kinship Past, Kinship Present: Bio-Essentialism in the Study of Kinship," *American Anthropologist* 118, no. 3 (2016): 570–84.

3. Travis H. Hedwig, "The Cultural Politics of Fetal Alcohol Spectrum Disorders and the Diagnosis of Difference" (PhD diss., University of Kentucky, 2013); Kelly Ray Knight, *addicted.pregnant.poor* (Durham, NC: Duke University Press, 2015); Lynn M. Paltrow and Jeanne Flavin, "Arrests of and Forced Interventions on Pregnant Women in the United States, 1973–2005: Implications for Women's Legal Status and Public Health," *Journal of Health Politics, Policy, and Law* 38, no. 2 (2013): 299–343; Leslie J. Reagan, *Dangerous Pregnancies: Mothers, Disabilities, and Abortion in Modern America* (Berkeley: University of California Press, 2010); Elyse Ona Singer, "From Reproductive Rights to Reponsibilization: Fashioning Liberal Subjects in Mexico City's New Public Sector Abortion Program," *Medical Anthropology Quarterly* 31, no. 4 (2017): 445–63; Michelle Stewart, "Fictions of Prevention: Fetal Alcohol Spectrum Disorder and Narratives of Responsibility," *North American Dialogue* 19, no. 1 (2016): 55–66.

4. Emmalee Bandstra et al., "Prenatal Drug Exposure: Infant and Toddler Outcomes," *Journal of Addictive Diseases* 29, no. 2 (2010): 245–58; Karol Kaltenbach et al., "Prenatal Exposure to Methadone and Buprenorphine: Early Childhood Developmental Outcomes," *Drug and Alcohol Dependence* 185 (2018): 40–49.

5. Bandstra et al., "Prenatal Drug Exposure."

6. Marylou Behnke and Vincent C. Smith, "Prenatal Substance Abuse: Short- and Long-Term Effects on the Exposed Fetus," *Pediatrics* 131, no. 3 (2013): 1009–24.

7. Kaltenbach et al., "Prenatal Exposure to Methadone."

8. Bandstra et al., "Prenatal Drug Exposure"; Behnke and Smith, "Prenatal Substance Abuse"; Amy S. Oro and Suzanne D. Dixon, "Perinatal Cocaine and Methamphetamine Exposure: Maternal and Neonatal Correlates," *Journal of Pediatrics* 111, no. 4 (1987): 571–78; Lynne M. Smith et al., "Effects of Prenatal Methamphetamine Exposure on Fetal Growth and Drug Withdrawal Symptoms in Infants Born at Term," *Journal of Developmental and Behavioral Pediatrics* 24, no. 1 (2003): 17–23; Lynne M. Smith et al., "The Infant Development, Environment, and Lifestyle

Study: Effects of Prenatal Methamphetamine Exposure, Polydrug Exposure, and Poverty on Intrauterine Growth," *Pediatrics* 118, no. 3 (2006): 1149–56.

9. Linda L. LaGasse et al., "Prenatal Methamphetamine Exposure and Childhood Behavior Problems at 3 and 5 Years of Age," *Pediatrics* 129, no. 4 (2012): 681–88.

10. Lynne M. Smith et al., "Motor and Cognitive Outcomes through Three Years of Age in Children Exposed to Prenatal Methamphetamine," *Neurobiology and Teratology* 33, no. 1 (2011): 176–84.

11. Rizwan Shah et al., "Prenatal Methamphetamine Exposure and Short-Term Maternal and Infant Medical Outcomes," *American Journal of Perinatology* 29, no. 5 (2012): 391–400.

12. Wilma A. Dunaway, *Women, Work, and Family in the Antebellum Mountain South* (New York: Cambridge University Press, 2008); Barbara Ellen Smith, "'Beyond the Mountains': The Paradox of Women's Place in Appalachian History," *NWSA Journal* 11, no. 3 (1999): 1–17.

13. Melanie Beals Goan, *Mary Breckinridge: The Frontier Nursing Service and Rural Health in Appalachia* (Chapel Hill: University of North Carolina Press, 2008).

14. Arline T. Geronimus, "Deep Integration: Letting the Epigenome out of the Bottle without Losing Sight of the Structural Origins of Population Health," *American Journal of Public Health* 103, no. S1 (2013): S56–S63; Margaret Lock, "Comprehending the Body in the Era of the Epigenome," *Current Anthropology* 56, no. 2 (2015): 151–77.

15. Maurizio Meloni, "Comments to: Comprehending the Body in the Era of the Epigenome," *Current Anthropology* 56, no. 2 (2015): 168 (emphasis in original).

16. Jeanne Flavin and Lynn M. Paltrow, "Punishing Pregnant Drug-Using Women: Defying Law, Medicine, and Common Sense," *Journal of Addictive Diseases* 29, no. 2 (2010): 231–44; Laury Oaks, "Smoke-Filled Wombs and Fragile Fetuses: The Social Politics of Fetal Representation," *Signs* 26, no. 1 (2000): 63–108; Reagan, *Dangerous Pregnancies*.

17. Lynn M. Morgan and Elizabeth F. S. Roberts, "Reproductive Governance in Latin America," *Anthropology & Medicine* 19, no. 2 (2012): 241–54; Elyse Ona Singer, "From Reproductive Rights."

18. James Rice and Hanna Björg Sigurjónsdóttir, "Notifying Neglect: Child Protection as an Application of Bureaucratic Power against Marginalized Parents," *Human Organization* 77, no. 2 (2018): 112–21.

19. Dorothy Roberts, "Prison, Foster Care, and the Systemic Punishment of

Black Mothers," *UCLA Law Review* 59 (2012): 1474–500.

20. Kathryn D. Chiplis, *Alternative Programs for Drug Offenders: An Evaluation of a Rural Drug Court* (MA thesis, Northern Illinois University, 2010); Jeanne Flavin, *Our Bodies, Our Crimes: The Policing of Women's Reproduction in America* (New York: New York University Press, 2009); Catherine Mitchell Fuentes, "Nobody's Child: The Role of Trauma and Interpersonal Violence in Women's Pathways to Incarceration and Resultant Service Needs," *Medical Anthropology Quarterly* 28, no. 1 (2014): 85–104.

21. Roberts, "Prison, Foster Care."

22. China Scherz, "Protecting Children, Preserving Families: Moral Conflict and Actuarial Science in a Problem of Contemporary Governance," *Political and Legal Anthropology Review* 34, no. 1 (2011): 33–50.

23. Matt Bevin, "State of the Commonwealth," Frankfort, Kentucky, January 16, 2018.

24. Bevin, "State of the Commonwealth."

Chapter 3: The Therapeutic State

1. United States Department of Health and Human Services, "Major Provisions of the Welfare Law," 1996, www.acf.hhs.gov/ofa/resource/law-reg/finalrule/aspesum.

2. Shana Harris, "The Social Practice of Harm Reduction in Argentina: A 'Latin' Kind of Intervention," *Human Organization* 75, no. 1 (2016): 1–9.

3. Elizabeth A. Hall, Dana M. Baldwin, and Michael L. Prendergast, "Women on Parole: Barriers to Success after Substance Abuse Treatment," *Human Organization* 60, no. 3 (2001): 225–33; Jennifer R. Wies, "Feminist Ethnography with Domestic Violence Shelter Advocates: Negotiating the Neoliberal Era," in *Feminist Activist Ethnography: Counterpoints to Neoliberalism in North America*, ed. Christa Craven and Dána-Ain Davis (New York: Lexington Books, 2013), 53–68.

4. Arline T. Geronimus, "Understanding and Eliminating Racial Inequalities in Women's Health in the United States: The Role of the Weathering Conceptual Framework," *Journal of American Medical Women's Association* 56, no. 4 (2001): 133–36.

Chapter 4: Punitive Rehabilitation

1. Kathryn D. Chiplis, "Alternative Programs for Drug Offenders: An Evaluation of a Rural Drug Court" (MA thesis, Northern Illinois University, 2010); Michael Wenzel et al., "Retributive and Restorative Justice," *Law and Human Behavior* 32, no. 5 (2008): 375–89.

2. Kimberle Crenshaw, "From Private Violence to Mass Incarceration: Thinking Intersectionally About Women, Race, and Social Control," *UCLA Law Review* 59 (2012): 1418–72.

3. Carole Cain, "Personal Stories: Identity Acquisition and Self-Understanding in Alcoholics Anonymous," *Ethos* 19, no. 2 (1991): 210–53; Erica Prussing, "Reconfiguring the Empty Center: Drinking, Sobriety, and Identity in Native American Women's Narratives," *Culture, Medicine, and Psychiatry* 31, no. 4 (2007): 499–526.

4. Max Weber, *The Protestant Ethic and the "Spirit" of Capitalism and Other Writings* (New York: Penguin Books, 2002).

5. Weber, *Protestant Ethic*, 78, 83.

6. Ann E. Kingsolver, "Neoliberal Governance and Faith-Based Initiatives: Agentive Cracks in the Logic Informing Homeless Sheltering in South Carolina's Capital," *Rethinking Marxism: A Journal of Economics, Culture, and Society* 24, no. 2 (2012): 202–14.

7. Sandra Teresa Hyde, "Migrations in Humanistic Therapy: Turning Drug Users into Patients and Patients into Healthy Citizens in Southwest China," *Body and Society* 17, no. 2/3 (2011): 183–204; Jarrett Zigon, *"HIV Is God's Blessing": Rehabilitating Morality in Neoliberal Russia* (Berkeley: University of California Press, 2011).

Chapter 5: The Pharmaceutical Approach: Suboxone

1. Shana Harris, "To Be Free and Normal: Addiction, Governance, and the Therapeutics of Buprenorphine," *Medical Anthropology Quarterly* 29, no. 4 (2015): 512–30; Anne M. Lovell, "Addiction Markets: The Case of High-Dose Buprenorphine in France," in *Global Pharmaceuticals: Ethics, Markets, and Practices*, ed. Andrew Lakoff, Adriana Petryna, and Arthur Kleinman (Durham, NC: Duke University Press, 2006), 136–69; Todd Meyers, "Promise and Deceit: Pharmakos, Drug Replacement Therapy, and the Perils of Experience," *Culture, Medicine, and Psychiatry* 38, no. 2 (2014): 182–96.

2. Annemarie Unger et al., "Gender Issues in the Pharmacotherapy of Opioid-Addicted Women: Buprenorphine," *Journal of Addictive Diseases* 29, no. 2 (2010): 217–30.

3. Susan Reynolds Whyte, Sjaak van der Geest, and Anita Hardon, *Social Lives of Medicines* (New York: Cambridge University Press, 2002).

4. Meyers, "Promise and Deceit."

5. Lovell, "Addiction Markets."

6. Michael Agar and Heather Schacht Reisinger, "A Tale of Two Policies: The French Connection, Methadone, and Heroin Epidemics," *Culture,*

Medicine, and Psychiatry 26, no. 3 (2002): 371–96.

7. Harris, "To Be Free and Normal"; Meyers, "Promise and Deceit."

8. Helena Hansen and Julie Netherland, "Is the Prescription Opioid Epidemic a White Problem?" *American Journal of Public Health* 106, no. 12 (2016): 2127–29.

9. Harris, "To Be Free and Normal."

10. Agar and Reisinger, "Tale of Two Policies."

11. Lesly-Marie Buer, Jennifer R. Havens, and Carl G. Leukefeld, "Does the New Formulation of Oxycontin Deter Misuse? A Qualitative Analysis," *Substance Use and Misuse* 49, no. 6 (2014): 770–74.

12. Agar and Reisinger, "Tale of Two Policies."

13. For the approach in France, see Lovell, "Addiction Markets"; for Baltimore, see Todd Meyers, *The Clinic and Elsewhere: Addiction, Adolescents, and the Afterlife of Therapy* (Seattle: University of Washington Press, 2013).

14. Lovell, "Addiction Markets"; A. Jamie Saris, "An Uncertain Dominion: Irish Psychiatry, Methadone, and the Treatment of Opiate Abuse," *Culture, Medicine, and Psychiatry* 32, no. 2 (2008): 259–77.

15. Judith S. Beck, *Cognitive Behavioral Therapy: Basics and Beyond,* 2nd ed. (New York: Guilford Press, 2011); Robert L. Leahy, *Cognitive Therapy Techniques: A Practitioner's Guide,* 2nd ed. (New York: Guilford Press, 2017).

16. Covidien, "About Covidien," April 28, 2013, www.covidien.com /covidien/pages.aspx?page=AboutUs; Steven B. Karch, "Is It Time to Reformulate Racemic Methadone?" *Journal of Addiction Medicine* 5, no. 3 (2011): 229–31. Buer et al., "Does the New Formulation?"

17. Zeba Siddiqui, "Covidien to Shutter South Carolina Plant, Lay Off 595," *Reuters,* September 13, 2012, www.reuters.com/article/2012 /09/13/us-covidien-plantclosure-idUSBRE88C1ES20120913.

18. Ed Silverman, "Reckitt's Suboxone Strategy Is Really About Patients or Profits," *Forbes,* October 12, 2012, www.forbes.com/sites /edsilverman/2012/10/12/reckitts-suboxone-strategy-is-really -about-patients-or-profits/#6aa3537b6c3f.

19. Katie Thomas and Charles Ornstein, "Amid Opioid Crisis, Insurers Restrict Pricey, Less Addictive Painkillers," *New York Times* and ProPublica, September 17, 2017; Ameet Sarpatwari, Michael S. Sinha, and Aaron S. Kesselheim, "The Opioid Epidemic: Fixing a Broken Pharmaceutical Market," *Harvard Law and Policy Review* 11, no. 2 (2017): 463–84.

20. Martin T. Hall et al., "Medication-Assisted Treatment Improves Child Permanency Outcomes for Opioid-Using Families in the Child Welfare

System," *Journal of Substance Abuse Treatment* 71 (2016): 63–67.

21. Philippe Bourgois, "Disciplining Addictions: The Bio-Politics of Methadone and Heroin in the United States," *Culture, Medicine, and Psychiatry* 24, no. 2 (2000): 165–95; Lovell, "Addiction Markets."

Chapter 6: Strategies for Making Do in Broken Systems

1. Kentucky Department for Community Based Services, "Division of Family Support," 2017, https://chfs.ky.gov/agencies/dcbs/dfs/fssb/Pages/ktap.aspx.

2. Rebecca Adkins Fletcher, "Keeping up with the Cadillacs: What Health Insurance Disparities, Moral Hazard, and the Cadillac Tax Mean to the Patient Protection and Affordable Care Act," *Medical Anthropology Quarterly* 30, no. 1 (2014): 18–36.

3. Appalachian Regional Commission, "Appalachian Apps: Transforming the Region's Economy Conference," Somerset, KY: October 14–15, 2015.

4. Appalachian Land Ownership Task Force, *Who Owns Appalachia? Landownership and Its Impact* (Lexington: University Press of Kentucky, 1983); Wilma A. Dunaway, "Speculators and Settler Capitalists: Unthinking the Mythology About Appalachian Landholding, 1790–1860," in *Appalachia in the Making: The Mountain South in the Nineteenth Century*, ed. Dwight B. Billings, Mary Beth Pudup, and Altina L. Waller (Chapel Hill: University of North Carolina Press, 1995), 50–75; Gordon B. McKinney, "The Civil War and Reconstruction," in *High Mountains Rising: Appalachia in Time and Place*, ed. Richard A. Straw, and H. Tyler Blethen (Chicago: University of Illinois Press, 2004), 46–58.

5. Nancy MacLean, *Democracy in Chains: The Deep History of the Radical Right's Stealth Plan for America* (New York: Penguin Books, 2017).

6. David Harvey, *A Brief History of Neoliberalism* (New York: Oxford University Press, 2007); Genevieve LeBaron and Adrienne Roberts, "Toward a Feminist Political Economy of Capitalism and Carcerality," *Signs* 36, no. 1 (2010): 19–44; Jeff Maskovsky, "The Other War at Home: The Geopolitics of US Poverty," *Urban Anthropology* 30, no. 2/3 (2001): 215–38.

7. Ann E. Kingsolver, "Farmers and Farmworkers: Two Centuries of Strategic Alterity in Kentucky's Tobacco Fields," *Critique of Anthropology* 27, no. 1 (2007): 87–102.

8. Ann M. Oberhauser, "Relocating Gender and Rural Economic Strategies," *Environment and Planning A: Economy and Space* 34, no. 7 (2002): 1221–37.

9. Oberhauser, "Relocating Gender and Rural Economic Strategies."

10. J. K. Gibson-Graham, "Building Community Economies: Women and the

Politics of Place," in *Women and the Politics of Place*, ed. Wendy Harcourt and Arturo Escobar (Bloomfield, CT: Kumarian Press, 2005), 130–57.

11. Mary K. Anglin, "Moving Forward: Gender and Globalization in/of Appalachian Studies," *Appalachian Journal* 37, no. 3/4 (2010): 286–300; LeBaron and Roberts, "Toward a Feminist Political Economy."

12. Allison Allbee, Rebecca Johnson, and Jeffrey Lubell, *Preserving, Protecting, and Expanding Affordable Housing: A Policy Toolkit for Public Health* (Oakland, CA: ChangeLab Solutions, 2015); Kelly Ray Knight, *addicted. pregnant.poor* (Durham, NC: Duke University Press, 2015).

13. E. Summerson Carr, *Scripting Addiction: The Politics of Therapeutic Talk and American Sobriety* (Princeton, NJ: Princeton University Press, 2011); Vincent Lyon-Callo, *Inequality, Poverty, and Neoliberal Governance: Activist Ethnography in the Homeless Sheltering Industry* (Toronto, Canada: University of Toronto Press, 2004); Ida Susser, "The Construction of Poverty and Homelessness in US Cities," *Annual Review of Anthropology* 25 (1996): 411–35.

14. Marilynne Robinson, *Gilead: A Novel* (New York: Picador, 2006), 98.

15. Ted Hawkins, "Sorry You're Sick," *Watch Your Step* (Nashville, TN: Rounder, 1982).

16. Kimya Dawson, "Loose Lips," *Remember That I Love You* (Olympia, WA: K Records, 2006).

17. Geoffrey R. Skoll, *Walk the Walk and Talk the Talk: An Ethnography of Drug Abuse Treatment Facility* (Philadelphia, PA: Temple University Press, 1992).

18. Patricia Hill Collins, *Black Feminist Thought: Knowledge, Consciousness, and the Politics of Empowerment.* 2nd ed. (New York: Routledge, 2000).

19. Erica Prussing, "Reconfiguring the Empty Center: Drinking, Sobriety, and Identity in Native American Women's Narratives," *Culture, Medicine, and Psychiatry* 31, no. 4 (2007): 499–526.

20. Lesly-Marie Buer, Carl G. Leukefeld, and Jennifer R. Havens, "'I'm Stuck': Women's Navigations of Social Networks and Prescription Drug Misuse in Central Appalachia," *North American Dialogue* 19, no. 2 (2016): 70–84.

21. Angela Garcia, *The Pastoral Clinic: Addiction and Dispossession Along the Rio Grande* (Berkeley: University of California Press, 2010).

22. Sharon G. Smith et al., *The National Intimate Partner and Sexual Violence Survey (NISVS): 2010–2012 State Report* (Atlanta: National Center for Injury Prevention and Control, Centers for Disease Control and Prevention, 2017).

23. Robert Gipe, *Trampoline: An Illustrated Novel* (Athens: Ohio University Press, 2015), 85.

24. Carr, *Scripting Addiction*.

25. Didier Fassin, "Inequality of Lives, Hierarchies of Humanity: Moral Commitments and Ethical Dilemmas of Humanitarianism," in *In the Name of Humanity: The Government of Threat and Care*, ed. Ilana Feldman and Miriam Ticktin (Durham, NC: Duke University Press, 2010), 238–55; Clara Han, *Life in Debt: Times of Care and Violence in Neoliberal Chile* (Berkeley: University of California Press, 2012); T. R. C. Hutton, *Bloody Breathitt: Politics and Violence in the Appalachian South* (Lexington: University Press of Kentucky, 2013); George Karandinos et al., "The Moral Economy of Violence in the US Inner City," *Current Anthropology* 55, no. 1 (2014): 1–22; Liisa Malkki, "When Humanity Sits in Judgement: Crimes against Humanity and the Conundrum of Race and Ethnicity at the International Criminal Tribunal for Rwanda," in *In the Name of Humanity*, 27–57.

26. Neil Websdale, "Rural Woman Abuse: The Voices of Kentucky Women," *Violence Against Women* 1, no. 4 (1995): 309–38.

27. Kimberle Crenshaw, "Mapping the Margins: Intersectionality, Identity Politics, and Violence against Women of Color," *Stanford Law Review* 43, no. 6 (1991): 1241–99; Carol Jacobsen and Lora Bex Lempert, "Institutional Disparities: Considerations of Gender in the Commutation Process for Incarcerated Women," *Signs* 39, no. 1 (2013): 265–89.

28. Crenshaw, "Mapping the Margins"; Sarah J. Hautzinger, *Violence in the City of Women: Police and Batterers in Bahia, Brazil* (Berkeley: University of California Press, 2007).

29. Gloria Anzaldúa, *Borderlands: La Frontera* (San Francisco: Spinsters/Aunt Lute, 1987); William L. Conwill, "Neoliberal Policy as Structural Violence: Its Links to Domestic Violence in Black Communities in the United States," in *The Gender of Globalization: Women Navigating Cultural and Economic Marginalities*, ed. Nandini Gunewardena and Ann Kingsolver (Santa Fe, NM: School for Advanced Research Press, 2007), 127–46.

30. Philippe Bourgois and Jeff Schonberg, *Righteous Dopefiend* (Berkeley: University of California Press, 2009).

31. Anzaldúa, *Borderlands*; Hautzinger, *Violence in the City of Women*.

32. Kimberle Crenshaw, "From Private Violence to Mass Incarceration: Thinking Intersectionally About Women, Race, and Social Control," *UCLA Law Review* 59 (2012): 1418–72; Jacobsen and Lembert, "Institutional Disparities"; Dorothy Roberts, "Prison, Foster Care, and the Systemic Punishment of Black Mothers," *UCLA Law Review* 59 (2012): 1474–1500.

33. Ann Pancake, *Strange as This Weather Has Been* (Berkeley: Counterpoint, 2007), 10.

34. Pancake, *Strange as This Weather Has Been*, 239.

35. Garcia, *Pastoral Clinic.*

36. Sally Ward Maggard, "Coalfield Women Making History," in *Back Talk from Appalachia: Confronting Stereotypes*, ed. Dwight B. Billings, Gurney Norman, and Katherine Ledford (Lexington: University Press of Kentucky, 1999), 228–50.

37. Shannon Elizabeth Bell, *Our Roots Run Deep as Ironweed: Appalachian Women and the Fight for Environmental Justice* (Urbana: University of Illinois Press, 2013); Silas House and Jason Howard, eds., *Something's Rising: Appalachians Fighting Mountaintop Removal* (Lexington: University Press of Kentucky, 2009).

38. bell hooks, *Belonging: A Culture of Place* (New York: Taylor and Francis, 2009); Crystal E. Wilkinson, "On Being 'Country': One Affrilachian Woman's Return Home," in *Back Talk from Appalachia: Confronting Stereotypes*, ed. Dwight B. Billings, Gurney Norman, and Katherine Ledford (Lexington: University Press of Kentucky, 1999), 184–86.

39. Sue Ellen Kobak, "OxyContin Flood in the Coalfields: 'Searching for Higher Ground,'" in *Transforming Places: Lessons from Appalachia*, ed. Stephen L. Fisher and Barbara Ellen Smith (Urbana: University of Illinois Press, 2012), 198–209; Maureen Mullinax, "Resistance through Community-Based Arts," in *Transforming Places*, 92–106.

40. J. K. Gibson-Graham, "Rethinking the Economy with Thick Description and Weak Theory," *Current Anthropology* 55, no. S9 (2014): S147–S53.

41. Benoît de L'Estoile, "'Money Is Good, but a Friend Is Better': Uncertainty, Orientation to the Future, and 'the Economy,'" *Current Anthropology* 55, no. S9 (2014): S62–S73.

Chapter 7: Moving Forward

1. James Still, *River of Earth* (Lexington: University Press of Kentucky, 1978), 76.

2. Paul Farmer, *Aids and Accusation: Haiti and the Geography of Blame* (Berkeley: University of California Press, 1992).

3. Robert Gipe, "In the Place I Live: Welcome to Rural Kentucky and 'Weedeater,'" *BookPage* Behind the Book, March 19, 2018, http://bookpage.com/behind-the-book/22490-place-i-live-welcome-to-rural-kentucky-weedeater#.WrKqbLpFyM_.

4. John Galtung, "Violence, Peace, and Peace Research," *Journal of Peace*

Research 6, no. 3 (1969): 167–91.

5. Paul Farmer, *Infections and Inequalities: The Modern Plagues* (Berkeley: University of California Press, 1999).
6. Galtung, "Violence, Peace, and Peace Research."·
7. Tax Cuts and Jobs Act of 2017, Pub. L. No. 115-97, 131 Stat. 2054 (2017).
8. Sarah Ogan Gunning, "Come All You Coal Miners" (New York: Alan Lomax, 1937).

Index

Abilify, 65
Adams County, 8–9, 13, 15, 33, 164
    Ashley's arrival in, 66, 82
    bupe in, 135, 140, 146
    DCBS in, 82, 147
    drug court in, 114–119, 121, 124
    economy of, 199
    fracking in, 35
    Horizons in, 100, 146
    housing in, 161–62
    inpatient detoxification services
        and, 50
    jail in, 54–57
    jobs in, 155
    Katie in, 66, 183
    Maggie's family in, 67
    methadone in, 131
    Narcotics Anonymous in, 173
    overdoses in, 176
    politicians in, 53, 56
Adderall, 2
Adoption and Safe Families Act of
    1997, 88–89
Affordable Care Act. *See* Patient
    Protection and Affordable Care
    Act
Aid to Families with Dependent
    Children, 93
Alaska, 182
Alcoholics Anonymous, 117, 125
Alisha, 57–59, 69–70, 75, 84,
    167–68, 176, 185, 188, 197
    bupe and, 148
    DCBS and, 86, 168

drug court and, 113–14, 117, 119,
    125–26, 172
    K-TAP and, 153
alprazolam, 2, 67, 70
American Pain Society, 40
Appalachia, 109–10, 197
    ADHD in, 77
    bupe in, 25, 129, 131–32, 145
    Christian missionaries and, 32, 111
    diversity in, 7, 22, 32–33, 185, 190
    economy of, 30–32, 155–157, 189,
        198–99
    education and, 52–53
    Gipe on, 189
    "hustling" in, 159
    interventions into, 3, 12, 23, 32, 191
    Mallinckrodt and, 137–38
    methadone in, 131
    migration and, 32
    organizations in, 25, 185
    OxyContin's emergence in, 2,
        27–29, 42, 45
    pain treatment in, 41
    Pancake on, 7–8, 28, 33, 183–84
    "poverty porn" and, 61–62
    power in, 9
    racism and, 33, 47
    reputations in, 50
    resistance in, 24, 30, 39, 185
    sexual assault in, 174
    stereotypes of, 2, 6–7, 21–22,
        27–30, 52–53, 59, 178,
        182–85, 188, 191–92, 197
    sterilizations in, 30, 75

257

About Haymarket Books

Haymarket Books is a radical, independent, nonprofit book publisher based in Chicago. Our mission is to publish books that contribute to struggles for social and economic justice. We strive to make our books a vibrant and organic part of social movements and the education and development of a critical, engaged, international left.

We take inspiration and courage from our namesakes, the Haymarket martyrs, who gave their lives fighting for a better world. Their 1886 struggle for the eight-hour day—which gave us May Day, the international workers' holiday—reminds workers around the world that ordinary people can organize and struggle for their own liberation. These struggles continue today across the globe—struggles against oppression, exploitation, poverty, and war.

Since our founding in 2001, Haymarket Books has published more than five hundred titles. Radically independent, we seek to drive a wedge into the risk-averse world of corporate book publishing. Our authors include Noam Chomsky, Arundhati Roy, Rebecca Solnit, Angela Y. Davis, Howard Zinn, Amy Goodman, Wallace Shawn, Mike Davis, Winona LaDuke, Ilan Pappé, Richard Wolff, Dave Zirin, Keeanga-Yamahtta Taylor, Nick Turse, Dahr Jamail, David Barsamian, Elizabeth Laird, Amira Hass, Mark Steel, Avi Lewis, Naomi Klein, and Neil Davidson. We are also the trade publishers of the acclaimed Historical Materialism Book Series and of Dispatch Books.